ASIA'S CRISIS AND NEW PARADIGM

Edited by

Walter Jung
Xiao-bing Li

University Press of America, ® Inc.
Lanham • New York • Oxford

Copyright © 2000 by
University Press of America, ® Inc.
4720 Boston Way
Lanham, Maryland 20706

12 Hid's Copse Rd.
Cumnor Hill, Oxford OX2 9JJ

Library of Congress Cataloging-in-Publication Data

Asia's crisis and new paradigm / edited by Walter Jung, Xiao-bing Li.
p.   cm.
1. Asia—Politics and government—1945-. 2. Financial crises—Asia. I. Jung,
Walter, 1942-. II. Li, Xiaobing, 1954-.
DS35.2 .A838 2000   950.4'29—dc21   00-030233 CIP

ISBN 0-7618-1728-X (cloth: alk. ppr.)

Contents

Acknowledgment

Asia's financial crisis which erupted in 1997 put our understanding and perception of the region to the test. Recent recoveries and new problems in Asian countries have aroused more concerns and interests for the future of Asia than ever before in America and in the world. Increasing attention demands re-assessment of the major issues of Asia through fresh intellectual engagement.

To make new academic efforts and enter scholarly input, the Western Pacific Institute at the University of Central Oklahoma (UCO) opened a new forum for discussions by holding its sixth annual Pacific Rim International Symposium on "Asian Crisis and New Opportunities" on March 23-25, 1999. The symposium addressed important topics on Asia's economy, finance, trade, international relations, domestic politics, education, culture, history, and society from a multi-disciplinary perspective and explored cooperative research efforts among scholars from all over the world. The scholarship makes a significant contribution through multi-faceted components represented by China's trade minister as the keynote speaker, Asian banks' CEO, government officials, business representatives, and more than 40 scholars. This book is the collection of the symposium papers. It offers Western readers a chance to view Asia's internal problems from an Asian perspective and makes an important contrast between the two very different cultures. The articles included here reflect the views of the contributors, which may or may not be supported by the Western Pacific Institute at UCO.

The volume acknowledges to the support from many people at the

University of Central Oklahoma. The co-editors wish to thank Dr. Roger Webb, UCO President, Dr. Don Betz, Vice President for Academic Affairs, and Dr. G. Douglas Fox, Executive in Residence of the President's Office. Their consistent and strong support for the Western Pacific Institute, its symposiums, and research projects is deeply appreciated.

A special appreciation goes to the Department of History and Geography which provided partial financial support and made the volume's publication possible. Dr. James F. Baker and Dr. Kenny Brown, chairmen of the department, supported both the symposium and the publication through the academic year.

We thank the Oklahoma Scholar-Leadership Enrichment Program (OSLEP) which provided three papers from its seminar, "Politics and Culture in China," at UCO on October 27-31, 1999. Helen DeBolt, OSLEP Director, and Dr. Diane Kremm, UCO Campus Coordinator for OSLEP, recruited these post-conference papers.

The co-editors are grateful to the professional support from their colleagues and staff members at UCO. Dr. Donald Duffy read and commented on part of the manuscript. Xiaoxiao Li and Liang Xu provided valuable computer technical assistance and edited final pages. Nancy J. Brewer and Ryan Paul Jones edited chapters written by international scholars. Joaneta Randell, Lasma Solita Siahaan, and Zhihong Chen provided secretarial assistance.

The final thanks have to go to Peter Cooper and Helen Hudson, editors of the University Press of America. Their commitment to academic excellence and professional guidance have helped make the publication a success.

Walter Jung
Xiao-bing Li

Chapter 1

Introduction:
Asia's Crisis and New Opportunity

Walter Jung

The crash of Thailand's financial market in 1997 was an ominous beginning for the most serious crisis Asia has faced in recent decades. The Thai debacle quickly spread to other Newly Industrializing Economies of Asia, like South Korea, Malaysia, and Indonesia, unleashing severe blows to most countries in the region. Though it came forth as an Asian problem, the Thai crash soon touched off serious financial distress in other regions such as Russia and Latin America. For a while, speculated was the fear that it would cast dark shadows on stock markets in the West, precipitating a global economic crisis. Indeed it was far more profound than an Asian financial problem; it was much broader in geographical scope and more severe in nature than any periodic economic downturn.

One of most remarkable aspects of the crisis was its rapid geographic proliferation; within three months after the currency crash in Thailand, stock markets had experienced free fall in Hong Kong and Indonesia.

Shortly after that, South Korea was forced to request massive International Monetary Fund's help. The crash was so severe and sudden that by the middle of 1998, it transformed into an acute political crisis in Indonesia; long-time strongman Suharto was forced to resign under the public pressure. The last half of 1998 ushered scarcely any slowdown of the worsening crisis; in June, the United States had to intervene to stop the Yen's skid, which in Japan led to the installment of the administration of Prime Minister Obuchi. In the meantime, Russia's economic crisis had reached a near meltdown point leaving Moscow no options but to declare a moratorium in August. Then the global community witnessed with growing uneasiness falling stock prices in Latin America and Europe. The Asian crisis appeared to bring down the economy of the entire world with it, initiating a global economic crisis.

The severe and swift geographical proliferation of the crisis indicates that its main causes were multidimensional in nature, representing both internal as well as external origins. The nation's internal conditions were a primary source, supplying a stage that had been ineffectual in blocking or even somewhat conducive to the externally transpired momentum. Yet the crisis itself was triggered by undertakings of external origin. Naturally, addressing the crisis calls for multidimensional approaches.

The crisis did not lead to world-wide economic disaster. Still the repercussions have been staggering. Thailand, Indonesia, and South Korea all needed IMF's massive bailout loans to stall the slide of their economies. Unemployment sky rocketed as thousands of big and small businesses failed. Overnight, the world's highest growth areas became the land of despair and disillusion. The economic hardship on the public was so intense that it led to an acute political crisis, and ugly racial conflicts resurfaced in Indonesia. In other countries, political unrest was kept in check, but even they did not escape the economic hardship the crisis had unleashed. Most common was falling currency values by 60 percent or more, which effectively demoted a middle class to a downright poor. It was the most serious social calamity the nations had suffered since the end of the Second World War.

The West's responses to this crisis have been intriguing. A seemingly wide-spread reaction was based on a typical view that such a crisis was inevitable, that the region's high growth rate was unsustainable for a long period. It has been no secret for the Western developed countries to harbor less than solid confidence in Asia's Newly Industrializing Economies. Apparently remaining unconvinced of the Asian tigers' stellar performance in the 80s and 90s, the West maintained that the area's new economic movers had not proved their ability to withstand the pressures of open international commerce. In a sense, the crisis proved that Western suspicion was solidly grounded. Yet it is a gross error to assume that the crisis was spawned solely by domestic shortcomings since the event was activated by volatile capital flows and currency speculation. It appears to be more logical for the West to share some responsibility for it is a principal player in the region's international capital market.

Causal factors responsible for the crisis vary depending on each country's economic approaches and development level. Nevertheless, some common features are easily identified. Internal factors include the nature of industry ownership, mode of industrial operation, and government-industry relations. Foot-loose international capital and Japan's long recession are prominent external factors.

Contemporary industrial culture is a fairly recent introduction to the developing countries in Asia. They had mostly adopted industrialization as the central piece of national development during the Cold War period under the encouragement of the West in general and the United States in particular. Although Japan supplied outstanding examples, their ambitious drive toward industrialization had encountered expected difficulties and hurdles. Only during the last few decades have most of these countries begun to enjoy the fruits of their hard work. Although they have accomplished some measurable success and have gained experience and confidence in themselves, the region's industrial economy is in essence still in its infancy. They have yet to undergo a full cycle of evolutionary transformation in their quest for world-class industrial economy. They have often insisted, with justification, that their economies still need some protective layers against highly sophisticated, experienced competitors in the developed world, and they were well aware that their infant industrial economies could not survive the onslaught of the well-established multinational corporations without some governmental protection. But in the 90s, the West insisted on the full and unconditional opening of Asian markets to its products fearing the emergence of a second Japan. As a result, most developing countries in the region were hardly ready for the global commerce when they were forced to embraced it.

The mode of industrial ownership and operation in the region had been far from achieving the level of the developed world in sophistication and rationality. In South Korea, ownership of major industries was, and still is, monopolized by the nation's handful of the *jaebuls,* or conglomerates, the rise of which was the direct result of the military government's aggressive drive for the rapid development of the nation's industrial sector during the 60s. It made the *jaebuls* locomotives for South Korea's industrialization and subsequent international commerce. Thus, the *jaebul* groups were directed to play pivotal roles in laying the nation's industrial infrastructure and accumulating valuable experience in international market places. The government, in turn, was prepared to overlook peculiarities of the *jaebuls*, including stringent family ownership, control-oriented management style, and often irrational expansion enthusiasm, the methods that are generally regarded as harmful to the free market economy. As a result, the *jaebuls* were instrumental in the nation's belated but promising debut in the most competitive sectors of international commerce. Unfortunately, their early competitive edge was provided by the nation's hard working labor and government-sponsored financing rather than their creativity and productivity.

To sustain large industries that generated typically meager profits, the *jaebul* groups needed almost unlimited bank credits, for which the government had exercised near exclusive influence. South Korea's government felt it had few options other than meeting the needs of the *jaebuls*, primary instruments for its economic development agenda. The failure of major *jaebul* groups would have been equivalent to the collapse of the government's principal economic goals, the very excuse for its authoritarian rule. Thus, a symbiotic relationship between the nation's power elites and the *jaebuls* was born and maintained for decades. Still, it is incorrect to portray the government as unaware of the undesirable aspects in the *jaebuls'* operation. In spite of their undeniable contribution to the nation's rapid rise in the industrial hierarchy of the world community, the *jaebuls'* penchant for monopoly and control had been constant irritations to the government. Every administration had proposed ambitious plans for reforming the *jaebuls*, but by then these powerful groups had acquired sufficient political skills to survive the administrations.

The *jaebuls'* excessive domination had been the cause for more than a few undesirables. First, it led to the nation's sagging productivity, thus losing competitiveness in the global market place. Second, the *jaebuls'* routine and assured access to the nation's banks meant the virtual shutout of access by the nation's small and mid-size industries, typically the most productive and creative segments of a national economy. Third, government-sponsored lending practices, both direct or indirect, inevitably became the major contributing factor to growing insolvency among the nation's financial institutions. Mounting nonperforming loans became common place and eventually became one of major triggers of the financial crisis.

An even more malicious alliance between government and leading industries prevailed in Indonesia. President Suharto's children and friends had monopolized control of the nation's major industries. In fact, the first family's monopoly was so extensive that it controlled most of the key manufacturing as well as service sector activities. This blatant nepotism and favoritism, irrefutable outgrowths of Suharto's long authoritarian rule, became serious barriers to Indonesia's entry to the West-dominated global commerce and thus the most direct causes of the crisis. Like South Korea, Indonesia was yet to graduate from the pseudo-industrial culture where politics ruled rather than safeguarded the national economy.

Industries heavily sheltered by a government are unlikely to have a strong desire to pursue competitive management. In South Korea, profits generated by most corporations under a *jaebul* ownership had been so meager that they did not even contemplate an expansion through internal funding. They had to turn to banks and other lending agencies for funds. The result was chronic low performance for financial institutions and an unacceptably high debt-to-equity ratio for corporations. The fact that in most Asian countries, excluding Hong Kong, Singapore, and Taiwan, nonperforming loans made by banks were over 30 percent of the total number of loans during the pre-crisis period illustrates the severity of the problem. Another financial practice common among Korea's *jaebuls* but which remains mostly prohibited in the West was the liberal application of cross-guarantee among institutions belonging to the same group, effectively concealing the true strengths and weaknesses of the corporation from the scrutiny of the public in general and the minority share holders in particular.

Furthermore, the practice of raising political funds has heavily contributed to shaping the region's unique political-industrial landscape in the region. The region's political establishments, unable to satisfy their financial needs through voluntary, transparent contributions, typically rely upon the corporate sector's generous and often illegal contributions. Such contributions are often made against regulations and without proper reporting. Moreover, these illegal, unethical contributions are likely to accompany certain political deals or favoritism. Although its downside is well publicized, close corporate-political collaboration has been a fixture as political campaigns become increasingly expensive. Requests by the political establishments for contributions are generally considered by the corporate sector a necessary evil since corporations need political backing on variety of issues. Consequently, the government's oversight role is often politically compromised and rarely effective in securing transparency in the corporate sector.

Illegal political contributions inevitably led to the practice of wanton favoritism, which enabled a few well-connected corporations to monopolize access to bank credits, the direct cause of often irrational expansion and reckless operation in spite of their sordid performance in market places. Corporate mismanagement and the ultimate squandering of public funds were the outcome of the corrupt politics, which remained blind to the brutal competition of the global market place. A case in point is the recent failure of South Korea's major steel maker, which was almost entirely funded by government-sponsored loans. This spectacular failure, which obviously cannot be considered limited to only one corporation, is widely presumed to have facilitated the nation's financial crisis. With legitimate justifications, the global capitalists had voiced their concerns over the practice and become cautious with their investments in the region. Insufficient foreign investments, a result of international investors' lukewarm enthusiasm, in turn had become a serious limitation to the region's achieving a confident, sophisticated industrial economy.

Japan's lingering recession, the worst since World War II, had been a major external contributor to the crisis. Although the nations in the region still harbor some painful emotions over Japan's colonial rule and wartime atrocities, they had come to accept Japan as the leading industrial power in the region. To the region's industrializing economies Japan had successfully proved the effectiveness of its development model, export-led industrial expansion. Japan also became an important supplier of critical capital, technology, and management skills. Moreover, in recent years, Japan had taken steps, however grudgingly, to open its markets to the region's exporters. Thus, Japan's debilitating recession had deprived the region's export-oriented economies of one of the key export markets. The recession also compelled the Japanese banks to find ways to utilize their huge capital resources in the region. Inexpensive Japanese capital, in turn, encouraged the region's banks to gamble on quick-profit ventures in Indonesia, Russia, and Latin countries with disastrous results. With some justification, Prime Minister Mahathir of Malaysia accused the international capital market of being the chief instigator of the crisis. Certainly, international capital, which had become far more footloose since the collapse of international socialism, had played a significant role in the crisis. Not subject to any enforced guidelines and regulations, international capital flow tends to be highly volatile, dictated only by profit-making opportunities and market share considerations. It is, in all practical sense, a simple profit raider, which simply chooses to disregard the welfare of a host market. Even George Soros, one of the best known international capitalists, does not refute the malevolent role played in this crisis by international capital in general and currency speculators in particular.

Asia's emerging economies reacted to the crisis with earnest determination and corresponding urgency. Their responses to the crisis were based on adequate comprehension of the problems at hand although the approaches and policies undertaken differed substantially. Even before various corrective steps were devised, however, failures of businesses and banks had skyrocketed followed by record high unemployment and drastic reduction of income. Most economies quickly sank to their lowest level in history, and the region seemed capable of doing only one thing, sinking to the bottom. Emergency measures and initiatives were hastily formulated and implemented. In spite of mounting business failures and soaring unemployment rates, the governments resolved to pursue extensive reform and restructuring of corporate and banking sectors for a long-term solution. But securing quickly some semblance of social stabilization was the most crucial task they faced.

In South Korea, major *jaebul* groups were under tremendous pressure from the new administration that inherited the crisis. As before, the *jaebuls'* initial responses were no more than lip service, probably intending to ride out the new storm with minimum disruption to their typical mode of operation. They remained highly protective of their market share in every strategic sector of the national economy. No more than cosmetic surgery were they willing to accept even though by then it was common knowledge that the *jaebul* operations shared the center stage of the national crisis. It was most brazen display of the *jaebuls'* selfishness and blatant disregard of the nation's welfare.

This time, however, the administration was determined to push as they were painfully aware of the gravity of the crisis. As the government made public that recovery from the crisis depended largely on successful, extensive reform of the *jaebuls*, serious confrontation between the administration and the *jaebuls* was inevitable. As powerful and influential as they were, however, the *jaebuls* realized that the government had exclusive regulatory powers. Although the *jaebuls* resisted the wholesale reform measures the administration favored, they gradually agreed to take some corrective steps. As a result, some corporations under *jaebul* control but with poor management records were either sold or closed down in an effort to streamline operations. It was largely a face-saving gesture but a symbolic step toward the systematic reform of the *jaebuls.* The government demanded each major *jaebul* group declare publicly its main areas of industrial operations, hoping that such restrictions would enhance productivity and thus improve global competitiveness by eliminating costly duplication in key sectors. Along with the restriction on each j*aebul's* operational territories, the administration demanded that the *jaebul* groups take concrete measures to lower their excessive equity-to-debt ratio. To achieve this goal, the government was willing to accept the *jaebuls'* restructuring measures including the reduction of work forces through layoffs. These reform measures were intended to bolster both productivity and managerial transparency so that badly needed foreign direct investment could be secured. For those industries for which domestic salvation was not feasible, the administration strongly recommended sale to foreign buyers.

Although the administration's efforts were extraordinary by any measure, the *jaebuls'* foot-dragging was stubborn. The modest results of reform the *jaebuls* have undertaken so far are contradictory to the strong society-wide pressures and demands for professional, not family, management. The nation's *jaebuls* have responded to the government and the public outcry with determined reluctance to undertake major reform and restructuring even under the darkest cloud the nation had experienced in recent history. The *jaebuls'* repeated claims of willingness to cooperate with the government continue, yet there seems to be growing skepticism that the *jaebuls'* dogged resistence may outlast the administration's political mandate.

Other nations in the region that had become victims of the crisis have formulated similarly ambitious reform measures to recover from the economic fallouts and have been eager to address the fundamental flaws responsible for the crisis. As they pursued various reform and restructuring initiatives, lay offs of large numbers of workers and significantly reduced earning became common features, which ignited in places violent labor protests and even political unrest. In Indonesia, the economic crisis quickly escalated into a societal breakdown, which shortly led to violent protests against the unpopular, authoritarian rule. A general election to be held in the late 1999 is considered favorable to the opposition party, a turn of events that is unimaginable in the pre-crisis period. In Thailand, reform initiatives have helped clean up the nation's banking sector, ushering in more a market-oriented, democratic society.

While the nations undertook various measures to overcome the crisis, the external factors of the crisis, the region's macroeconomics and the basic tenets of an international capital market, still remain virtually unchanged. In Japan, recession lingers as the government has yet to devise and implement effective recovery programs. While the threat of volatile capital flows remains unabated, the global community is yet to agree on measures regarding key questions like currency speculation. More than anything, the region seriously lacks a common voice that is respected in the global community.

Japan, the region's economic powerhouse, has yet to recover from its historic recession. Tokyo has periodically advanced recovery measures, but they have typically fallen short. Frequent leadership changes in recent years have made categorical reform of Japan's economic system nearly impossible. The Obuchi administration has unveiled another series of measures to boost its sagging economy, and although the new policy package includes programs similar to those proved in the past to be piecemeal and thus ineffective, new initiatives are regarded as more realistic and therefore promising as they rely more on the works of invisible hands, the market forces. Japan's full recovery from the recession should not be the sole answer to the Asian crisis, but it is certain that the region's battle against the crisis would be far more difficult without the full recovery of the Japanese economy.

International capital flow remains footloose more than ever. Market forces are only directives it understands and obeys. Dictated by the market forces, international capital not only precipitated the crisis but became the force that took most advantage of the crisis. The crisis opened for Western capital an unprecedented horizon of profit making and market control in the region. Its dramatic economic downturn was indeed an unprecedented opportunity of high profit making for those sophisticated, well-versed Western capitalists. A number of Asian firms were sold to Western buyers at bargain prices, a direct benefit of extremely favorable exchange rates. Foreign capital had deserted the region by throngs when profit-making opportunities looked unfavorable, but it reentered the region with enthusiasm when the crisis-devastated region presented an excellent environment for its profits. It was but a simple display of free market dynamics in which international capital flow was being controlled by profit prospects alone. Still there is yet to be any worldwide movement devoted to safeguarding weak and unsophisticated economies from predatory raids by international capital. The world community must remind itself that such unrestrained capital movement could easily create havoc to even developed markets under certain circumstances. Moreover, it would be most illogical to assume that the victims of international capital's unrestrained mobility are limited to developing economies of Asia.

Initiatives and measures the nations have devised and implemented are generally focused and reasonably effective, considering the serious nature of the crisis. Industrial sectors have been asked to undertake extensive reform and restructuring, which would have been most difficult and costly even under normal conditions. Their responses have fallen short of what the government desires. It is the general public that has suffered the brunt of the economic collapse by losing jobs and by earning far less. Nevertheless, the efforts have achieved some positive results in every country. Reportedly, some of these nations are near to declaring their victory over the unprecedented crisis. It seems that they do deserve hearty compliments for their focused drive and perseverence. But the crisis is not over by any means. Reform has a long way to go in both corporate and government sectors. Naturally, investor confidence remains at a less than desirable level. Investors are encouraging by their actions deeper and more extensive reform. One can hardly escape the nagging feelings of some deficiency if a careful survey is made of the region's overall reform efforts. Granted that the reforms undertaken are arduous and time-consuming; some are closely tied to external conditions, too. So some tardiness and incompleteness are expected and easily understandable. But there remain some serious fundamental challenges.

The basic framework of Asian economy is significantly different from that of the Western economy. More than anything, societal evolutionary processes in the East and the West have been essentially dissimilar. While the West had been the early beneficiary of the free market concept following the tradition of mercantilism, the East in general was left struggling with the traditional way of life for a long period. In fact, the concept of a free market economy is fairly new to most Asian nations. The tradition of the free market system is yet to be deeply rooted even in Asia's emerging economies. What the region's industrializing economies practice is thus close to a pseudo-free market system at best. In this system, government interventions are not only fairly routine but also widely expected. The fact that the region as a whole has adopted government-led economic expansion as a national development plan is highly indicative, for instance. Differences between the two systems are not subtle but extensive.

Yet, in searching for correct answers to the crisis, the nations have failed to pay necessary attention to more fundamental society-wide issues. Instead of focusing on broader fronts, their efforts so far have been directed mostly to financial and/or management aspects of corporate culture. Granted, reforms of streamlining less competitive industries, reduction of high equity-to-debt ratio, rationality, and transparency in loan management are critical and deserve serious attention, yet such approaches are likely to produce results more superficial in nature than systematic solutions unless more fundamental reform measures are implemented simultaneously. The fact that current reform efforts are being seriously undermined by corporate sectors and their traditional allies may justify the point further.

Asia's financial crisis was not just a simple foreign currency reserve problem. It was a general failure of the nations' economic systems, products of the nations' political cultures. Thus, it should have been relatively simple to identify the root causes of the failure in the corporate sector as the unique nature of the relationship between politics and industrial economy. Therefore, most sensible, effective approaches to the crisis should have included extensive reform measures of the nations' political sector. On the other hand, it would be most futile and myopic to address the problem with measures to correct only the symptoms but leaving the unstable, badly arranged foundation nearly intact.

Asia's crisis-stricken countries should have first surveyed their political landscape. Had they done that, they would have been overwhelmed by most inefficient, old-fashioned party politics. Their lack of policy-oriented statesmanship would be troublesome to any fair-minded observers, but even more serious findings would be that such backward politics had been responsible for the system-wide failures.

It is by no means trivial that the region's prevailing mode of leadership remains highly authoritarian, only a few steps away from a full-blown dictatorship. In South Korea, a mixture of authoritarian rule and old-fashioned backroom power politics prevailed for decades. In Indonesia and Thailand, the military still plays a powerful role, known to be ready to intervene whenever their views are not fully respected. As a whole, the Asian political landscape is best described as an industrial feudalism although the region has aggressively adopted the Western style economic development model. This serious mismatch has allowed political establishments total domination over industrial institutions, creating friction and fallout. Most serious efforts thus have to comprehend the implications of the immature political system on the crisis.

An economic crisis of this proportion is not likely to be vanquished through economic initiatives alone, no matter how comprehensive they may be. A system-wide failure has to be dealt with both extensive and intensive measures including radical reform and the restructuring of the nation's political establishments. So far, there has been little indication that individual nations of the region are taking meaningful steps to reform their troublesome political sector. Admittedly, it would be an extraordinary feat for the political establishments to take such self-defeating measures. Yet it should have been evident to even self-interest driven political establishments that the crisis the nation faces is serious enough to justify even the most drastic countermeasures. However unlikely it may be, the momentum for this critical reform movement has to come from the political sector itself, for the public in the region as a whole has yet to prove its ability to mobilize itself for such broad issues. Regardless, without the political establishment's full support, any grass-roots reform drive could hardly make a riffle in most countries.

In South Korea, the election of long-time opposition leader and committed democratic leader Kim Dae Jung was heralded as the opening of a new era. By inheriting the nation's most serious crisis since the civil war of 1950, his administration took immediate measures to combat the nation's overnight economic free fall. At the same time, he realized that the extensive reform of banks and major *jaebul* groups could not be completed without corresponding reform in the political sphere. But his political reform drives were met by stonewalling from the nation's old-fashioned political establishments. Even facing a disastrous crisis, the nation's political establishments still remain unwilling to surrender their political interests and privileges. The result shows a political reality that a democratic leader is not sufficient in reforming the political practices deeply rooted in the nation's temperament and tradition.

Even in Japan, the political system has yet to be fully liberated from an old-fashioned boss-system, often tainted by sensational corruption cases. It also has been largely ineffective in combating the nation's longest recession in the postwar period. Moreover, the liberal democrats, the party of traditional power brokers, have lost the overwhelming mandate enjoyed since the end of the war. As a result, Japan has suffered serious political instability as the frequent leadership changes have signified. Even when Obuchi was elected the prime minister, he was expected to last a short while as another transition figure. He has, however, proven that he is the man of substance, contrary to the earlier general perceptions. Still, he is regarded as a somewhat long-term transition figure. In the meantime, long-established, conservative bureaucrats continue to exercise their powerful influence, which accompanies no political accountability, however.

In Indonesia, a free but heavily contested presidential election is to be held at the end of 1999. The most consequential factor in this unprecedented transition remains to be politically-sensitive and powerful military and police forces, which are feared to be capable of ignoring even the democratic process if their own interests are at stake. Even if the opposition wins the general election, Indonesia's political future is likely to remain in balance for some time to come as the nation is facing the lofty task of reforming its entire politico-economic culture. It would be a historic challenge for Indonesia to formulate and adopt a new political framework that promotes national unity through harmony among groups of different racial origins and religious beliefs.

Internal friction among ethnic groups and vocal squabbles over the leadership slow down the economic recovery in Malaysia. Its political framework is based on the delicate arrangement of power sharing among many tribal groups, hardly an ideal format in overcoming the national crisis. Instead of crippling infighting, the entire nation should have rallied around the capable leadership for the successful resolution of the crisis and for safe journey in global waters for years to come. Prime Minister Mohammed Mahathir's extreme views on the West and its harmful influence in the region are not impossible to grasp, but such dogmatism could very well backfire in the long run. In Thailand, the tenure of civilian governments still remains tentative as the military continues as the power behind the scene. Even the monarchy, a well respected and generally productive national icon, seems unable to convince the military to stay in its barracks. It is unfortunate that Thailand is in such a predicament, in which any meaningful reform even in industrial sectors would need at least the tacit support of the nation's defense forces. In Thailand, priority must be given to military reform before both political and industrial reforms. Thus, Thailand has the dubious distinction of facing three excruciatingly challenging fronts simultaneously, a task that appears to be beyond the realm of speedy resolution.

One of the positive factors of the crisis has been the relative stability of the Chinese economy for the last several years. Thus, Beijing has been able to steadfastly resist growing pressure to devalue its currency. This, however, does not imply that the Chinese decision not to devalue its currency was based on its considerations for the region's economic crisis alone. Still, it is certain that any sizable devaluation of the Yuan must have been a damaging development for the region's efforts to recover from the crisis. Beijing could not be a savior but could easily have been a spoiler in the crisis. It is rather unlikely that China can resist the devaluation pressure indefinitely as it is under mounting pressure from many domestic elements including a high unemployment rate and a worsening recessionary trend. The region, however, could withstand the fallout of the Chinese devaluation somewhat better now than in the recent past.

It is most likely that China will become an even more powerful player in the region's security-trade spheres. Thus, politico-economic developments in Beijing will have direct repercussions on the region including the full recovery from the ongoing crisis. Beijing's rulers are communists, members of the nation's sole political party, the Chinese Communist Party. They have openly committed to one socialist capitalism, a smartly conceived, sensibly implemented, and fairly effective system. They seem to have every intention of extending the party's exclusive political tenure for decades to come. But the ruling party's wishes may become no more than simple wishes after all. There are increasing indications that the public regards the hybrid market system as no more than an elaborate transition that relates defunct socialism to the globally prevailing free market economy. Beijing has yet to devise an effective response to the growing public sentiment. Moreover, the Chinese economy, seemingly finding no serious barriers in its way to becoming one of the newly industrializing economies, is about to outgrow its rigid, half-baked politico-economic framework. Unless Beijing undertakes revolutionary measures for system-wide reform rather quickly, the economy of the world's most populous nation may crash, generating severe reverberations on the region and the world.

Currently, China suffers an acute dual economy. The nation harbors simultaneously two entirely different economic regions: coastal zones are open and dominated by high growth rate industries while inner land zones are stagnant, housing old low-productivity industries. Its industrial sector is a mixture of most advanced, productive segments and the backward, low productive sectors. This dual economy could become a poignant centrifugal factor and an ultimate reminder of the one-party system's limitations. Growing gaps in income and standard of living between urban-coastal zones and rural-inner zones are bound to spark a serious political unrest that could certainly invite dangerous political interventions. For a society with a rapidly expanding middle class that thirsts for more open, free venues of free expression, no amount of government pressure will be able to suppress what is essentially a natural process of societal development.

Beijing's recent harsh crackdown on the nation's apolitical meditation group Falun Gong indicates that the Chinese communist party remains unwilling to allow any alternative venues even if it is a relatively harmless group. It appears that Beijing unequivocally wishes to continue its present political setup. Yet the number of citizens who value highly a more open society with a multi-party political system will grow as their contacts with outside world expand through various means including satellite transmissions and the Internet. They are quite unlikely to acquiesce to Beijing's authoritarian rule for much longer. However painful it may be to the ruling party, Beijing must heed the irreversible trend of the market economy and participatory democracy the rest of the world community has already embraced. Even the middle kingdom may not be an exemption in this regard.

China remains the pivotal element in the region's long-term stability. As long as it is unwilling to change the one party rule, China will continue to be the simmering volcano ready to erupt any moment. Of course, there is no assurance that profound political reform will not touch off an empire-destroying civil unrest. Nonetheless, judicious but revolutionary political reform seems to be the only logical course to follow for history's longest unbroken civilization.

The financial crisis that hit Asia's many emerging economies hard and extensively should not be considered a simple failure of a region's economic system or policy. It was not. Although the crisis was kindled by unsound loan management, large corporations' poor performances, the political institutions' unwarranted interferences, and predatory raids by international capital, the roots of the crisis run much deeper. In effect, it was damaging fallout of the latest paradigmatic change of the 20th century. It was not even isolated. Even in Europe the fallout of the profound shift has been evident since 1990.

A paradigmatic shift should be met by equally profound society-wide responses, not by piecemeal symptomatic treatments. Such a shift requires a comprehensive approach, of which the central theme should have been radical political reform. Not just the cosmetic reconfiguration of a system but a wholesale reorganization of the entire system including mental framework is what a long-term response to the global paradigmatic shift should have been.

At the end of the 20th century, East Asian nations encountered the last paradigmatic shift, to which each nation's response was quite dissimilar. The consequences were truly profound. Japan seized the crisis as an opportunity to transform its feudal society to a western-style more science-based society. It had had quickly accomplished its hastily formulated goals, reaching the plateau of modern society first in the region. Both China and Korea had not been able to comprehend the shift adequately and in time badly squandered the opportunity. Both countries paid high prices for their failure for many decades. Southeast Asian nations fared no better. Historically, those who were imprudent in responding to a profound crisis such as a paradigm shift were forced to suffer consequences later, and these nations are not exceptions.

Asian nations, those affected by the crisis in particular and others in general, should be well advised to heed the ongoing paradigm shift. That may be the most important lesson they could learn from the financial crisis that has left such unpleasant footprints in the region.

Chapter 2

China: an Active and Stable Factor in Asia and Western Pacific Region

Haoruo Zhang

The Asian financial crisis has seriously affected the economy of Asian countries. Countries in the western Pacific rim were also hit in different degrees. China was not an exception: Its export growth momentum has weakened, foreign capital inflow reduced and economic growth slowed down. It also suffered a severe flooding last summer. However, China did not fall in economic contraction nor stagnation. Its economy still maintained a high growth, a fairly good grain production, a steady increase of industrial production, a favorable balance of international payments, a stability of Chinese currency, and a continuous increase of foreign reserves.

The above is proven by the fact that China is an active and stable factor in Asia and Western Pacific Rim. The question today is: what are the trends of the Chinese Economy? Some predicted that China would be the next target to be hit by the crisis, that China would fall in contraction, and that the Chinese economy would even collapse. I do not want to minimize difficulties and problems that China faces today. After twenty years of economic reform and open-door policy, China indeed encounters a rather big and unprecedented economic readjustment, whose outcome will determine China's future fate. I am not pessimistic but let us first look at the following three preoccupying issues: first, whether the rapid economic growth rate can be maintained; second, whether the Chinese currency will devalue or not; and third, whether China will slow the process of reform under pressure inside and outside China.

1. China's Economy Will Maintain a Fast Growth

In the past twenty years of economic reform and opening up, the annual growth rate of China's national economy has averaged 9.8%. Since 1995 the growth rate began to slow down; and in 1998 the growth rate dropped to 7.8% due to the Asian financial crisis and flooding. Nevertheless, this growth rate is still 5% higher than the average world level in the same period. I believe that China's economy will maintain a comparatively fast growth this year and in the years ahead. The main reason is that the implementation of the past twenty years' reform and opening-up has laid a solid foundation. China has also accumulated various experiences in dealing with issues like the economy's over-heating or sliding, inflation or deflation. Also, China's market potential, consumption and investment demand are very big; furthermore, China needs a fast growth to solve unemployment, get rid of poverty, and catch up with moderately developed countries in the middle of the next century. Chinese people have the confidence and determination to achieve this goal and overcome any difficulties lying ahead.

Under present international conditions, China has to rely on its domestic market and actively expand domestic demand to realize a sustained economic growth. Since the last half of 1998, the Chinese government has adopted a set of anti-cycle economic policies to pull up the economy. The following measures will guarantee a relatively long-term sustained economic growth.

(1) Pursue an active fiscal policy

This year China will continue to carry out an active fiscal policy. The state will issue long-term bonds to commercial banks to strengthen the country's infrastructure construction. China's present infrastructure is backward, and there is a big gap between demand and supply. Therefore, to increase the investment will not lead to any overcapacity. Indeed, it can improve economic environment and lay down a foundation for further development. At present the ratio of China's government debts and deficits to its GDP is lower than the international warning line. The debt ratio is expected for 1999 to be around 9.9%, and a deficit ratio around 1.7%.

Therefore, there is room for maneuvering policy. State investment is concentrated on agriculture, irrigation, water conservation, transportation, telecommunication, and environmental protection. The effects are evident. This year, investments made by the state in the first two months came to 85 billion yuan (those made by collective and private economies were not included), an increase of 28.3% compared with the same period as last year. Pulled up by investment, China's industrial production went up by 10.6%, in which state companies increased by 8.8%, the collective economy by 8.6%, shareholding companies by 14.4%, and foreign-funded companies by 15.3%. Industries like cement, plate glass, and nonferrous metals experienced the fastest growth by 15-20%. Nevertheless, seeing from a long-term prospective, major investments should be made by the private sector and by the whole society. China has already set up mutual funds and plans to develop an industrial investment fund.

(2) Expand consumption demand

In recent years China has changed from a scarcity economy to a buyer's market, but this equilibrium between supply and demand is achieved at a low level and with irrational structure, and is bounded by the present system. China has an immense consumption demand and market potential. The government is now adopting measures to stimulate consumption: reduce three times interest rates, eliminate restrictions on private consumption; allow people to open up bank consumer credit; encourage individuals to purchase housing, cars, and other durable consumer goods; and develop new consumption highlights such as culture, education, medical and health care, tourism, entertainment, and insurance. In China's telecommunication sector, for example, the business expands by 40% a year, and China ranks third in the world in the number of mobile telephone users.

(3) Push forward housing reform and promote housing consumption

The Chinese government has set housing industry as a new economic growth point. Since the 1990's the housing system reform has been carried out. China will stop the welfare housing distribution system, turn to monetization of housing distribution, develop the housing market, reduce housing prices, and establish a public housing accumulation fund system.

(4) Develop rural markets

There are 900 million farmers in China now. After twenty years of economic reform and opening-up, the income of farmers has greatly increased and their purchasing power enhanced, and the potential of the rural market is immense. China will soon become the world's number two beer consuming country only because Chinese farmers have begun to drink beer in addition to spirits. They will then need TV sets, refrigerators, and washing machines. Washing machines are used not only for clothes but also to wash potatoes. To further expand the consumption demand of rural residents, the government is accelerating the construction of public utilities and infrastructure in rural areas, constructing electric transmission networks in rural areas so that electric appliances can go into every household, and modernizing agriculture to increase the farmer's income and enhance their purchasing power, developing small towns, and promoting the process of urbanization. It is expected that the expansion of domestic demand will make the possibility of economic growth 7% or even higher.

2. The Exchange Rate of Chinese Currency Will Remain Stable

The currencies of southeast Asian countries have depreciated by a large margin since the breakout of the financial crisis. The depreciation of the Japanese yen in the late half of 1998, triggered another round of competitive devaluation. It is popularly said that Chinese currency will depreciate. In 1998, Chinese succeeded in implementing its non-devaluation policy and has stabilized the exchange rate of its currency. This success is attributed to the following factors: a stable economic growth base; favorable balance of payments and large foreign reserves; timely macroeconomic adjustment such as reduction in interest rates, and increases in export rebates. China also takes a responsible position in helping to reduce the pressure of the financial crisis on countries in the region and stabilizing their economies and financial markets.

Last year the aggravation of the Asian financial crisis also imposed negative effects on the Chinese economy, especially on China's exports. Exports to southeast Asia, Japan, and South Korea fell by a large margin due to declining purchasing power of residents in these countries and shrinking market demand. The exchange rate could be one factor, but looking at the export commodity structure, it is found that devaluation may not be a necessary determining factor to increase exports.

The devaluation may work temporarily but cannot last long. The key to increase exports is to adjust export structure. To stop declining trends, measures have been taken such as adopting better quality and market diversification strategy; adjusting export commodities structure, increasing high value added and brand name exports; improving export management, and enhancing the competitiveness of exports, etc.

The exchange rate of Chinese currency is determined by fundamentals of China's economy (economic growth, balance of payments, level of foreign reserves, price parity between home and abroad, etc.). At present, China's economic fundamentals are good. With current active fiscal policy put in place and further expanded domestic consumption, it is predicted that in 1999 China will still maintain a fairly high economic growth of 7% or higher, favorable balance of payments, and further increased foreign reserves. Under these circumstances it is unlikely that Chinese currency will depreciate. It will continue to be stable

It is necessary at the moment, in order to avoid the financial crisis, that China's currency be convertible under the current account, but not yet under the capital account. Along with further financial reform and increased supervision capability, China's final goal is to make its currency fully convertible.

3. China Will Not Slow Down the Pace of Its Reform

Though China still encounters many difficulties and problems, it will not stop nor slow down the pace of reform. Experiences over the past twenty years have shown that the reform is a driving force for development. Without reform there is no development, and many contradictions and problems in economic life can hardly be resolved. Therefore, China will continue to carry out its reform. Its goal is to establish a fairly perfect socialist market economy in the length of approximately ten years. Following are some major ongoing reforms in China:

(1) Reform of state owned enterprises

The state economy is still the pillar of China's national economy. The reform of state owned enterprises is to transform them into corporate legal entities. Up to now, China has set up or reorganized 523,000 shareholding companies. By the end of last year, 851 companies were listed on the Shanghai and Shen Zhen stock exchanges with total market value exceeding 2 trillion yuan and accounting for 25% of China's GDP; 43 companies were listed in Hong Kong, New York and other parts of the world, raising capital of $10 billion. After being converted into a shareholding system, companies have seen their performance and efficiency much enhanced.

A shareholding cooperative system, leasing, contracting-out, merger and acquisition, and bankruptcy have been introduced and applied to a variety of state-owned small and medium sized enterprises.

Private business is encouraged and supported. Besides the public sector, private business is encouraged and supported.

(2) Reform of the social security system

Since the early 1990s, the reform of the social security system has been accelerated and substantial progress achieved in pensions, medical insurance, unemployment, etc. The basic pension and medical insurance have been established. It is featured by a combination of social pooling and individual accounts. Contributions are shared among state, enterprises, and individuals. The pay-as-you-go system is being replaced progressively by a partially funded system. By the end of 1997, 96.7% of workers and employees in the public sector participated in the basic pension scheme. New reform efforts will be focused on further expanding the coverage of the basic pension and medical insurance so that all the labor force in state enterprises, collective economy, private business, and foreign-funded companies will be covered by the social security system. Collection of contributions and fund management are to be improved.

(3) Reform of agriculture and the rural economy

China began its economic reform in rural areas. At present further reform is still needed to promote the modernization of agriculture and to readjust and optimize the agricultural structure; improve the quality of produce; enhance efficiency; integrate farming, processing, and marketing; extend farming scale and increase farmers' revenues; upgrade the township enterprises to get better performance and change farmers' residential status system and their living style; and develop small cities and towns to accelerate the process of urbanization and narrow down the gap between urban and rural areas.

(4) Development of non-public economy

The individual and private economy has been recognized recently by China's constitution as an important integral part of the national economy. Its significance is historical. Over the past twenty years, China's non-public economy has played an important role. It developed productivity, satisfied people's various demands, offered jobs, and also brought changes to China's ownership structure. China's non-public economy accounts now for 24.2% of the GDP. It has a huge potential and constitutes a new growth point in China's economy in future.

(5) Further expanding the opening-up to the outside world

China has carried out an all-dimensional open-door policy. Fields open to foreign investors are extended from primary and secondary sectors to the tertiary sector, including banking, insurance, telecommunication, commerce and retail sales, foreign trade, tourism and real estate, and so on. By the end of 1998, China set up 320,000 Sino-foreign-funded enterprises; the actual use of foreign capital amounted to $407.2 billion. There are 174 foreign funded financial institutions now operating in China offering foreign currency and Chinese currency transaction business; 14 foreign-funded insurance companies offer their life and non-life insurance service; and more than 100 joint ventures deal in retail sales, etc.

The Chinese government has recently decided to open further fields and areas to foreign business. More foreign banks will be allowed to set their branches in major cities to do business, including Chinese currency business; more joint venture insurance companies will be set up; domestic telecommunication will be opened to foreign company step by step; more joint ventures will operate in the retail sales sector; and more joint trading companies will do business in a number of cities. The proportion of shares held by foreign investors in China's air transport companies will increase, encouraging multinational companies to invest in high technology, and establish R & D centers in China. All of these promote cooperation between domestic and foreign small business, encouraging private companies to cooperate with foreign firms. Thus, China remains a good place for investment, and foreign capital will continue to flow in.

In conclusion, I fully believe that Asian countries and countries in the western Pacific rim will recover from the current crisis though they still face difficulties. Their economies will regain momentum as the most dynamic area in the world. China will continue to play an active and stable role in this region. In the short run, the greatest contributions China could make to the Asian and Western Pacific economy are a continuous rapid economic growth and the stability of Chinese currency. To achieve this, China must consistently carry out its economic reforms and opening up.

Chapter 3

Export Performance and Trade Conflict Resolutions: South Korea's Experience

Yong U. Glasure and Aie-Rie Lee

Rapid modernization and high sustained economic growth of Korea from the mid-1960s to the late-1970s had benefitted from U.S. global policy of maintaining the cohesion of the Western coalition against the socialist block. In the early-1960s, the United States opened its markets to imports from Korea and other allied countries while allowing these countries to be largely negligent in opening their own markets to U.S. products (Sato 1984). By the late-1970s and the 1980s, however, Korea's external and internal environments had been drastically transformed. Korea's key assets during the earlier periods of high-speed growth began increasingly more like liabilities. By the late 1980s, the United States revoked the tariff-free entry of selected Korean imports, imposed voluntary export restraints on Korea while forcing to appreciate the Korean won and to open Korea's domestic markets.

Thus, Korea had become a prime target of protectionist policies of the

United States (Bello and Rosenfeld 1990). A recent GATT study reports that the bilateral voluntary export restraint arrangements (VERs), known to have been in effect at the end of 1987, protect the E.C. market or the market of one of its member states, followed by the U.S. market. The arrangements mainly limit exports from Japan (38 arrangements) and Korea (35), in addition to voluntary export restraints (GATT 1988). Moreover, estimates of developed countries' tariff and non-tariff barriers for 1986 show that these barriers applied to 20-22 percent of world exports, but for Korean exports, these barriers were 35-38 percent (Petri 1988).

The consequences of changes in U.S. goals from long-term global political objectives to specific national economic interests had precipitated numerous trade conflicts between the United States and Korea, with greater frequency and intensity. This article attempts to empirically link the effects of trade conflict resolutions involving export commodity groups from Korea on the economic and export performances of Korea within the "export-led growth hypothesis" framework for the period 1973-1994.[1] Also examined is the export-led growth hypothesis for Korea. The methods used are five-variable vector autoregressive (VAR) and vector error-correction (VEC) models.

The paper proceeds with a discussion on trade conflicts and their respective resolutions. Section 3 presents the empirical models and their results. The last section is summary and conclusions.

Trade Conflicts and Their Resolutions

Korean Products in the U.S. Markets

Trade conflicts between the United States and Korea in the 1970s and the early-1980s arose mainly in three sectors: textiles and apparel, footwear, and television sets (see Table 1).[2] In all sectors, the U.S. government initiated the complaints, stating that Korean products, albeit a minuscule portion of the U.S. market, were disrupting the American market. The first American ploy in the 1970s was to suggest a multilateral agreement covering all the fibers. The U.S. proposed to Korea that a new comprehensive bilateral five-year restraint accord would limit synthetics' growth to 11 percent in the first year and 1 percent less in each subsequent year, and would calculate limits starting with the level of trade in a base period of April 1970 through March 1971 (Odell 1984, 128). While resisting the new proposal maintaining that the United States failed to show that exports in these additional areas were disrupting the U.S. market, Korea counter-offered to accept a growth limit of 40 percent per year, the level of recent actual growth. The final agreement reached was Korea's reducing this synthetics' growth to 25 percent, the rate assumed in the national development plan.[3]

In September 1971, President Nixon threatened Korea with unilateral quotas unless Korea accepted U.S. terms by October 15. Korea yielded to this intense pressure. The agreement sharply widened restrictions against Korean exports, where the number of controlled products jumped from eighteen to thirty five, and these limits were to be in effect for five years. Growth for man-made fibers was limited on the sliding scale, starting at 10 rather than 11 percent. Korea, in return, secured major offsetting gains from the United States, which agreed to provide Korea with a $100 million concessional loan plus $275 million worth of food aid over the next five years. The United States also boosted Korea's quota for cotton products (Odell 1984, 129). At the expiration of the five-year export restraint agreement in 1977 and also in 1979, the United States under pressure from the American clothing and textile complex of credible threat of jeopardizing the entire Tokyo Round trade negotiation renegotiated the five-year agreement, seeking Korea to forgo the use of its provisions for carryover and carryforward during that one year.

Soon after signing the new five-year restraint agreement, the U.S. in 1979 sought further new concessions from Korea, demanding that the 1980 settlement eliminated carryover and carryforward for 1980, reduced swing by 1 percent on eleven clothing items, including four of the most important ones, and cut sharply the quota on sweaters. In 1981, the same scenario was replayed a third time. The United States sought and received reductions in Korean flexibility for 1981 trade. Korea gave up carryover, carryforward, and 1 percent of swing for eleven apparel items, including four major products and relinquished all flexibility for sweaters. Lastly, on August 4, 1986, Korea agreed to U.S. demand that it limit export growth of textiles and apparel to 0.8 percent per year.

In regard to footwear, in March 1973 the Korean government had eliminated its footwear export promotional policies and imposed voluntary quantitative limits on exports of rubber footwear from 1973 through 1975. In July 1975 the U.S. Treasury Department ruled that the Korean government was granting a 1 percent subsidy on shoe exports through a program of preferential export financing. The U.S. wanted Korea to end the subsidy or to offset its effects on the U.S. economy. In January 1976, the U.S. imposed a countervailing duty of 0.7 percent on non-rubber shoe imports from Korea. With respect to rubber shoes, Korea agreed to extend its voluntary restraint through 1976, and the U.S. waived the imposition of this countervailing duty on rubber shoes.[4]

In the winter of 1977, the U.S. International Trade Commission concurred with the American industry in the second dispute, ruling that Korea's exports of non-rubber shoes were causing the American industry serious damage. The United States asked Korea for a massive cutback from the 1976 shipment level of 44 million pairs to the 16 million pairs that Korea had shipped in 1975 (Yoffie 1983). Because of Korea's resistance, the U.S. proposed to increase the limit to 30 million pairs the first year and the possibility of some growth thereafter or a flat limit of 34 million over a five-year agreement, at Seoul's option. The final outcome was Korean exports were to set at 33 million pairs for the first year and at an average of 36.25 million over the life of the agreement (Odell 1984, 131-132).

The other conflict involved was Korea's color TV receivers. In March 1977 the International Trade Commission (ITC), under pressure from Zenith Radio Corporation and a coalition of labor unions to curb imports, held that imports of color TV sets were causing serious injury to the American industry.[5] In fact, Korea just began to build a color TV export industry in 1976. Thus, Korean firms exported a negligible amount in 1976 but the amount increased to $72 million in 1978. Recognizing the fact that the United States will target Korean TV receivers, Korean firms expanded their production capacity threefold in 1978 to 1.1 million units per year to establish foothold in the American market (Odell 1984, 133). Because of this rapid increase of Korean exports, the Japanese government and other American companies complained that Korea, along with Taiwan, was undermining the 1977 arrangement between the United States and Japan that limited Japan's exports.[6]

In November 1978, the United States started to pressure the Korean government to cut back TV exports. Although the Korean government presented its case that no American companies were producing the TV sets with small screens and also stated that any restrictions that reduced the level of recent trade would be inconsistent with GATT and threatened to boycott American nuclear energy and aircraft exports in retaliation if Korean interests were not protected,[7] these had little effect. Korea complied with the U.S. demand and signed the December 1978 agreement that drastically limited Korea's color TV exports. The agreement called for Korea's cutting back its exports to 204,000 units for the next twelve months or half of the expanded 1978 level. The self-restraints were to remain in effect until June 1980.[8] As a result of this agreement, capacity utilization in Korean factories fell to 34 percent in 1979 (Odell 1984, 134). The second agreement of July 1980 extended but loosened restrictions on Korean TV exports. The new limits did exempt small screen sets and the ceiling on others was set at 385,000 for the next twelve months and 565,000 for the year beginning July 1981 (Odell 1984, 131).

Besides the three main sectors above, trade conflicts also arose in steel products between 1986 and 1993, of which the U.S. ITC investigated under the Tariff Act of 1930 and found that Korea was dumping certain steel, brass, and plastic products such as carbon steel pipes and tubes, cold-rolled carbon steel sheet and carbon steel structural shapes in U.S. markets. The United States imposed antidumping duties accordingly.

U.S. Products in the Korean Markets

In spite of the insurmountable trade barriers for Korean exports, in November 1988 U.S. Congress and the President signed "the Trade Protection Act", under which the President could seek retaliation for trade barriers imposed by U.S. primary trading partners. This is called the Super 301 provision of the Omnibus Trade and Competitiveness Act of 1988 requiring the identification of trade liberalization priorities. The act requires the listing of foreign countries where trade barriers and distortive trade practices are pervasive and significantly impede U.S. exports. Section 301 gives the administration broad powers to act against practices determined unilaterally to be unjustifiable, unreasonable, or discriminatory. Discriminatory implies the denial of national or most-favored-nation treatment for U.S. goods, services, or investment.

Korea managed to escape Super 301 designation by promising to liberalize imports, especially imports of agricultural products, by increasing public investment to expand aggregate demand, and by employing buying missions to reduce its bilateral surplus with the U.S. Furthermore, the Korean government in August 1986 decided to divert imports of 235 products from Japan particularly to the U.S. as part of its on-going efforts to achieve a more balanced pattern of bilateral trade with the U.S. In actuality, Korea's market diversification plan encouraged more imports from Japan. The United States perceived the market diversification plan to be directly inimical to the interests of U.S. exporters and strongly advocated some limit on its scope and its ultimate elimination. The initial response to U.S. pressure by the Korean government was to announce a trade diversification program that would encourage expenditures in the United States (USITC 1987).

Table 2 presents some specific trade conflicts between the two countries that involve U.S. firms' access to the Korean markets. In response to the American Meat Institute's filing a Section 301 complaint in February 1988, the United States requested in March 1988 GATT arbitration to settle the beef dispute. In April 1989, GATT found that Korean import restrictions are inconsistent with GATT, and Korea complied with the GATT finding by pledging to open its beef market fully over the following three years (USITC 1988). In fact, before the GATT finding against Korea, Korea, despite the political sensitivity, lifted the import ban in June 1988 as a result of beef shortages. Thus, in 1988 U.S. exporters sold about $37 million of high quality beef in Korea.

In January 1988, the U.S. Cigarette Association filed a Section 301 complaint against Korea, alleging unfair trade practices that shut U.S. companies out of the Korean market. In response, in February 1988 the USTR launched an investigation. Succumbing to U.S. pressure, in May 1988, the Korean government agreed to reduce the tax on imported cigarettes about $1.50 to $0.49. Also, the Korean government allowed firms to sell imported cigarettes independent of the Korea Monopoly Corporation. This agreement went into effect on July 1, 1988.

Similar to the cigarette case, in April 1988 the Wine Institute and the Association of American Vintners filed a complaint, alleging that Korea's 100 percent wine tariff and quota on table wine effectively kept U.S. wines from being price competitive with Korean wines. On July 8, 1988, the USTR initiated a Section 301 investigation. Under pressure from the U.S., Korea agreed to fully open its wine market for U.S. table wine and other wine products. In September 1988, the Motion Picture Export Association of America (MPEAA) filed a complaint, and Korea's response was similar to the cigarette and wine cases. Again, the United States using a Section 301 pried open Korea's insurance market. The outcome of that dispute was Korea's granting a larger share of the domestic market to two U.S. companies (Cho, 1987).

Korea was placed on the U.S. "priority watch list" in telecommunications and insufficient protection of intellectual property rights in April 1994. In November 1994, the USTR initiated a Section 301 investigation of Korea's practices regarding the importation of U.S. beef and pork. Also, in 1994 the U.S. intensified its pressure to open up the Korean automobile market, given the fact that the Korean auto market is the second largest in Asia after that of Japan. On September 29, 1995, Korea agreed to reduce specified taxes against imported cars and to liberalize certification procedures.[9]

$$(1) \quad \Delta y = \alpha + \sum_{i=1}^{4} \beta_i \Delta y_{t-i} + \sum_{i=1}^{4} \gamma_i \Delta e_{t-i} + \sum_{i=1}^{4} \delta_i \Delta g_{t-i} + \sum_{i=1}^{4} \pi_i \Delta m2_{t-i} +$$

Lastly, Korea's import ban on rice was one of the most contentious topics of bilateral dispute between Korea and the United States in the 1990s. Negotiating pressure on Korea to remove the rice ban was focused in 1991 on the Uruguay Round of GATT negotiations. The United States tried to encourage Korea to end its import ban on rice and replace the ban with a tariff. The 1993 GATT agreement in agriculture, together with bilateral negotiations which provided the United States with greater leverage to achieve its objectives with Korea, would have devastated effects on Korea's food self-sufficiency by reducing the self-sufficiency ratio from 65 to 14 (Goldin and Knudsen 1990).

Other side effects of complete liberalization of the Korean rice market would not only put subsistence family farmers, most of them operating on a less than one-hectare farmland, out of business but also displace the farming population, which accounts 13.1 percent of the total population in 1992. Despite these fatalistic outcomes towards food security and self-sufficiency, and devastating effects on the farming population, Korea decided to open up its rice market to the U.S. starting in 1995 to import 3-5 percent of its rice requirement for 10 years and by the year 2005 completely liberalizing the rice market (Glasure and Lee 1995). This complete liberalization of the rice market was, in fact, quite contrary to President Kim's presidential campaign promise:[10] "I am going to stop the rice import at the cost of my presidency." At the end of the GATT agreement, President Kim fired two agricultural ministers for failing to protect farmers' interests while drawing up market opening measures. This action by Kim was precipitated by the opposition Democratic Party's accusation that Kim had traded the rice issue for a tougher U.S. stand on the inspection of North Korea's nuclear facilities after meeting with President Clinton in November 1993 and continued demonstration by farmers and students, who claimed that Kim succumbed to U.S. pressure.

Methods and Results

Vector Autoregressive Tests

Glasure and Lee (1999) show that the export-led growth hypothesis should be examined in the framework of the real exchange rate, monetary policy and fiscal policy, in the context of the export-led growth hypothesis model to empirically link the effects of trade conflict resolutions on Korea's economic and export performances. Following their approach, this paper develops a five-variable, first difference vector autoregressive (VAR) model.

where Δy, Δe, Δg, Δm, and Δxp respectively are real GDP, real exchange rate, real government spending, m2, and real exports in the first differences. D_i is a dummy variable i, where i = textiles and apparel, footwear, electronics, and steel products. α, β_i, γ_i, δ_i, π_i, ψ_i, and ω_i are coefficients to be estimated, and μ_t is a disturbance term. All the variables are in natural logarithms.

Table 3 presents results of the VAR in levels. Note that the VARs in levels are a valid specification for cointegrated systems and also are an alternative to the VARs in first differences with an error-correction term (Glasure and Lee 1997).[11] When real income is a dependent variable, only real exchange rates and money are significant at the 1% level, while government expenditure and exports are not even marginally significant. This implies that in the short-run, real exchange rates and money contain information on future movements in income, while government expenditures and exports do not. More interesting findings are dummy variables for electronics and textiles and apparel which have negative coefficients and are significant at the 5% level. The findings on those two dummies are consistent with Korea's market penetration strategy. As discussed earlier, Korea's exports of color TV receivers started in 1976, with a negligible amount. However, in 1978 Korean firms increased their production capacity by threefold to 1.1 million units per year to establish foothold in the U.S. market. When the U.S. put restraints on Korean exports of color TV receivers, capacity utilization fell to 34 percent in 1979. Similarly, textiles and apparel were major export items to the U.S. in the 1970s. In consequence, any major hindrance caused negative effects on income.

Also shown in Table 3 are results of the VAR in levels with real exports as a dependent variable. Here, exchange rates, government expenditure, real income are significant at the 1% level, thus signifying strong effects on exports. Hence, the finding on government expenditure supports the prevalent view among economists and policy-makers that Korea's rapid modernization and high sustained economic growth in the 1970s and 1980s are attributable to government intervention and guidance in the export markets with subsidy, tax reduction and low interest rates. Moreover, because of Korea's small, open economy which lacks natural resources such as oil and relies heavily on exports for its economic development, fluctuations in the real exchange rate had major impacts on both exports and income. Of the four dummy variables, only footwear is marginally significant at the 10% level with a positive coefficient. Although the U.S. restricted number of footwear exports from Korea, the final outcome called for increasing the number of pairs of shoes exported over the life of the agreement.

Vector Error Correction Tests

Although individual time series that contain stochastic trends are non-stationary in their levels, it is possible that stochastic trends are common across series, thus rendering stationary combinations of the levels. This is known as cointegration, which requires stationary residuals. To examine whether the five variables in the model are related in a long-run equilibrium manner, cointegration tests are performed for all five variables. The test statistics reveal that the non-stationarity of the residual of the five variables can be rejected at the 5% level.[12] We thus use the VECM model below to test for causality.

$$(2) \qquad A(L)\Delta x_t = \beta\delta' x_{t-1} + d(L)$$

where x is the n-vector of variables in the model, Δ is the first difference operator, δ is the n X r matrix of cointegrating vectors, β is an n X r matrix of coefficients, A(L) and d(L) are matrix polynomials in the lag operator L with A(0)=I, and ϵ_t is a zero-mean n-vector of white noise disturbances.

The procedure used here is the two-step procedure applied by Hall (1986). The model includes the lagged error correction term to capture the current period response of the cointegrated series to the prior period's disequilibrium. This establishes the long-run relationship, while the coefficients on the first difference variables capture the short-run dynamic response.

Table 4 reports results of the VECMs. With real income as a dependent variable, neither the macroeconomic variables nor the error-correction term is significant even at the 10% level. Moreover, only the dummy variable for electronics is marginally significant at the 10% level with a negative sign, thus negatively impacting income growth. When the dependent variable is exports, however, exchange rates, government expenditures and real income are significant either at the 5% or 1% level, but the error-correction term is not significant even at the 10% level. Of the dummy variables, only the dummy variable for electronics is significant at the 5% level and has a positive sign.

Summary and Conclusion

Trade conflict resolutions on textiles and apparel and electronics negatively impacted the Korean economy in the short-run, while resolutions on electronics had negative effects on income in the long-run. When the dependent variable is exports, trade resolutions on footwear positively influenced exports in the short-run and resolutions on electronics had a positive impact on export growth in the long-run. Also, government activities on export promotion through subsidy, tax reduction and low interest rates contributed to Korea's rapid modernization and high sustained economic growth in the 1970s and 1980s. Moreover, the exchange rate was an important factor in exports and income for Korea.

References

Ahsan, Syed M., Andy C. Kwan and Balbir S. Sahni, "Public Expenditure and National Income Causality: Further Evidence on the Role of Omitted Variables," Southern Economic Journal 59, January 1992, 623-34.

Bello, W. and S. Rosenfeld, "Dragons in Distress: The Crises of the NICs," World Policy Journal 7, 1990, 431-68.

Cheng, Benjamin S. and Tin Wei Lai, "Government Expenditures and Economic Growth in South Korea: A VAR Approach," Journal of Economic Development 22, June 1997, 11-24.

Cho, Yoon-Je, "How the United States Broke into Korea's Insurance Market," The World   Economy 10, December 1987, 483-96.

Far Eastern Economic Review, July 25, 1963; November 24, 1963.

GATT, Review of Developments in the Trading System, General Agreement on Tariffs and Trade, Geneva, 1988.

Glasure, Yong U. and Aie-Rie Lee, "The U.S.-Korea Conflict over Rice Liberalization: A Korean Perspective," Journal of Northeast Asian Studies 13(4), Winter 1994, 3-20.

Glasure, Y.U and A.R. Lee, "The Export-Led Growth Hypothesis: The Role of the Exchange Rate, Money and Government Expenditures from Korea," Atlantic Economic Journal, 27(3), forthcoming, September 1999.

Goldin, Ian and Odin Knudsen, "How Developing Countries Could Gain from Agricultural Trade Liberalization in the Uruguay Round", in Ian Goldin and Odin Knudsen (Eds.), Agricultural Trade Liberalization: Implications for Developing Countries, Washington, DC: The World Bank, 1990, 41-76.

Grier, Kevin B. and G. Tullock, "An Empirical Analysis of Cross-National

Economic Growth, 1951-80," Journal of Monetary Economics September 1989, 259-76.

Hall, S.G., "An Application of the Granger and Engle Two-Step Procedure to United Kingdom Aggregate Wage Data, Oxford Bulletin of Economics and Statistics 46, August 1986, 229-39.

Lee, Aie-Rie and Yong U. Glasure, "The Political Dynamics of Trade Negotiation: The Korea-U.S. Experience between 1960 and 1990," in Jung, Water and Xiao-Bing Li (eds.), Korea and Regional Geopolitics, 1999, 15-35.

Lim, Y., Government Policy and Private Enterprise: Korean Experience in Industrialization, Berkeley, CA: University of California Press, 1985.

Odell, John S, "The Outcomes of International Trade Conflicts: The US and South Korea," International Studies Quarterly 29, September 1985, 263-86.

Odell, John S, "Growing Trade and Growing Conflict between the Republic of Korea and the United States," in Karl Moskowitz (Ed.), From Patron to Partner: The Development of U.S.-Korean Business and Trade Relations, Lexington, MA: D.C. Heath and Company, 1984.

Petri, Peter A., "Korea's Export Niche: Origins and Prospects," World Development 16, January, 1988, 47-63.

Piazolo, Marc, "Determinants of South Korean Economic Growth, 1955-1990," International Economic Journal 9, winter 1995, 109-33.

Sato, Hideo, "The Political Dynamics of US-Japan Economic Conflicts," Journal of North East Asian Studies 3, Winter 1984, 3-24.

USDC, US Foreign Trade Highlights, various issues.

USITC, Operation of the Trade Agreements Program, 39th-45th Reports, 1988-1995.

U.S. Federal Register, January 9, 1976, 1587-89.

Yoffie, David, <u>Power and Protectionism</u>, New York: Columbia University Press, 1983, 183.

Appendix

Variables

The variables in the model are: rgdp, real GDP; rexch, real exchange rate; rgov, real government spending (a proxy for government activities, following Cheng and Lai (1997), Ahsan, *et al.* (1992), Piazolo (1995), and Grier and Tullock (1989); m2, money supply; and rxpt, real exports. The real exchange rate is defined as rexch $= e(p^f/p)$, where e is the nominal exchange rate, expressed as Korean wons per U.S. dollar, p^f is the U.S. gdp deflator and p is the Korean gdp deflator. All the variables are in natural logarithm.

Data

Seasonally adjusted quarterly Korean data are from The Bank of Korea's Historical Statistics diskette, 1995. The U.S. GDP deflator (base year=1987) is from the Federal Reserve Bank of Saint Louis. To be consistent with the Korean data, the U.S. GDP deflator is converted to base year 1990.

The effects of trade conflict resolutions are measured by dummy variables. This articles underscores four dummy variables based upon groups of products involved in the U.S. market -- textiles and apparel (text), footwear (foot), electronics (elect), and steel products (steel). The duration of a resolution on the commodity group is coded as 1 and otherwise, 0. In other words, if the restraint on the commodity group starts from January 1973 to December 1975, the dummy variable takes a value of 1 from 1973:1 to 1975:4, otherwise, 0.

TABLE 1

TRADE DISPUTES INVOLVING KOREAN PRODUCTS IN U.S.
MARKET, 1960-1992

Outcome	Disputes
More favorable to Korean initial position	None initial
Intermediate	1972 textiles and apparels 1974 textiles and apparels 1977 footwear orderly marketing agreement 1986 textiles and apparels
More favorable to U.S. initial position	1976 footwear countervailing duty case 1977 textiles and apparels 1979 color television receivers 1979 textiles and apparels 1980 color television receivers 1980 textiles and apparels 1981 textiles and apparels 1986 pipe fittings 1987 stainless steel cookware 1987 brass sheet and strip 1988 color picture tubes 1992 television receiving sets

Sources: Odell (1984, Table 7-3, 127); various issues of USITC publications.

TABLE 2

TRADE DISPUTES INVOLVING U.S. PRODUCTS IN
KOREAN MARKETS

1979-1994

Outcome	Disputes
More favorable to Korean initial position	None
Intermediate	1979 insurance market share 1989 telecommunications (tariffs, government procurement, market access)
More favorable to U.S. initial position	1988 beef import restriction 1988 cigarettes import restriction and tariff reduction 1988 wine import restriction 1988 motion pictures import restriction 1989 intellectual property rights protection 1991 rice ban 1994 beef-pork import restriction 1994 automobile market access

Sources: USDC, US Foreign Trade Highlights, various issues; Far Eastern
Economic Review.

Asia's Crisis and New Paradigm

TABLE 3

RESULTS OF THE LEVEL VECTOR
AUTOREGRESSIVE MODELS

Variable	F-value	t-value
Dependent variable = rgdp		
rexch	3.89^c	
rgov	0.48	
m2	3.86^c	
rxpt	0.69	
steel		-0.23
elect		-2.54^b
foot		1.32
text		-1.86^b
Dependent variable = rxpt		
rexch	3.79^c	
rgov	4.64^c	
m2	1.87	
rgdp	2.69^b	
steel		-0.67
elect		-0.65
foot		1.76^a
text		0.27

Note: [a,b,c] denote significance at the 10%, 5% and 1% levels, respectively.

TABLE 4

RESULTS OF THE VECTOR
ERROR-CORRECTION MODELS

Variable	F-value	t-value
Dependent variable = drgdp		
drexch	0.49	
drgov	0.26	
dm2	1.48	
drxpt	0.54	
ec		-0.35
steel		0.33
elect		-1.61[a]
foot		-0.36
text		0.57
Dependent variable = drxpt		
drexch	2.76[b]	
drgov	4.48[c]	
dm2	0.67	
drgdp	2.71[b]	
ec		-0.81
steel		-1.15
elect		2.09[b]
foot		0.68
text		0.27

Note: [a,b,c] denote significance at the 10%, 5% and 1% levels, respectively.
ec is an error-correction term.

Endnotes

1. The effects of trade conflict resolutions involving U.S. products in the Korean market are not examined; however, this article fully discusses the resolutions for completeness.

2. The authors update Lee and Glasure's (1999) work on this area. The interested audience should refer to "The Political Dynamics of Trade Negotiation: The Korea-U.S. Experience between 1960 and 1990," in Jung, Water and Xiao-Bing Li (eds.), Korea and Regional Geopolitics, 1999, 15-35.

3. Journal of Commerce, March 11, 1971.

4. U.S. Federal Register, January 9, 1976, 1587-89.

5. In 1976, the TV import market share was up to 33 percent, mostly from Japan and some from Taiwan.

6. Wall Street Journal, October 14, 1978.

7. Wall Street Journal, October 14 and November 24, 1978.

8. Wall Street Journal, January 9, 1979.

9. Lubbock Avalanch-Journal, September 29, 1995, C9.

10. Far Eastern Economic Review, December 16, 1993, 13.

11. For cointegration tests, see the section on Error-Correction Tests.

12. The estimated statistics for the cointegration equations respectively are -3.02 and -2.91 when the dependent variables are rgdp and rxpt. The critical value from Fuller (1976, p.373) is -2.89 with the intercept when the sample size is 100.

Chapter 4

An Analysis of the Asian Financial Crisis

Yajie Wang

The Asian Financial Crisis that broke out in July of 1997 was and is the most serious financial upheaval since the Great Depression of the 30's. It will have a profound affect on the world economy as a whole. This essay, from the point of view of China and other Pacific Rim countries, shall attempt to disclose and prove that the source of the Crisis lies in deficiencies with the existing International Monetary System. Moreover, we shall discuss the necessity for reform of the System, with emphasis on the key position by the United States.

The structure of the paper will be as follows: Section 1 will present a description of the Asian Financial Crisis; its background and its diffusion. Section 2 gives some analysis in the necessity for the System's restructuring. Section 3 emphasizes the key role that America should play in the reform of the System.

Background of the Asian Financial Crisis and its Diffusion

Background

The international environment of free finance and the distempered Asian economic construction consists of the background of Asian Monetary Crisis.

First, let us view from the aspect of international environment: In the past thirty years, there appeared in the global financial field a wave of financial innovation and deregulation. It is now growing stronger and stronger, which can be taken as main characteristics of the current international economic environment.

The so-called financial deregulation actually suggests loosening the financial control, namely the governmental behavior of supervising capital movement, which chiefly involves the loosening of exchange rate. The main body of financial innovation is financial instrument innovation, which in turn, is closely related to the financial control evasion. While in a furious and competitive financial environment is full of risks, the banking authorities will enact certain decrees so as to supervise financial institutions, while the latter, driven by the profitability, can continuously create some financial tools which are beyond the reach of financial control. Therefore, the process of financial innovation is indeed a gaming of deregulation and control. Meanwhile, the innovation of financial tools compel the government to loosen its supervision, thereby, financial deregulation is an inevitable result of financial innovation.

The US Dollar-leading international monetary system ultimately results in the financial deregulation.

Financial deregulation originated in the U.S. in the 1960's. The U.S. dollar-centered Bretton Woods system enabled the United States to be a main supplier of international currency. In order to meet the great domestic and overseas demand for dollars, the U.S. government increasingly issued dollar, which consequently brought down on currency inflation. Under such a high inflation, Both enterprises and individuals begun to maintain value for the nominal earning of their assets in possession, hereby the capital mobility went down. For financial institutions, a declining mobility meant a descending profitability. Hence, they adopted a dear- money policy accordingly so as to put the high inflation under control, which was the most effective method.

But, owing to the existence of the American banking Financial Code, Regulation Q, the upper limit of bank savings was set, sequentially embarrassing the efforts of those monetary financial intermediary organs, such as banks, to absorb deposits and scramble for funds. Under such high inflation and high exchange rate, both enterprises and residents have been gradually shrinking their investments on those financial assets whose earning rate is declining, whereas, they are paying more and more attention on those with high exchange rate and strong liquidity. Hence, the innovation of the financial instruments appeared, which can avoid supervision. The increase of financial transaction instruments, types and channels further stimulated the development and integration of financial market. Accompanying the integration, the international capital mobility grew. Under such a global environment, the fusty laws and regulations financial administration had become obstacles for global economic development. Leading under developed countries, the financial control stepped down, while the deregulation wave swept the entire globe, which inevitably impacted on those newly developed industrial countries swiftly growing up in Asia.

In a word, the characteristics of the monetary system that focused on U.S. dollars is to unceasingly supply U.S. dollars and eventually incurred a higher velocity of increase of the dollars than that of the U.S. economy. Thus, the inflation was inevitable, or, we can say that it was the system that initiated the inflation. The current international monetary system is still an U.S. dollar leading one. It acted actively in the process of financial deregulation.

Secondly, let us view from the aspect of Asian economy: Fairly speaking, the economic development situation of each country in Asia cannot adapt, or cannot wholly adapt such an international environment. In order to get rid of their backward and impoverished condition and to realize economic leap at an early date, many Asian countries are in pursuit of the velocity of economic increase and the expansion of scale. The path they followed was an extensive one; the things they depended on were massive input of foreign and domestic funds instead of adjusting the industrial structure in time. They relied too much on tourism, services, real estate and securities industry, thus, bubble economy and temporary prosperity occurred.

For the fast growth of economy caused by high input, the world had once looked upon Asia with new eyes and over-expected its prospect. A large sum of fund poured into this area and there was not any advanced and strict system of finance and supervision. This plus the labor-intensive structure of industry made the countries in Southeast Asia tied heavily on foreign capital. Early entrance into deregulation array of the developed financial countries and the adoption of fixed exchange rate with U.S. dollars brought about dilemma when they tried to keep international payment balance and to keep domestic economy balance. However, the best way out is to declare currency depreciation and give up fixed rate system, hence solicit crisis. In a word, the fix rate mechanism under current floating exchange rate system was the source and focus of crisis. The financial crisis was spreading in almost all the countries that the fixed rate system.

Diffusion of the Crisis

Asian monetary crisis first started from Thailand, a Southeast Asian country and it quickly spread out to its surrounding countries. From July to September 1997, Thailand, Singapore, Malaysia and Philippines bogged down into crisis; from October to November, the crisis effected Taiwan and Hong Kong; in December Indonesia joined the group. Meanwhile Japan and South Korea in East Asia got involved and it impacted Mainland China, Latin American countries like Mexico and Columbia. At the end of April 1998, Japanese economy was in confronted with hot potato that it had never had before. Following that, in August, Russian Ruble depreciated half of its value.

After the placidity during the second half of the year 1998, when people begun to expect that the economy in Asian countries would make a recovery, financial turbulence emerged in Brazil, economically speaking the world eighth strongest country and the most strongest in Latin America. The depreciation of the currency cruzeiro reached as high as 30%. Again the stock market fluctuated, and it fluctuated to such an extent that the U.S. and West European stock markets suffered seriously. Consequently, it became another focus of the world financial community. Brazil is called as " the backyard of U.S.A. " or " the rear area ". Its financial fluctuation directly threatens the U.S. and what we should worry about is that the victim seemed to be in next in line. And the fluctuation of U.S. shocked the entire globe.

Viewing through the spread of Asian financial crisis, every country tried to give up fixed exchange rate system. This showed that the current monetary system is on the verge of death and destruction. A revolution is imperative under the situation.

The Necessity for Reform of the International Monetary System

Now let us discuss the abuses of current international monetary system and the necessity for its reform. The main abuses are:

1). The current International Monetary System is the floating Exchange Rate System which is to some extent an alternative to the fixed one for Asian developing countries, namely, is a pegged exchange rate system.

In order to make a better explanation on the essences of the current international monetary system, it is necessary for us to run back over the history of international monetary system. Before World War I, Britain was extremely influential in the world economy. Sterling became the sole reserve currency. The gold standard system era before 1914 has been viewed as the typical fixed exchange rate system. Since the outbreak of World War I in 1914 as country after country suspended the convertibility of its currency into gold, gold standard system gave way to gold bullion standard system and gold exchange standard system. After World War II, the international monetary system that led by the U.S. dollars was also a kind of fixed exchange rate system.

However, there lied a significant difference that under gold standard system the fixed exchange rate system came into being unprompted. As gold was imported and exported permissively, with gold export point serving as the ceiling of the market exchange rate and gold import point as the floor, the fixed exchange rate could be realized automatically, hence such an exchange rate system was rather stable. Under the fixed exchange rate system that led by the U.S. dollars, the exchange rate mechanism was man-made, which was greatly influenced by man-induced factors and could probably be not in conformity with the economic development in reality. The value of the currency could be overestimated or underestimated. When the currency was overvalued, there would exist the crisis of depreciation. The disintegration of the Bretton Woods system verified it.

In 1970's, Jamaica System was established. It was nothing but an extension of the Bretton Woods system born in 1944 that led by the U.S. dollars. Although floating rate was extensively implemented. Such a floating system was a patent for developed countries. For the large group of developing countries, especially for those emerging industrial countries in Asia, it was a pegged exchange rate system bound with the U.S. dollars, which bore with itself the characteristics of fixed exchange rate. When such a system first came into being in Asian countries, governments of each country would keep a fixed parity between the U.S. dollars and their own currencies, based on practical situation of local economy. It could, in some way, suit the export-oriented economic pattern of Asian countries and promote economy expansion. But once currency overvaluation occurred in the rigid exchange rate system, it would add to the export cost and cause deficit in current account.

What is more? An even worse defect in the pegged exchange rate was that the Central Bank could have no independent monetary policy. In order to keep a static exchange rate, the Central Bank had to passively buy in and sell out foreign exchange in the exchange market and try to keep the change of interest rate coincident between their local currency and the U.S. dollars. Thus, the inherent discrepancies in local economy were piled up and enlarged and the vulnerability of local economy was intensified and expanded.

Under the flag of deregulation, such a system allowed the international capital that was in pursuit of exorbitant profits to flow in and out of the countries ceaselessly, thereby, bubble economy broke down in good time and financial crisis engendered. Take Thailand for example, on one hand, currency was overvalued and current account endured unfavorable balance. However, in order to maintain exterior balance and keep conformity with the interest rate of the U.S. dollars, Thailand raised its exchange rate to absorb foreign investment. According to macro-economical analysis under closed economic condition, high interest rate will lead to deflationary domestic economy. However, with an inflow of large sum of foreign funds, slackened credit and high interest rate were co-existent inside the country and interior unbalance occurred. Consequently, bubble economy yielded.

This pegged exchange rate system was based on the stability of the U.S. dollars and that the pegging currency depended on the pegged currency. Eventually, the unbalanced domestic and foreign economy was induced and became a hidden trouble for the crisis.

2). The current international monetary system is regarded as a three-pole system. By December 31, 1998, U.S. dollar, Japanese Yen and Deutsche mark had been considered as the three poles. From January 1, 1999, Eurodollar took the place of Deutsche mark. But can Eurodollar possibly become a pole of international monetary system and what influence will the start-up of Eurodollar bring about to the entire international exchange rate mechanism?

With the collapse of the Bretton Woods System, global exchange rate system entered into a disorderly and unsystematic floating rate stage. The launch of Eurodollar indicated unification of the currencies in various European countries and in nature, it actualized the union of fixed rate system. The persistent rapid growth of trade surplus in European Union and the much higher gross assets deposits than those of the U.S. dollars provided solid foundation for the rise of Eurodollars.

However, there still existed a lot of factors that constrained its stability:

Owing to historical reasons the leading position of the U.S. dollars can hardly be altered. Firstly, the U.S. economy has remained mighty influence in global economy. Secondly, the inertia of investment that is led by the U.S. dollar can hardly be modified.

The mightiness of European Political Union is the key to restrict the stability of Eurodollars.

Because of the differences in the economical development level and price level of the 11 countries in Europe, the substantial factor for the stability of Eurodollars is whether a stable and uniform price system is to be formed. Therefore, The Eurodollars still can not stand against the U.S. dollars at present or even within a period of time, and obviously, its function in international monetary system is weaker than the U.S. dollars. Take Japanese yen for example. Intervened by the finance ministers of the Five West Countries, the exchange rate of Japanese yen began to rise in 1985, while the exchange rate of U.S. dollars declined; and the exchange rate once reached to as high as 83.65 Japanese yen for one U.S. dollar.

This increase had lasted out for 10 years that it was said that the 21st century would be the era of Japanese yen. However, from the end of 1980s' to the beginning of 90s', the bubble economy led to an economic depression that lasted for 6 years. Finally the Japanese yen was depreciated so seriously that the Japanese yen declined to 146 yen for one U.S. dollar, and the Asian Monetary Crisis was restarted. Japanese economy is, in one way or another, similar to that of those new industrial countries in Asia except that defects appeared in the economic structure while being transformed from manufacturing to a higher level---financial deregulation was implemented in a distempered financial system---thus, bubble economy came into being.

There will be a long way to go for Japanese economy to recover and Japanese yen is between the beetle and the block in international monetary system. Thereby, among the three poles in international monetary system, U.S. dollar still remains its prevailing situation. Meanwhile the developing countries can not shake off their dependence on the U.S. dollars. Apparently, it is a sign of unsuitability that the focal point of international monetary system inclines toward the U.S.A. It indicates that the current international monetary system is nothing but a reprint of the Bretton Woods system.

3). The financial deregulation pursued by the System encourages international speculative capital to run rampant. In addition, speculative capital avails itself of loopholes in the pegged system, thus leading to the inevitability of the Crisis occurring.

International hot money, or the international speculative capital, the flows of it can reach very large proportions mainly in pursuit of higher profits or exorbitant profits. Under the international environment of financial deregulation, large flows of hot money poured into southeastern countries and combined with local economy, hence induced financial turbulence.

According to the estimates made by International Monetary Fund, the international speculative capital that frequently flow into and out of each market is approximately 7,200 billion U.S. dollars which equals to 20% of annual gross global economic output. In 1997, the total amount of exchange in the eight major foreign exchange markets reaches to as high as 1300 billion U.S. dollars. If we double the world economic growth rate, which is 3%, the growth rate of international capital flows would become over 6% in 1997.

The main source of world speculative capital is U.S.A., with the gross U.S. funds as a proof. Before the breakdown of stock catastrophe in 1987, there were 812 joint stock funds all over the U.S.A. the capital they were in charge of amounted to 241.9 billion U.S. dollars. By the end of June 1997, the figures had increased to 2,855 and 2,310 billion respectively. Since the U.S. funds account for more than half of the entire world funds, and the U.S. government carries out loose administration over them from the legal point of view. We can see the prospect of the international capital market through the development of U.S. funds.

How much on earth is the international capital? There is as prolific as a country. It is not egregious to say that it can put any central bank or the economy of any single country to rout.

In an open financial market, people can not identify investment capital from speculative capital among the mammoth of international capital. When investment capital is introduced into southeastern countries in the form of direct investment, it could transform into speculative capital. Then, how have they been transformed? One is sufficient financial freedom; the other is the pegged exchange rate system in southeastern countries. Under such a system, when individual capital flowed into the countries, it is allowed to exchange into much more local currencies on the basis of illicit market. Whereas, when individual capital flowed out of the countries, it could exchange more foreign currencies based on the pegged rate. Moreover, the capital was loosely supervised in local area. It could easily be invested in real estate, thus, fosterage bubble economy in these countries and eventually made the breakout of crisis unavoidable.

4). The organization and institution of the System, the IMF's "post-coordination" and its "common prescription for various ailment", make people lose confidence in the System.

IMF has in many ways bestowed aids to Indonesia, Thailand and South Korea and the aids had made, to some effect, positive impact. However, negative effect had offset the positive one. People are more willingly to see IMF, with abundant experiments, establish a monitoring mechanism and alarm or warn the countries or areas that are on the edge of crisis and avert the burst of crisis. Besides, IMF has put forward identical blueprint for the Asian countries to reform, for example, deflationary monetary and fiscal policies.

As a result, contrary to their anticipation, the economic recession emerged. According to classical economics formula, deflationary monetary and fiscal policies can dispel trade deficit and maintain international balance of payments. However, for Asia, since the economic crisis has brought about austerity, it will doubtlessly result in economic recession if the restraining policy is implemented in these countries.

5). The System cannot be corrected through the "Triffin Problem". The U.S. dollar's stability is the key factor in stabilizing the System, while inherent contradictions within the System pose a serious threat to America itself.

The existence of "Triffin Problem" lying in the international monetary system that is based on the U.S. dollar finally disintegrated the system. However, the shadow of this Problem still exists in the present international monetary system. Viewing from the current international reserves in various countries, there are multiplex international reserves. However, viewing from a global aspect, the U.S. dollars dominates the reserves, with a share of about 60%. The stability of the U.S. dollars becomes a key to the stability of the international reserves in every other country. Thus, those countries whose reserves currency is the U.S. dollars have no choice but to be manipulated by American economic policy.

In particular, those Dollar-pegging Asian countries which, in one way or the other, depended on the U.S.A., when under the pressure of whether dollars could be stable or not, more often than not, they would formulate policies to maintain a balance between the U.S. dollars and the currencies of their own. Therefore, as a result, either the binding force of local economic policy on local economy has been lightened or the policy is so much self-concerned that it may be detrimental to other countries. In the course of time, the complete international monetary system would trap in chaos.

The mechanism of the system requires the U.S.A. to undertake a responsibility of maintaining the integrity and stability of the international monetary system. IMF has contributed a great deal of assistance so as to stick up for a stable Asian economy. Since the U.S.A. is the largest partner in IMF, it has also got a commitment to Asia. But once the crisis bursts out for a second time, the cost of the American assistance will definitely increase, capital provided through IMF will run out at last, and the U.S.A. itself will strike a bad patch.

Just because there are abuses in present international monetary system, it is necessary to carry out reform, and the U.S.A. should set the pace for the world.

America's Key Role in
Reforming the International Monetary System

Owing to the its position in international monetary system, the U.S.A. is expected to assume more in reforming present international monetary system.

This means that, first of all, the U.S.A. should play a crucial role in intensifying the super-national financial supervisory function if IMF:

1). Financial deregulation is a trend that does not preclude the sequenced administration of international capital's speculative flow. The

U.S.A. should take the lead to change the dominant idea that the higher the degree of freedom is the better the finance will be and to urge IMF to carry on supervisory mechanism.

a). Bring under control the entrance of international hot money into other countries, esp. the developing countries, by means of laws and decrees or suitable policy. Since the U.S.A. is the maker of various financial innovation instruments which enter into other countries with various style. It is a strike to these countries and will eventually impair America itself.

b). The great amount flows of foreign direct investment into the developing countries should be also under strict supervision so as to prevent conversion into speculative capital.

2). The effects of the administrative floating system will be chronic, and every nation will set their own exchange rate policies on a case by case basis.

For example, exchange rate of RMB is based on the supply and demand of market. It is a single, administered floating exchange rate system. Since the breakout of financial crisis in 1997, esp. the devaluation of Japanese Yen, induced tremendous negative effect on the Chinese economy. Firstly, the devaluation of currencies in the surrounding countries imposed massive concussion on the export of Chinese goods. As RMB managed not to depreciate, the cost of export increased, thereby, Chinese export took up inferior position in international competition. Secondly, currency depreciation in surrounding countries imposed great pressure on China when she competed with other countries for foreign direct investment. However, in order to maintain economic stability in Asia and reduce impact of financial crisis on other Asian countries, Chinese government insisted her commitment of non-depreciation of RMB and kept the rate of RMB to the U.S. dollars at a level of 8.27: 1. China contributed a great deal for that and for the stability of Asian and global economy. In the year 1999, China will keep on with its policy of a steady exchange rate for RMB. She will carry out appropriate monetary policy, intensify financial supervision and stimulate the development of economy.

Similar to RMB, linked exchange rate system of Hongkong dollar, with its unique exchange rate mechanism, withstood with the two strikes of international hot money. In the Defense of Hongkong Stock Market in Sep 1998, one eighth of its foreign exchange reserves were lost, manifesting the stability of its exchange rate mechanism and the strength of its economy and a necessity of governmental intervention in maintaining a stable exchange rate. But, if no restraint is imposed on international hot money and Hongkong will have to pay much more for the victory of an anti-snipe, the world will see an unprecedented financial turbulence and the world foreign exchange reserves will be exhausted.

If the U.S.A. could promote ordered administration of international hot money, it will become a magnificent assistance for stabilizing the Asian or even the global finance. The effect of such a backing is going to surpass the function of aids from IMF after the crisis.

3). When extending credits and aids to the developing countries, if IMF can modify its original rules and prerequisites, it will surely receive warm welcome from Asian countries. The credits or aids extended by IMF to its member countries are limited by the amount of shares the member countries render. Since developing countries render fewer shares, they can get comparatively fewer loans, which are of no help. Besides, there are rigorous conditions along with the rendered aids that operate negatively on the economic growth of developing countries. Hereby, it is time for the U.S.A. to take a global viewpoint and offer the developing countries with support, an air a world power should have.

Second, with a viewpoint to reform international monetary system, it is necessary for America to further strengthen its administration on domestic short-term capital and hot money. Special legal restriction should also be imposed on funds and black money so as to float rationally.

Third, IMF and WTO should render assistance according to the situation and sovereign rights of various countries instead of the practice that exchanges assistance with commitments for a highly deregulated financial mechanism. Intensified administration is also required so that international capital can float orderly under control.

Finally, establishment of an international monetary system that coordinates multilaterally will be a trend for the reform. Active propelling for its realization will help the U.S.A. gain world's respect. The Asian Financial Storm shows that there is no other way out but to remodel the international monetary system. But the reform can not accomplish immediately. Before fundamental reform, we should at first constrain the hot money to do harm to the world. America should take the leading in associating with other great countries and each monetary group in the world so as to establish a harmonious multilateral monetary system and poise the relationship among the interest groups of America, developed countries and developing countries.

Conclusion: The Asian Financial Crisis still threatens to spread. The United States must play an active leadership role in the reformation of the International Monetary System, otherwise it too could be engulfed, leading to a global calamity of the first order.

Chapter 5

The Touchstone:
Southeast Asian Financial Crisis

Xiaoxiao Li

On September 26,1995, at the capital city of South Africa, Dr. Zunyi Liu from Stanford University predicted in his analysis of the financial activities of the world that there would be a "Next Mexico" in Southeast Asia. Despite the disputes of scholars from some of the Southeast Asian Countries, a thunderstorm of financial turmoil swept all over Thailand, Malaysia, Indonesia, the Philippines, and South Korea with strong waves striking Japan, Singapore, Hong Kong, even affecting American west coast exports in July, 1997.

The influences of the financial crisis are great and continuing. The world sees big currency devaluation in Thailand, Malaysia, and Indonesia, and has experienced wide stock market fluctuations in Hong Kong, Japan, and Singapore. Bankruptcies of giant steel plants such as Dawoo as well as the economic difficulties in South Korea have made us look more into negative impacts and to understand better that financial crisis in one region directly and indirectly influences other regions, especially those which have close trade contacts with each other. The global economy has been damaged badly by bank disasters in Japan, where people's dreams have been broken with the explosion of the typical bubble economy. Setback of exports as well as imports in many countries dependent on Southeast Asia's economy such as Australia and New Zealand have laid dark shadow on these countries' economic development. The activities of the directors of the World Bank and the International Monetary Fund regarding Southeast Asian countries have attracted much scientific analysis investigating the Asian crisis and offering theories for its solution. The whole world was astonished by this economic downpour which almost destroyed the total regional economy, whose growth rare formerly amazed the world. The shocked world turned its eyes to China. How and when China would react and respond to this crisis has become a serious question.

This article will review the Chinese viewpoint immediately after the financial crisis and during the process of its spreading all over the world and try to clarify the reasons why China has been so confident and consistent in its methods of tackling this financial problem. Furthermore, this paper will also suggest some points about what should be done to prevent this kind of financial crisis so as to make the gap between the rich and poor countries closer, to allocate world resources more efficiently, and to bring about more real benefits as well as an essential improvement of the world economy as a whole.

First of all, during and after the Southeast Asian financial crisis, China does and will have a lot of choices based on its steadily improving economy. Standing at the front line of the Chinese economic reform, Chinese leaders see clearly the negative impacts of the crisis on the competitiveness of Chinese exports, which will directly influence the government's economic growth target: an 8 percent growth rate in the total 1998 economy.

Actually, China has experienced more difficulties caused by this crisis than any other country in the world. The real economic growth rate in 1998 was 7.8%, slightly lower than expected. Exports dropped greatly compared with the previous period. The increasing numbers of laid-off workers from state-owned companies and factories have threatened potential harm to the political stability. Foreign investments have diminished. The cost of exports has been rising so much that the Chinese government has had to reinstate the Value-Added-Tax-Return policy, which was originallyy supposed to be eliminated gradually and finally discontinued in 1998. The Value-Added-Tax-Return policy supports the companies and manufacturers in China with a returnable tax rate from 13 percent to 17 percent, a great increase compared to that of the time before the Asian crisis. That means the government will give back the tax it first takes from companies and manufacturers for the goods that have been exported as a compensation to the companies and manufacturers to cover probable increased export costs. The purpose of the tax return is to offset the pressure of the Southeast Asian financial crisis and to encourage businesses to maintain and even enlarge exports. Furthermore, China has suffered in 1998 the most serious flooding in several hundred years. The direct losses were more than $40 billion. To sum up, all these problems provided good excuses for the Chinese government to shift its burdens caused by the financial crisis.

However, despite these difficulties the Chinese government declared again and again that the Chinese currency (the Renminbi) would stay firm and not devaluate. Not long ago the vice-minister of the Finance Ministry of China said in Singapore that the Renminbi would stay fixed despite the pressures caused by the incorrect expectations for the Renminbi. The same idea was expressed by Li Ruogu, director of the department of the International Financial Organization of the Bank of China. He said, "We need to correct some wrong perception for Renminbi. Its value is decided by the economic foundational structure. Now the rate has already confirmed this support."[1] He also added that China has accepted other means to strengthen exports instead of devaluating the Renminbi, mainly by increasing the market demand and reinstating the Value-Added-Tax-Return policy.

He pointed out that some people believe the only way and the main factor to expanding exports is by devaluation of its currency. But if countries try to devaluate their currencies, there will be no way or any possibility of solving the problem. According to a statistics report exports from January to July 1999 have been recovering from a decline in China: 10.8%, 10.5%, 7.9%, 7.8%, 5.3%, 4.6%, and 2.8% (The percentage of decline becomes smaller every month onward). As we can project here, if China had devaluated its currency plus employed the government policy support, the state-owned import and export companies and the manufacturers of export products would have never had problems of export growth and profitability.

Besides this the Chinese government offered a $1 billion loan to Thailand and more than $2 billion to the International Monetary Fund

(IMF) for IMF's emergency-support plan. The world is very much impressed by China's attitude towards this financial crisis. It is said that this has shown to some extent the maturity of China to deal with the economic and market problems under its reform to shift from a centrally planned economic system to a free market system. Now it has become very clear that the positive aspects of China's insistence not to depreciate its currency are much stronger than the negative impacts.

First, this attitude of not devaluating showed the strong confidence of the Chinese government in its political stability, continuing economic growth, and determination for the success of the targeted economic reform. When re-elected, the president of the People's Republic of China, Jiang Zemin, said, "The people will highly hold the great banner of Deng Xiaoping's economic theory; continuously liberate our thoughts; be more practical and realistic; intensify our economic reform; expand more openly our gate towards the outside world; speed up to transfer from the old centrally controlled economy to a new market based economic system and new type of economic growth; stick to the policy to run our country by law, and greatly develop science and technology."2 He also expressed his hope that when the Chinese people celebrate the country's one hundred-year anniversary, the country will be modernized, prosperous, civilized, and democratic.

At that time China will be one of the medium developed countries, and the Chinese people will reach a higher standard of living based on modernization. The Chinese people will welcome the country's rejuvenation. During the press conference, the newly elected premier Zhu Rongji said, "The Asian financial crisis will not influence the development of our reform of government-owned enterprises and the increased pace of Chinese financial reform either."3   All these manifested China's responsibility and growing importance in regional affairs. On September 28,1998, Lins Rohner said in an article published in Fortune that "China is the real economic wild card. In the wars of nerves between bulls and bears, China is the key. If it stays strong, another round of currency collapses can be avoided."4

Secondly, the Chinese government declared its currency would not depreciate because of the clearly practical factors of macro economic development and favorable trend in its international balance of payment. At present China's macro economic situation is good. The financial movement is stable, and grain storage is at its highest record in history. The foreign exchange reserve is also at its largest amount in history, sufficient enough to back up the bad influence of the financial crisis. These gains are a result of government macro- control and the policy of high growth rate and low inflation, which is quite different from that of Southeast Asian countries. As reported by Elaine Kurtenbach on March 8,1998, "To overcome Asia's financial upheavals, China is stepping up investment, easing controls on banks and getting its finances in order."5 She also stated that the central bank governor Dai Xianglong said China would tap its underdeveloped market of 1.3 billion people to weather the Asian crisis, while avoiding moves such as a depreciation of its currency that might worsen the situation elsewhere. The economic turmoil in neighboring countries has dimmed prospects for China's exports and foreign investments at a time when its own growth is slowing and millions of workers are losing their jobs in downsizing state-owned industries.

Also, as predicted by the Political and Economic Risk Consultancy, Ltd. on October 25, 1997, the economic risk of China continues to lessen. One big challenge for the Chinese leadership in the short term probably lies in its ability to continue to attract foreign investment into the country in sufficient amounts to sustain modernization momentum. Direct investment has already showed signs of weakening this year. In recognition of this, Zhu Rongji, the premier minister, announced that some investment incentives for foreign companies that were abolished in 1996 would be re-introduced. In particular, import tax breaks on equipment needed by businesses are likely to be restored on a case-by-case basis. The continued inflow of indirect investment capital into China also cannot be taken for granted; Hong Kong's share market, which is the main vehicle through which this capital is being raised, is bound to suffer setbacks periodically.

Some of them--such as the plunge on October 23--could be very steep and quite prolonged, which would be bad news for a China which has grown dependent on this well of funds. The reports from other channels also show China in a worried mood. Seth Faison, in the New York Times on January 15,1998, said that the pressures on the Beijing authorities are strong. Chinese banks are saddled with untold billions of dollars in bad debt and are caught in a wrenching shift from a planned economy to one driven by market forces. Should depositors lose confidence in China's state-run banks, which depend on the nation's 40 percent savings rate to function, the financial system could falter. In 1998, China is trying to engineer a big sell-off of state-owned industries, and there is a pressing need for domestic and foreign investment, both of which seem to be receding. Should the financial crisis spread to China, tens of millions of urban workers may well be unemployed.

Further pessimistic views conclude that China, conspicuously immune so far during the crisis, won't escape unscathed. Beijing's industrial modernization drive is largely financed by investors from Hong Kong, Southeast Asia, and Taiwan-places where many companies suddenly have less capital to put into the mainland. Adding to the squeeze, sharp currency devaluation is making such countries as Thailand and Indonesia more formidable export competitors to China. Thailand's 54 percent surge in exports in September 1997 may well be a hint of what lies ahead for the region as a whole.

Despite all these problems the Chinese leadership has insisted on increasing its investments in agriculture, science and technology, and fundamental infrastructures as highways, railroads, and energy sources, etc. Dai Xianglong, central bank governor, asserted that China will still keep its currency firm, an ethical and moral responsibility that a big country like China should sustain. Dai said that capital spending-investment in roads, ports, housing, factories and equipment-would climb 15 percent in 1998.

Overall, China plans to spend the equivalent of about $1 trillion to stimulate the economy. Dai said that the figure included both public and private investments and that it would be spread over the next three years. The adjustment outlined by Dai is evidence of a broad program to fortify the economy and wean it from central planning. At the same time China also announced reforms to curb bureaucratic meddling in the economy, fight waste and corruption, and halve the country's total of 8 million civil servants. So in this way the reform of state-owned enterprises is speeded up and exports are expanded for the purpose of maintaining high economic growth. Such are the actions taken by the Chinese leadership to stabilize its currency exchange rate from devaluation.

This is what China has been doing to offset the influence of the financial crisis. It is estimated that with the improving economic atmosphere in Southeast Asian countries, China would keep its annual growth rate around 6.5%. The Chinese economy now is still stagnating. Although the government has spent large sums of money to stimulate consumption, the peoples' expectation about future spending is much bigger and this encourages them to keep a large portion of their savings in the bank even when the central bank has reduced the interest rate to an unexpectedly low level. And some of the government spending is like spreading pepper. You can feel it everywhere, but without concentration on the most urgent objects, one can hardly see the quick results of this big spending.

Also the people in China have been worrying about the depreciation of the currency and are concerned that the devaluation of currencies in Southeast Asian countries and regions would cause serious competitive disadvantage to Chinese exports. Currency depreciation would reduce the total amount of foreign investment to China and bring about imbalance of payments. Frankly speaking, China's exports are facing a rigorous situation. Export growth has slowed down heavily. The Asian financial crisis caused a decline of international demand and raised many more difficulties for Chinese exports, whose lowered growth rate adversely influences the whole economy. In the meantime, trade protectionism is spreading worldwide, trade disputes have become more frequent and much stronger, and international competition has become much more intense. The global loss of confidence in Chinese currency has resulted in negative expectations and built up barriers against attracting foreign investment. Even so, China is still optimistic about its export trend.

The devaluation of currencies in Southeast Asian countries and regions increases import costs while stimulating their exports. This offsets the advantages of their currency devaluation. On the other hand, we can trace the good effects of growing Chinese exports in the past few years. Chinese companies' and manufacturers' price competitiveness has been strengthened by changes in their management system, improvement in the quality of their products, stepped up in technological advancement, and building up a favorable export product structure, all of which have greatly reduced the cost of production and strengthened competitive capability dealing with foreign companies. China's international trade has been gaining a continuous balance of payment surplus in the past few years. In spite of these efforts taken by the companies and manufacturers, the government also has increased bank loans to those that have export contracts and can make profits from fulfilling these contracts. Financial as well as new and restored tax policies have given higher return to the value added tax for the exported products.

According to customs statistics, in the first seven months of 1999, China's foreign trade was $189.10 billion, increasing 5.4%, with exports of $100.20 billion, a 2.8 percent drop compared to the same period of the previous year, while imports were $88.90 billion, a 16.6 percent increase compared to the same period of the previous year. We can also see the positive changes of China's exports through the International Monetary Fund's global economic expectation report based on the PPP calculation the China is ranked the number two economic unit in the world. And according to the China National Statistics Bureau's report, China is ranked number seven in total GNP.

Turning from exports, let us examine the influence of the financial crisis on foreign investments in China. The investments from Southeast Asian countries and regions, which occupy nearly two-thirds of China's total foreign investment, have decreased without any doubt. But European and North American countries are still optimistic about the Asian economy. To respond to foreigners' strong interests, China has resumed many favorable regulations to support and encourage foreign companies to invest in China.

Thus the total volume of foreign investment has not decreased greatly. Since China's economy is strong enough to support the stability of its currency, foreign investments will not have any danger of losing profits. Li Ruogu, the director of the International Financial Organization Department of the Bank of China, estimated that in 1999 there will be more than $30 billion foreign investment in China, and he noted that China also has an even balance of payments. Also one should never forget the fact that China has a big foreign exchange reserve of $146 billion, the second largest in the world. Specialists in this field have predicted the growing reserve trend would weaken and the revaluation of China's currency would be sustained, but there is no danger of devaluation.

Third, China's responses to the Asian financial crisis have gained the great trust of those countries suffering from the influences of the crisis. China has become a more important and decisive factor in Asia's stability. Since China has shown its strong desire and determination to keep a suitable and stable progressive environment for economic reform and development, the world should cooperate and concentrate on the settlement of Southeast Asian financial problems, such as the fundamental financial structure, stock market policy, and the monetary control system. As for this matter, Wang Yajie, the director of Finance at the University of Northeast China, suggested that the U.S. should play a major role in the reform and functional changes of the International Monetary Fund (IMF) so as to enable it to react more promptly and efficiently to tackle the serious drawbacks and problems caused by the financial crisis all around the world. As the world economy is more and more internationalized, this globalization has already become the decisive trend for today's business. This trend offers both chances and challenges.

In 1998, total volume of world trade was $6.5 trillion, a drop of 2 percent compared to that of 1997. The reason is that the Asian financial crisis influenced the whole world and restrained the overall development of world trade. Taking again the Asian financial crisis, for instance, the fact that the crisis caused sharp devaluation of Southeast Asian countries' currencies should have increased their competitiveness of export products and Asian countries have put great hope in offsetting the declining domestic demand in their economies with the stimulus of immediate, expanding exports.

But since the largest part of exports is among the Asian countries themselves, with imports among these countries dropping by 25 percent, as well as the Japanese economic recession and declining of international demand, the Asian " Prosperous Export Ship" stalled and never appeared on the horizon. They all hoped in vain. At any rate, in the past two years, with the rapidly spreading influence of the Asian financial crisis and economic collapse in Russia, financial crisis in Brazil, and the stagnation of the Japanese economy, most of the countries now recognize the risks brought forth by globalization. At the same time the tremendous advantages of globalization have also made broader space for further development of the world economy.

The trade of services, high technology, and environmental products has been developing so greatly that it is offering good chances for world trade. Accompanying economic globalization, capital internationalization, and fast development of modern technology, global trade is also spreading from product trade to services, information technology, and its products. According to the report of the World Trade Organization, the total exports of world service trade in 1998 was $1.29 trillion, nearly 20 percent of the total annual world trade. Experts estimate global service trade volume will reach $2 trillion by end of this century. In 1998, environmental products also reached a high record. Now the market scale is about $450 billion, and this figure will be $500 billion in the year 2000 for environmental equipment and services.

More than one and half years have passed since the financial crisis first appeared in Thailand. Now the stern situation in Southeast Asian countries and regions has given a sign of positive improvement. The director of the International Monetary Fund considered that because of the vigorous efforts of Southeast Asian countries and regions in their reform of monetary and financial systems, they will overcome the present difficulties and regain their economic power early in the next century.

So we can believe that having seen the seriousness of the financial crisis in one area and its bad influence on the total development of the world economy, every responsible country and international organization will pay more attention to the stability of its own financial and monetary system while developing its economy. Without a high alertness to the different signs of potential crisis, and strong and efficient action toward this potentiality, world trade will never develop to reach expectations. The Asian financial crisis is a touchstone for every government to be more prepared for the future, especially in the coming new century.

Endnotes

1. Li Ruogu, director of the department of International Financial Organization of Bank of China, Phoenix Report, September 9,1999.

2. Jiang Zemin, president of the People's Republic of China, speech at the opening session of 15th Chinese Communist Party National Congress.

3. Zhu Rongji, premier of the People's Republic of China, CCTV report on the Press Conference held by the Ministry of State.

4. Lins Rohner, Fortune, September 28,1998.

5. Elaine Kurtenbach, "China Easing Bank Curbs to Deal with Asian Crisis," Wall Street Journal.

References

Beijing Tianze Economic Research Academy, Report on Market System of Chinese Economy, 1998.

China Foreign Trade: 1999, China National Statistics Bureau.

Elaine Kurtenbach, "China Easing Bank Curbs to Deal with Asian Crisis",

Wall Street Journal.

Guangming Daily, "21th Century: Chances and Challenges", June, 1999.

George Soros, "The Global Crisis of Capitalism and China," Strategy and Management, vol. 1, 1999.

Hu Angang, "Step-On Domestic Demand", Wenhui Daily.

Jiang Qiping, "21th Century On-Line Economy", Strategy and Management, vol. 5, 1998.

Jim Rohner, "China: The Real Economic Wild Card", Nanyang Zaobao, August 23,1999.

Jin Liqun, vice minister of Ministry of Finance, speech at press conference in Singapore, Ming Bao Daily, September 3,1999.

Jinan University, "How to Deal with the Bad Debt of State-Owned Banks", Guangzhou Daily, September 6,1999.

Neel Chowd and Antony Paul, "Where Asia Goes from Here," Political and Economic Risk Consultancy, Ltd., A Risk Report, 1998.

Seth Faison, "Chinese Economic Leaders Read A Warning in Asian Crisis", Xingdao Daily, October 4,1999.

United Nations, "Humanity Development, Annual Report" 1998.

Wen Tian, "China's Choice in the World Economic Crisis", Strategy and Management, vol. 1, 1999.

Wu Yi, "Report on Foreign Trade and Investment", Renmin Daily, November 22, 1999.

Yue Jian Yong and Chen Man, "The Current Challenge to China's Export and the Solution-on the Strategy of Devaluation of RMB", Economic Research Journal, October, 1999.

Chapter 6

New Direction in China-U.S. Economic and Trade Partnerships

Yue Yang

China's tremendous achievements such as continued economic growth, price stability, rich foreign exchange reserve, and high quality of life during the last 20 years of reforms as well as being the Equilibrium or Stabilizer in the Asian Financial Crisis have shown its strength, vigor and attraction. Recently, China successfully issued 10-year term Yangki Bonds on the basis of holding 140 billion foreign exchange reserves in International Capital Market, and collected at least 5 billion dollars in more Asian countries suffering their serious financial crisis, it's strength showed once again. It can safely be said that China is getting stronger and stronger, a huge dragon is jumping up in Asian economy.

China's large market potential, successful reforms, and opening policies are attracting many countries, such as America, Japan, Canada, Russia, and so on. America, the strongest developed country, leads an important role in the Asian Pacific Area. What direction will the China-

U.S. economic and trade relations go in the 21st century? I think that should be a matter of common interest and effort to us all. We need each other. This paper briefly analyses the above question.

This paper reviewed briefly the status quo of China-U.S. economic and trade partnerships. In the course of rearranging the New Economic Order of Asian Pacific Area, it was suggested that the new direction of China-U.S. economic and trade partnership should develop omni-directional economic and trade partnership, that is to say, further expanding bilateral trade, laying a tress on mutual direct investments, opening cooperative fields, strengthening cooperation of capital market and so on. Having analyzed this way, China and America are faced with some opportunities and challenges in developing new partnership. The end of this paper will show that our two countries should seize these opportunities and greet these challenges.

So far, China-U.S. economic & trading partnership has three main categories: bilateral trade, direct investment, and financial services. In recent years, bilateral trade has been increasing. According to new official statistics, America is China's second largest trading partner and China is the fourth that of America. Two countries trading volume is as below: (Unit: billion dollars)

	China	Statistics		America	Statistics	
Year	Total Sum	Export	Import	Total Sum	Import	Export
1995	408.30	247.10	161.20	573.03	455.55	117.48
1996	428.40	299.85	161.55	634.60	514.90	119.70
1997	489.93	326.95	162.98	753.00	625.00	128.00

China and America's direct investments have been developing slowly. The direct investment utilization of America is increasing in China, however,'s it is still below 1% of the whole America's investment abroad. The direct investment of China is less in U.S. Especially two countries, which have insufficient mutual large-scale fixed assets investments, which can build a long-term and steady bilateral relationship.

1. Financial services is a field with the largest magnifying effects and the strongest chain reactions. Opening up this field in China is prudent.

Until now, Merrill Lynch, Goldman Sachs, CS First Boston and First Bank of America have been managing limited businesses. According to China's situation, it is urgent that this service be encouraged and so strengthen capital market cooperation. As noted previously, China-U.S. economic and trade partnership is only beginning, with many opportunities for development.

I put forward this view on the basis of equality and mutual benefits, which will further expand bilateral trade, lay a tress on mutual direct investments, open cooperative fields, such as transportation services, communication facilities, energy development, automotive, green agriculture, environment protection, high scientific and technological products, infrastructure construction, annexations of enterprises, finance and insurance, and so on. In a word, developing omni-directional partnership in China-U.S. economy and trade. This conclusion comes from some opportunities and challenges facing the two countries.

2. Economic development of China is facing some opportunities . First, China is carrying out further reforms in many respects. On one hand, China will give preferential policies in loans, lower prices and duties to new consumer products including telephone, housing, personal car, Internet, personal computers, and so on, to stimulate consumer demand with the result of increased economic growth. On the other hand, government will adopt financial and monetary policies, issuing treasury bonds RMB3,165 billion in 1999 plus the balance of 500 billion last year, total sum 3,665 billion, investing in areas having truck with infrastructures construction for solving investment shortage, unemployment problems, and infrastructure environment.

The Asia Crisis resulted in a decrease of China's export; meanwhile with difficulties in areas such as state-enterprise, unemployment, bad bank debt, government reforms, and other difficult questions, the government has to be working along two lines. One of these is further reform inside while another is opening more fields to the outside, creating favorable policies and investment circumstances for foreign investors.

China's reform will be stressing middle and small enterprises and private businesses in the 21st century, the first time that China has written it into the constitution since China was founded. In addition, the government has established a special department to administrate middle and small enterprises and private businesses. According to the State Economic and Trade Commission, by the end of 1998 there were over 10 million small, medium, and private companies being 99% whole enterprises, with finished gross value of industrial output and profits tax being 60% and 40% whole state's, finished employment posts being 75% whole state cities and towns employment.

The data shows reforming big state enterprises at the same time as developing middle, small, and private businesses is a great strategy for settling unemployment, driving economic growth, and adjusting economic structure. In my opinion, groups by joint stock system formed in China is a trend. When the government gives private businesses more preferential policies and encourages them to cooperate with foreign enterprises, it is a good beginning for developing omni-directional partnerships in China and U.S. economy and trade; however, it is necessary for China to perfect further rules and laws in bilateral cooperation .

China has been opening up some new fields and providing preferential policies to attract foreign investors. Perhaps, specific contents will be published later. Some information shows our two countries have made an effort for securing market cooperation. China's enterprises have planned to solve problems of fund shortage in U.S. capital market. Mr. Suber (transliteration) as Chairman of U.S. Securities Exchange Association at NASDAQ Market Parent Company took great interest in cooperation of securities market between China and America when he visited Shanghai Securities Exchange in January, 1999. Shanghai Exchange and NASDAQ Exchange have kept in touch. China must open this field step by step on the basis of further reforming the financial system and perfecting rules and laws

China's commitment to its reforms, such as State enterprises, financial system, government setup, social security system, administrating the country by law, punishing corruption, social justice, and opening up new fields are the most important guarantee for developing omni-directional partnerships in China and U.S. economy and trade.

Second, 1998 was a year that saw a decrease in growth since 1993, but it will recover from this slowdown by the fourth economic cycle in 1999. As a result, the reforms that have begun will play a more important role.

(1). Spending of government, enterprise and family after 5 years decreasing has gone up, which is a key to driving investment growth. According to State Statistical Bureau data, fixed capital investment of state and state holdings reached a low point (10.3%) in the first quarter of 1998, but it began to go up the second quarter of 1998, especially the third quarter, with government expanded direct investment by increasing treasury bonds, this target has remained over 20%. Investment growth of government, state enterprises, middle and small enterprises, and private businesses will increase economic growth within several years, which is inevitable.

Financial Crisis of Asia has continued for two years. With Asian states adopting vigorous measures, the Asian economy will go up slowly in 1999. America, European Monetary Area and other states have adopted measures to avoid crisis. As a result, China's export environment has remained sluggish, however with its incentives, plus government preferential policies of enterprises for increase exports, we estimate this year's exports to be better than that of 1998's, which is one of the facts to promote economic growth.

Estimated total volume of social goods and retail sales in 1999 will go up 2-3 percentage higher than 1998's 6.8%. This result comes from these following reasons.

First, deflation expectancy of enterprise and resident have changed, which have brought about purchase wants for enterprises and residents to consumer goods and investment products such as household appliances especially in countryside, personal computers, telephones, cement, glass, steel products etc.

Second, resident's salary has gone up from the third quarter of 1998, with government increasing salary for residents in 1999, which will increase residents purchasing power. To sum up, economic growth of China will increase. China's good fortune is an opportunity for economic growth in America.

Third, our two countries must work together in our areas of strength. The 21st century is a century on the basis of high science and technology. China's choice of key industry, which must consider both domestic and international in two respects. Premier Zhu Rongji said that information and communication are key industries of China in the 21st century, which has invested over RMB1,600 billion every year, putting a stress on telephone lines, portable telephones, data communication, striving to reach output values of RMB1,200 billion for information and communication products in 2000, it will offer a wide market for China and America.

Key industries of China need American technology. According to the America Present Science and Technology, which submitted a report in March 1995, as compared with Japan, America was in the head in twenty-seven main technology fields, that information and communication fields held a safe lead among them, and had an advantage in biology, medicine, agriculture and food, and was equal in energy and manufacturing, and reduced disparity in environment protection. In addition, China and

America in many fields still exist complementary, such as green agriculture, utilization of natural resources, development of energy resources, biological products, pharmaceuticals and so on. Cooperating in these fields means our two countries benefits.

Fourth, China, as a rapidly growing country carrying out all its reforms, is faced with a favorable situation which rearranges the New Economic Order of Asian Pacific Area in the 21st century. This is a golden opportunity. Many events have happened to prove China's leaders are a strong collective who are possessed of creative and forward ideas. They have been doing their best for global problems which perfect marketing economy systems, solve unemployment and inflation, promote economic growth, adjust economic construction, reform financial system, control pollution of environment, and so on.

3. Economic development of America is faced with some challenges During Clinton's tenure of office, economic development of America has been prosperous, but they have ignored some warning signs. First, America's economy is moving too fast, with the possibility of economic recession in late 2000 year. Some reasons are:

(1). From economic cycle view, economic growth of America has been going up for 7 years. Whether it can break the record 105 months in the 1960's is uncertain. According to Schumpeter's Middle Cycle Theory in which cycles of economic growth last 9-10 years, America's economic growth will reach the minimum of Middle Cycle Theory in 2000, but the longest cycle in the 1960's still didn't reach its minimum after World War II.

(2). Value of Stock Market is expanding rapidly. Dow Jones Index has been going up 300% from 1990 to 1998, especially the last 3 years, where there have been many billion dollar mergers. For example, H&Q company, price of stock went up 2.5 times within one year, from less 10 dollar per share in April of 1997 to 35 dollar per share in March 1998. Super-high stock prices stimulated a lot of American families to put their savings in the stock market. Low-interest rate monetary policies have impelled some people to invest in the stock market so that super-high stock prices are pushed up further, value of stock market is been expanding. In my estimation, Clinton's allowing the social pension fund about 7000 billion dollars to invest in the stock market in State of the Union Message of 1999 will be a great problem. The bigger value, the bigger damage. Isn't the lesson of Japan's "broken bubble" of stock market brought about economic damage since 90's? Some economists of America think of the most valuable lesson is in 1929, when American economist, Owen Fisher, had hardly finished speaking Stock Market had gone into a long time and stead term. Wall Street stock market fell apart.

(3). Excessive real estate investment and credit expansion has hidden inflation. According to the report of U.S. Department of Commerce on January 20, 1999, last month housing starts were up 3.5% than the month before, last year up 9.6% than 1997, the highest since 1987. China's a lesson because of excess-demand inflation over 20% several years ago should be drawn.

(4). Fierce mergers. In the 20th century, America ever had 4 times annexation waves which was early this century, the 1920's , 1960's, and 1980's, all of them accompanied a powerful economic growth, rapid credit expansion, stock market increase, but their results were economic crisis in 1904, 1929, 1969, and economic recession in 1990. History frequently repeats.

(5). Trade deficit continue to increase. U.S. Department of Commerce reported, unfavorable balance of trade went up to 14%, $1,550 billion in November 1998 than last month. From international circumstance view, American deficit in 1999 still will be expanded, not only causing financial deficit and inflation, but also certainly affecting economic growth. Because Americas economic growth depends on exports. Sum up above all analyses lead up to the same result, America economy is faced with recessive challenge.

The second challenge, negative world circumstance will outweigh the advantages to economic growth of America. Influence of main trade partners such as Japan, Brazil, and European Monetary Area on economic growth of America is disadvantageous.

(1). According to Ducang province of Japan, a report on January 25, 1999, Japan's balance of trade 130.9851 thousand billion Japanese Yan in 1998, up 40.1% than last year, over the history top of 1996, with Japan pushed new measures for solving bank problems and recovering economy, it will change the negative growth which has continued 3 years in 1999, but it can not go into prosperity within a short time. As I see it, the worsening economy of Japan failed to influence America's economy during the Asian Crisis, but once Japan's economy heats up, it will drive the Asian economy forward and unless America raises its interest rate in time it will follow into recession.

Brazil is the most powerful state among Latin American countries. Brazil's financial crisis directly controls the trend of Latin America economy. Most analysts believe that Brazil's economy will shrink this year. Brazil's crisis directly influences trade of America which buys 20% export goods to America and manufacturers. According to data shown, businesses like General Motors Corporation ,Ford Motor Company, Xerox, and other manufacturers of high scientific and technological equipment in Brazil have been seriously affected.

European Monetary Area. The lasted financial crisis have weakened economic growth of European Monetary Area. For example, industrial production of Germany is going down, unemployment rate is up, economic growth looks as if will be 2% below in 1999. France and Italy are the same too. A lot of proofs showed, Economic growth of European Monetary Area suffering bad international environment will go down in 1999, which is sure to restrict economic growth of America

(2). European Monetary pins down American dollars. European Monetary has affected strength of dollars. According to China's official said, China will change about 1/3 dollars foreign exchange reserve into European Monetary. Part foreign exchange reserves of all nations, a rough estimate $5,000-10,000 billion will be changed into European Monetary in 2000 year. If a great quantity of settling accounts of trade and securities use European Monetary, dollar demand would be reduced and exchange rate of dollar dropped. In order to prevent this case happen, America has to raise interest rates, but it will cause the stock market to go down, investment and consumer reduce, inflation and economic recession. Some Economists of America think, if inflation happened, U.S. Federal Reserve Board may drop by a range interest rate, which will be pinned down by European Monetary and other facts, such as above mentioned, it is afraid incapable of action in the end.

(3). Speculative capitals in America will probably back-flow. Asia high rate of economic growth was ever an important investment place of international capitals, where attracted a great quantity of international capitals. During Asian Financial Crisis, a large amount of capital was invested in the American Capital Market to avoid losses. According to statistics, $10000 billion speculative funds , about $7,000 billion from Asia among them, have pushed Capital Market of America going up. Until now, the Capital Market of America's unprecedented prosperity comes in two ways. One way is that they originate from the economic structure adjusted for positive results. The other way results when there is a serious loss of confidence in the world and people invest in the American market. Asia Crisis escaped, with Asia states recovering economy and expanding value of stock market in America, these capitals must be back-flow unless interest rate, the most sensitive as capital is risen by a large margin by U.S. Federal Reserve Board, but it will cause same violent turbulence of Capital Market of America. Once Capital Market of America shows a violent fluctuation, it is self-evident to influence of economy of America.

Above analyses in many respects show, during rearranging New Economic Order of Asia in the 21st century, our two countries to develop omni-directional partnerships in economy and trade, America to take China's favorable advantages, such as steady social environment, continued economic growth, low salary and price of raw and processed materials, preferential policies, reform inefficient of government and punish rotten, perfect market economic system, and so on, to avoid influences from domestic economic recession, that is the most wise decision which will benefits overall to promote America's competition ability in the 21st century. China develop and expand itself power meanwhile reform and opening up, too. China and America are faced with a global opportunities and challenges in the 21stcentury. Whoever seizes these opportunities and greets these challenges, will be winner in the 21st century.

References

Schumpeter, Theory of Economic Cycle.
Reference News Daily.
News Page -Direct(Internet).
WSRN News(Internet).
Statistics of China Customs and Statistics of U.S. Department of Commerce
Economy Daily, December 1998.
News of China Department of Information Industry, December 1998.
"Foreign Situation of Social Science," no.2, 1998.
World Economy Digest, no. 4, 1998.
Reference News Daily, January 1999.

Chapter 7

North Korea's Secret Wars and Foreign Policy in the Post-Cold War Era

Anthony Song and Xiaobing Li

In August 1998, North Korea launched a crude three-stage rocket -- a step toward developing an intercontinental ballistic missile. U.S. intelligence is concerned about Pyongyang's building a plant to make plutonium, the essential ingredient of nuclear weapons.[1] In February 1999, North Korean troops again crossed the 38th parallel and raided South Korean army. The conflict claimed a couple of dozen deaths. The Korean Peninsular has remained one of the most unstable and troublesome hot spots since the Cold War ended in 1990.

The fact that the Democratic People's Republic of Korea (DPRK or North Korea) now has operational military nuclear capability, imperils not only its neighbors, the Republic of Korea (ROK or South Korea) and Japan but also the rest of the world. In 1998, North Korea had over 1.2 million standing forces, the fourth largest army in the world, and over 5 million reservist. In other words, 6% of the population are in uniform, and in emergency, 32%. The United States deploys 37,000 troops in South Korea. U.S. Congressman Bill McCollum warns that "North Korea's unstable economic situation and impending power shift from Kim Il-Song to his son has the potential to start another war in that region."[2] Byung Chul Koh points out that "In terms of track record and potential alike, the DPRK is a key player in Northeast Asia. Its formidable military capability and deep-seated hostility toward ROK, coupled with the awesome military might of both the ROK and the United States arrayed against it, ensure that the Korean Peninsula will remain a potential tinderbox."[3]

North Korea is certainly the most dangerous and mysterious communist state in today's world. This paper tries to make a breakthrough by the following three efforts: First of all, it elucidates Pyongyang's post-cold war policy-making through primary communist sources and personal interviews in order to document the major events and to identify a new pattern of North Korea's military and diplomatic behaviors. Second, our analysis moves away from the usual Korean-American or North-South rivalry and instead focuses on the relatively unknown area of Pyongyang-Beijing-Moscow interactions and interest conflicts. The tremendous changes and developments in their relations which have been all but hidden behind have not yet explored. With a critical look into the activities and transition between the two generations of the North Korean leaders, especially between Kim Il Sung and his son Kim Jong Il, we believe that Chinese and Russian factors, not American, strongly influenced Pyongyang's strategic thinking and post-cold war foreign policy-making. Third, our analysis focuses on relatively unknown areas of Pyongyang-Beijing-Moscow interactions such as intelligent services and military exchanges like nuclear technology programs.

1. Communist Sources and Analytic Framework

Although the newly available Communist sources shed light on some of the questions, they do not necessarily offer automatic answers and interpretations. They of course provide new research opportunities, but they also require that historians and scholars of political science and international relations take greater care in the treatment of unfamiliar Communist sources and be more creative in the construction of new conceptual and analytical framework. The study on the North Korean intentions and others' understanding of the intentions in the mid-1990s not only requires relevant evidence, but also challenges the conventional methods in international crisis historiography and East Asian studies. Few issues in international crisis research are more pivotal and difficult than the identification of motivation or intent behind a crisis. And to study a nation without any diplomatic relation presents even more difficulties to American students.

In the recent years, some interpretations on the identification of North Korean strategic thinking employ different methods and conflicting hypotheses, producing diverse results.

(1) *Sovereignty and Territorial Integrity* Some research works have tried to draw a different picture through new approach, the Korean point of view. The sacred task of defending their own country and unifying the nation seems the first consideration of the DPRK. Geoff Simons points out that Pyongyang was pushed to the concern since its sovereign rights and "the sovereign equality" have been violated frequently by bigger states like the U.S.[4] It furthers searches for the subject and provides a better understanding of international tension over the peninsula. The interpretation, however, desalinizes different characteristics between the two Koreas and assumes an American-North Korean strategic confrontation as the essential prerequisite for the civil struggles between the North and South. The main problem of inquiring North Korean intentions to resort use of force along the 38th Parallel remains at large.

(2) *Juche as the Central Guideline for Policies* Juche is commonly translated as "self-reliance" which has become a philosophy and political belief system in North Korea. In his well written article, Park considers the Juche as the "central guideline for policies" in Pyongyang. "All policies are given justification as concrete manifestations of Juche philosophy.... The self-reliance idea has become the underlying principle of all areas of public policy ranging from economic plans to cultural life."[5] Although the interpretation provides a very important analytic framework for our foreign policy research, the question remains at large: why Kim wanted a war at that particular time. Such a broad and general search may also lead to a simple conclusion of an inevitable clash between the two countries with two different ideas: "self-reliant" North Korea and "globalized" America.

(3) *Response to the Threats* This interpretation has made a valuable contribution to the subject. It, however, views the North Korean considerations as a psychologically conditioned reflex of a passive reply in kind to the U.S. policy or South Korea's actions. It skips the North Korean

initiative in the international affairs and their perception of the post-cold war world. The interpretation, taken to its logical conclusion, gives external elements and influence rather than an internal development of the DPRK policy as the original reasons.

(4) *Domestic Mobilization* Among the analyses is the domestic political and economic variables seems very much involved in making of North Korean policy toward the world, especially toward the U.S. It explains the North Korean motivation in using forces in a view of the internal political mobilization. Yossef Bodansky views North Korea as "an impoverished country on the brink of total economic collapse. It is in this abnormal situation that the key to the crisis lies."[6] It is likely the case that North Korea's strategic thinking is determined by its domestic political and economic demands as well as by their international interests and concerns. One, however, must ask an immediate question about what kind of political needs the DPRK had in the mid-1990s. Our evidence shows that generating a serious international crisis for political mobilization is not the case in this period.

(5) *Competing against South Korea in the World* It points out an international competition between the North and the South, and therefore Pyongyang have tried everything it could to undermine the ROK status and reputation in world arena to demonstrate its disapproval of Seoul's actions and a pretext for it to throw the South Korean regime off-balance politically. Andrew C. Nahm concludes that what North Korea had done is to "bring about the collapse of the South Korean government" and the "reunification of a divided Korea."[7] The interpretation seems missing a connection between the intention and results of North Korea's actions. Pyongyang has paid a big price in the international community for its nuclear programs and war preparation. Its aggressive policy aroused the anxieties and concerns of world opinion, particularly Asian opinion, which worried about the spectra of another Korean War. It also caused great fear and apprehensions among the neutral countries in the Third World which desired a stable and peaceful international environment after the end of the Cold War. As non-popular moves, even Russia and China hesitated to support North Korea's war plans. The crisis did not undermined the relations between Seoul and Washington, but instead resulted in a closer relationship which Pyongyang did not want to see.

Our intention is to depict the main significations that shaped the war crises and describe the nature of major policy decisions in the mid-1990s in

Pyongyang. This paper focuses on the policy problems which occurred during the 1990s and then developed a momentum of their own. These problems can be identified when we look through the changes in relations between Pyongyang and Beijing and between Pyongyang and Moscow. The three neighboring countries could not concealed their own concerns and interests when they communicated with each other through meetings, treaties, signals, and use of clear or ambiguous threats or commitments.

2. A Communist Brother for Sale

Because of the strength and territorial size of their mighty neighbors, China and Russia, North Korean leaders have repeatedly tried to ally themselves with one of them for protection or support. Koh points out that "Insofar as its international behavior is concerned, North Korea has had a fair amount of success in steering an independent course thanks largely to the fortuitous dynamics of the dispute between the former Soviet Union and the People's Republic of China (PRC)."[8] One of the most important Chinese contributions regarding security concerns is that China was the principal intelligence source for North Korea during the Cold War. After the founding of the PRC in 1949, Beijing trained Korean agents, provided equipment, and shared information with the Democratic People's Republic of Korea. The cooperation in espionage helped the two countries achieve their foreign policy goals, thus aiding in the formation and maintenance of their alliance.

During the early Korean War, for example, Chinese agents reported from Japan that a large number of American and British warships were concentrated in the Tsushima Straits and seemed to be preparing a new landing in Korea. On August 22, 1950, the Operations Department of the General Staff of the Chinese People's Liberation Army (PLA) held a staff meeting at Beijing and discussed UN forces' landing points, scale, and impact. The PLA staff concluded that MacArthur would land behind the North Korean People's Army (KPA) lines in order to cut off north-south logistical supplies and strategic communication and then launch a northward counteroffensive. Among the four possible landing points, Lei Yingfu believed that Inchon could be the "most likely" landing place.[9] As the head of the Operations Department, Lei briefed Zhou Enlai, PRC Premier and chief of the PLA General Staff, on August 23 and in the same evening also briefed Mao Zedong, chairman of the Chinese Communist Party (CCP). Mao warned General Lee Sang Cho, head of the Intelligence Bureau of the

KPA General Staff, about a possible UN forces landing when Lee met Mao in early September 1950. PRC Ambassador to Pyongyang Ni Zhiliang also informed both North Korean Workers' Party (KWP) Chairman Kim Il Sung and his Russian advisors of a possible MacArthur landing. Throughout the war, Kim Il Sung depended on Chinese intelligence. Kim knew the fact, as Koh emphasizes, that it was Mao who helped the North Koreans prevent a humiliating defeat during the Korean War.[10]

Although swinging between Beijing and Moscow in a cyclical pattern for many reasons, Pyongyang managed to maintain a close brotherly cooperation in intelligence service with the Chinese through the 1960s and 1970s. Their chiefs and high-level agents' visits took place virtually every year. Their exchanges of information were on a regular basis. The Chinese helped the KPA air force shoot down a U.S. EC-121 reconnaissance plane in 1969; trained Kim Jong Il, Kim Il Sung's son, in both Chinese language and intelligence from 1974 when he began to work at the National Security Department (KNSD), North Korea's intelligence service; and provided the KPA with Chinese reconnaissance submarines and airplanes in the late 1970s.[11] The Chinese also agreed that KPA naval reconnaissance ships could use Qingdao, a seaport in North China, as North Korea's naval reconnaissance base. The Korean ships were allowed to pretend to be Chinese fishing boats in the Yellow Sea and use their electronic listening devices to spy on the movements of U.S. and South Korean naval vessels.[12] Kim Il Sung appreciated China's cooperation and described in 1982 the DPRK-PRC friendship as "an invincible force that no one can ever break.... It will last as long as the mountains and rivers in the two countries exist."[13] As Don Oberdorfer describes, "China had been the foreign nation with the greatest importance in the Korean world."[14]

In September 1990, the establishment of diplomatic relations between South Korea and the Soviet Union was certainly a heavy blow to Pyongyang. Thereafter, North Korean intelligence suffered a major setback when the Soviet leader made a secret deal with South Korea. In 1991, Soviet President Mikhail Gorbachev met ROK President Roh Tae Woo at the UN conference in New York City. Gorbachev requested South Korea's economic aid. Roh did not decline his request but asked Moscow to provide Seoul with Pyongyang's military, political, and intelligence information on a regular basis in exchange for South Korea's aid. On his return, Gorbachev instructed KGB Director Bakatin to provide the ROK with a large amount of classified information on the DPRK.[15] After the dissolution of the Soviet Union, Russian President Boris Yeltsin continued the same policy and therefore received a badly needed loan of US$1.5 billion from the new leader in South Korea.

After the collapse of the Soviet Union, North Korea sped up their own research and development of nuclear technology in order to cope with possible post-cold war military threats without Russian nuclear protection. In 1991-92, Pyongyang paid very high salaries to employ about 50 former Soviet nuclear experts and engineers while smuggling nuclear materials from Russia, into North Korea, including 239 and 235. Kim believed that North Korea's access to the nuclear weapons should reduce its dependence on Russia, gain political independence in international affairs, and increase its deterrent force. Although he promised South Korea that his nuclear weapons would never be used on the Korean people in the South, he used American deployment of tactical nuclear weapons in South Korea as a reason to justify his rapid nuclear development. Since 1992, the began their talks with Kim Jong Il regarding the international inspection of North Korea's nuclear facilities. Kim refused their request and announced their withdrawal from the organization as an aggressive move to protect his nuclear secrets on March 12, 1993.

3. From Internationalism to Regionalism: No More Swing

When the Cold War reached the end, however, political developments in the Soviet Union and Eastern Europe did not automatically bring Beijing and Pyongyang closer together. Our findings contradict to much research on this topic.[16] Pyongyang no longer swung between Beijing and Moscow. First, the bi-polar world order as an institutional constraint during the Cold War on North Korea disappeared. The DPRK gained more freedom and confidence in expanding its relations with South Korea, Japan, and even Taiwan. Second, while free of an international communist camp, Pyongyang also lost former Soviet nuclear protection. Beginning in the late 1980s, Pyongyang has had strong incentives to develop relations with the United States, because a working relationship might increase North Korea's leverage in dealing with the Korean problem and with East Asia as a whole. Third, geo-politics and regional concerns have become more important since they have an immediate impact and direct bearing upon the Korean Peninsula. Having good relations with all neighboring countries, including both China and Russia, may put North Korea in the best possible situation in regional affairs. When Pyongyang has struggled for a more independent foreign policy, its national interests and security concerns have increasingly differed from those of Beijing. North Korea's differing political needs, uneven economic development, and own consistent inner logic and dynamics have caused new problems in PRC-DPRK relations.

The two countries' intelligence services experienced sour relations when North Korea began to recruit its own agents in China. In early 1989, for instance, the KNSD recruited a PLA colonel, Gao Yongnan, deputy director of the Third Bureau of PLA Nanjing Regional Command. As a Korean national, Gao agreed to pass classified Chinese military information to a North Korean military representative to China. After being discovered and jailed in Nanjing, Gao was able to escaped with the help of North Korean agents. To find out the Chinese leaders' new strategic thinking, Kim Il Sung visited Beijing again in October 1991 to discuss a new strategic partnership with China in a rapidly changing world. Kim argued that after the collapse of the Soviet Union, China should lead the world communist movement joined by North Korea, Vietnam, Cuba, and Iran to fight back capitalism. He also asked China to help North Korea develop its own ballistic missiles. Jiang Zemin, the new CCP Chairman and the PRC President, explained Deng's current foreign policy that China does not intend to take a lead in world affairs. Jiang also declined Kim's request for advanced missile technology, and only agreed to assist in a defensive weapon system if North Korea faces a possible foreign invasion. Kim was disappointed by Beijing's new position and called for a more independent foreign policy after his return back to Pyongyang. "The present era is an era of independence," emphasized by *Rodong sinmun*, the party official newspaper and the KWP's organ. "No matter how serious the twists and turns may be, we will go our own way to the end, overcoming whatever obstacles that may lie in our path."[17]

The new leadership in Beijing had their own agenda by the end of the Cold War. Quansheng Zhao points out that while being much less concerned about ideological differences than ever since 1949, the Chinese leaders have experienced a transition from dogmatism to pragmatism in their foreign policy-making.[18] According to Zhao, this new pragmatism can be found in China's policy toward South Korea. To normalize its relationship with Seoul, Beijing could (1) achieve initiatives in the major issues regarding the Korean Peninsula; (2) have Seoul on its side to counter Japan's power in East Asia because of high anti-Japanese sentiment in South Korea; (3) isolate Taiwan; and (4) attract more investments and have direct trade with South Korea.

In May 1992, the PRC and ROK foreign ministers held negotiations in Beijing to finalize full diplomatic relations. In June, PRC President Yang Shangkun visited Pyongyang, supposedly to inform Kim of the PRC-ROK negotiations. But he found it very difficult to talk without hurting his Korean comrades' feeling. He did not say anything until 30 minutes before his train's departure. Kim was shocked and called for an emergency Politburo meeting after Yang left for Beijing. He was very frustrated and said that he was prepared when Russians sold him out, but he did not worry too much since North Korea still had China. The relationship between the Chinese and North Korean parties seemed to him as the same as that between father and son. He never thought that China could turn its back against North Korea.[19]

At the meeting, the KWP Central Committee decided that Kim Jong Il should prepare three immediate measures to deal with China-South Korea relations. First, Kim drafted a KWP Central Committee document to prepare party leaders and members psychologically for the negative impact of the Beijing-Seoul cooperation and educate them to recognize the capitalist nature of China's so-called "reforms." Second, the KPA should reinforce two divisions at the Chinese-North Korean borders for a possible military conflict. Third, given the fact that China was playing the two Koreas, North Korea could play the "Taiwan card" against the "Seoul card."

On August 24, 1992, China and South Korea announced their official diplomatic relationship. In September, ROC President Roh visited Beijing as the first South Korean president ever to Communist China. Economic development was one of Beijing's primary incentives for normalizing relations with South Korea. Since normalization, South Korea has become increasingly important as a trading partner for China. According to Zhao, in 1993, Sino-South Korean trade reached US$8.2 billion, far exceeding trade with North Korea of US$899.6 million. In his November 1995 state visit to South Korea, President Jiang Zemin re-emphasized the importance of China's ties with South Korea, and projected that bilateral trade in 1995 would reach the level of US$15 billion.[20]

4. Reinventing the Cold War

In the fall of 1993, negotiations on nuclear weapon between the U.S. and North Korea was under way. Facing tremendous pressure from Washington, Kim instructed the Korean delegation that they should take the initiative, buy more time, and hold on their principles to the end even at risk of war with the U.S.

In the spring of 1994, for example, North Korea refused to permit outsiders to inspect their nuclear plants. The UN and the US put more pressures on Pyongyang, including possible economic sanctions, in order to keep North Korea in line with the nuclear control agreements by the International Atomic Energy Agency (IAEA). Beijing failed to publicly support Pyongyang's position, and expressed its desire to see a nuclear-free Korean Peninsula. Thereafter, the North Korean Ambassador to China declared on June 2 that any imposed international economic sanction "would be regarded as a declaration of war."[21] Pyongyang deployed additional troops along the 38th Parallel and replaced spent fuel rods from the five-megawatt reactor in Yongbyon. Then, in the same month, as Andrew Nahm demonstrates, American policy-makers in Washington "considered a plan to apply military means to eliminate North Korea's nuclear facilities."[22] Shortly after that, on June 15 former American President Jimmy Carter entered North Korea and met North Korean leaders. Fortunately, the 1994 crisis did not lead to another war between North Korea and the United States.

Thereafter, the situation in the Korean Peninsular maintains explosive because the North Korean forces created by Russia and China before the transformations are no longer controlled by the third generation of Chinese leaders or post-Soviet Union Moscow.

In the summer of 1994, three unexpected events eventually took away the life of Kim Il Sung. The first major event that in fact excited the party chairman and republic president was the visit by Jimmy Carter to Pyongyang, the first important American leader to travel to the communist state since its founding in 1948. It was too important for Kim to miss the opportunity for a possible national reunification for which he had been fighting during his entire revolutionary career. Thus, he negotiated with Carter on America's mediation of the summit between North and South. Though at 82, he participated in every major event during Carter's visit. The First Lady complained to American reporters who came with Carter that Kim never listened to her and ignored his age. The second event was a heavy blow to him during his visit to the summer harvest right after his meeting with Carter. Upset by the provincial government's inability to reach its plan of grain production, Kim went to a village and wanted to see the reality. Even though farmers told their president how happy they were, Kim could easily see for himself those pale, sick-looking faces, and hungry, dying kids, and very poor living conditions in the village. He was shocked and said, "I can't imagine any worse of a life than this. When I started our revolution [in 1938], village life was just like this. It was why we wanted to have a revolutionary change. But after so many years of revolution, your life is still the same. It is I who am not a wise leader. I should apologize." His tears fell down. Everybody around him cried with him, and the provincial governor was on his knee and asked for punishment. The last traumatic event was the death of General Zhao Minxuan. As soon as he was back in his office, Kim requested his secretaries' briefing. The first news was bad: General Zhao Minxuan, 75, had died, the third general who had died in one month. It was the final blow to Kim's extremely exhausted and tired heart. Zhao began his revolutionary career at 14 and had followed Kim everywhere as a brother for more than 60 years. Shaking and shouting while his staff tried to calm him, suddenly Kim stopped breathing and fainted to the ground.

Kim Jong Il was so shocked that he could not face the reality and handle daily routines. His father's funeral was scheduled for July 17, but it had to be postponed to July 20 because of his inability to recover from the shock. The sudden death of Kim Il-Song made the Korean Peninsula more uncertain and unstable than ever before. Kim Chong-Il claimed that he would follow his father's domestic and foreign policy in major issues such as national reunification, relations with the United Sates, and nuclear development, and he has employed more aggressive and assertive approaches. He wants his small backward state to become the most active and assertive communist state in the world and achieve the unification of Korea by force of arms. "Through the ruthless implementation of *Juche*-based policies, North Korea has evolved into an aggressive military power, and, at the same time, is an impoverished country on the brink of total economic collapse," as Yossef Bodansky, director of the House Republican Task Force on Terrorism and Unconventional Warfare, points out that "It is in this abnormal situation that the key to the crisis lies."

5. The Communist Last Stand

Kim Jong Il carried on his father's legacy–strong military, national unification, and independent foreign policy. His father prepared his son as his successor. In December 1990, Kim Jong Il was appointed as the KPA Supreme Commander, and in April 1992, he became KPA marshal.

Kim Jong Il showed his different approaches from his father's in pursuing their political goals. Noting the changing world politics and political damage to the KWP, Kim Jong Il imported Russian-made equipment and weapons and employed Chinese-trained experts and commanders to limit Russian and Chinese influences. The most advanced weapons of the KPA came from Russia. There wouldn't have been any way to get rid of Russian influence and control if he had trained his technicians in Russia. Instead, Kim sent his young commanders to China, Cuba, and some Southeast Asian countries for military technology training. In the fall of 1992, Kim led an investigation committee to identify and purge a pro-Russian group inside the KPA, including 12 generals headed by deputy commander of the KPA navy who studied in the Soviet Union before.

By 1992, North Korea had over 1.2 million standing military forces, the fourth largest army in the world, and over 5 million reservists. In other words, 6% of the population are in uniform, and in an emergency, 32%. Bill McCollum warns that "North Korea's ... impending power shift from Kim Il Sung to his son has the potential to start another war in that region."[23]

The transfer of power in Pyongyang has been completed. The new leadership is now even more determined to live up to what they believe to be their responsibility. Understandably, Korea's tremendous strategic importance increased after events like the reform and opening-up of China and the collapse of the Soviet Union.

After the death of Kim Il Sung, China-North Korean relations reached a low point again. Kim Jong Il launched another propaganda campaign against China, criticizing Beijing's leadership as "modern revisionists." He did not get all the economic aid he needed from Beijing. As a retaliation, in 1996, the DPRK International Travel Bureau opened its office at Taipei, Taiwan. In May, several Taiwanese officials visited Pyongyang. In June, a high level North Korean trade delegation visited Taipei. What upset Beijing the most is an agreement between the Republic of China and North Korea that Pyongyang is willing to store Taiwan's nuclear waste in North Korea in exchange for financial assistance. These may give Beijing another good reason to continue a health relationship with South Korea. In November 1995, Jiang Zemin visited Seoul. In 1996, China-South Korean trade reached US$20 billion.

Pyongyang made another drastic move in 1996. North Korea announced that it unilaterally terminated the Korea Truce Treaty, which was signed by the U.S., the PRC, the ROK, and the DPRK in July 1953 to end the Korean War. In other word, North Korea is no longer responsible or obligated to maintain any peace agreement in the Demilitarized Zone (DMZ). Without informing Beijing, North Korea asked the Polish representatives to leave the DMZ, who had been there as truce inspectors since the end of the Korean War in 1953. Then, the Chinese representatives had to leave Panmunjom since the termination also ended their mission there.

Pyongyang's actions really upset the leaders in Beijing, especially the PLA high command. But Beijing has since been patient without direct retaliation. China needs North Korea in Northeast Asia to check on Japan and keep a regional balance while Russia is declining in the Far East. The KPA as a major military force in Northeast Asia should play an important role in dealing with America in Asia. Beijing still keeps a close working relationship and a military alliance with Pyongyang, the only one military alliance Beijing has in the world. In July 1996, the PLA sent its naval fleet delegation to North Korea led by General Wang Jiying, commander of PLAN Northern Seas Fleet. In November 1997, General Tang Tianbiao, deputy director of the PLA General Political Department, visited Pyongyang. In August 1998, General Xiong Guangkai, PLA intelligence chief and deputy chief of the General Staff, led a high ranking military delegation to visit the KPA. Such a working relationship and a military alliance fit into China's interests in Northeast Asia and maintain a status quo in the region. China is neither ready for a united Korea, nor willing to be involved in a major crisis or another Korean war.

Endnotes

1. Gregory L. Vistica and Melinda Liu, "The showdown Ahead," Newsweek (September 28, 1998), 50.

2. Bill McCollum, "Introduction" to Yossef Bodansky, Crisis in Korea-- The Emergence of a New and Dangerous Nuclear Power (New York: S.P.I. Books, 1994), 7.

3. Byung Chul Koh, University of Illinois at Chicago, "Foreign Policy Goals, Constraints, and Prospects," in Han S. Park, North Korea: Ideology, Politics, Economy (Englewood Cliffs, New Jersey: Prentice Hall, 1996), 176.

4. Geoff Simons, <u>Korea: The Search for Sovereignty</u> (London, England: MacMillan Press, 1995), 59.

5. Han S. Park, "The Nature and Evolution of Juche Ideology," in Park ed., <u>North Korea: Ideology, Politics, Economy</u>, 10.

6. Yossef Bodansky, <u>Crisis in Korea: the Emergence of a New and Dangerous Nuclear Power</u> (New York, NY: S.P.I. Books, 1994), 11.

7. Andrew C. Nahm, "The United States and North Korea since 1945," in Yur-Bok Lee and Wayne Patterson eds., <u>Korean-American Relations, 1866-1997</u> (Albany, New York: State University of New York Press, 1999), 141.

8. Byung Chul Koh, "Foreign Policy Goals, Constraints, and Prospects," in Park ed., <u>North Korea: Ideology, Politics, Economy</u>, 178.

9. Lei Yingfu, "Recollections of Several Important Decisions during the War to Resist America and Assist Korea," <u>Dang de wenxian</u> (Party History Archives) (Beijing, no. 6, 1993), 76-78. Lei was director of the Operation Department of the PLA General Staff and military secretary of Zhou Enlai, PRC Premier and the chief of the PLA General Staff during the Korean War. The English translation of Lei's recollection is from "Chinese Generals Recall the Korean War," translated by Xiaobing Li, Don Duffy, Zujian Zhang, and Glenn Tracy, in <u>Chinese Historians</u> (vol. Vii, no. 1-2, spring and fall 1994), 133-5.

10. Koh, "Foreign Policy Goals, Constraints, and Prospects," 182.

11. Interview with a retired PLA general by author, Beijing, July 1998. For some understandable reasons, this paper does not give some names of the persons with whom we agreed to have an off-record interview in China and North Korea.

12. Zhang Wenjin, interview by author, Beijing, August 1986. Zhang was vice minister of the PRC Foreign Ministry in 1978-83 and PRC Ambassador to the U.S. in 1983-88.

13. Kim's words from Don Oberdorfer, The Two Koreas; A Contemporary History (Basic Books, 1997), 231.

14. Oberdorfer, *ibid.*, 230.

15. Interview with a DPRK diplomat by author, Beijing, October 1995.

16. For example, Quansheng Zhao points out in his research that "Political development in China and Eastern Europe since the late 1980s brought Beijing and Pyongyang closer together." See Zhao, Interpreting Chinese Foreign Policy (New York, NY: Oxford University Press, 1996), 197.

17. The quotation from Koh, "Foreign Policy Goals, Constraints, and Prospects," 183.

18. Zhao, Interpreting Chinese Foreign Policy, 67-8.

19.   Interview with a DPRK diplomat by author, Beijing, October 1995.

20. Zhao, Interpreting Chinese Foreign Policy, 198-9.

21. The quotation from Nahm, "The United States and North Korea since 1945," 135.

22. Nahm, *ibid.*, 136.

23. U.S. Congressman Bill McCollum, Introduction to Yossef Bodansky, Crisis in Korea-The Emergence of A New and Dangerous Nuclear Power (New York, NY: SPI Books, 1994), 7.

Chapter 8

Taiwan's Struggle for Independence

Nancy J. Waldenville-Brewer

On October 1, 1949, after several years of Civil War between Mao Zedong's Communist Party and Chiang Kai-shek's Kuomintang (or Guomindang) or Nationalist Party, Mao declared a victory for the People's Republic of China. It was proclaimed in Beijing on Tiananmen Square.[1] Chiang Kai-shek at the same time was gathering millions of his supporters and crowded onto ships bound for the Island of Formosa, later to be known as Taiwan.[2]

Chiang Kai-shek established an authoritarian dictatorship on Taiwan, which was adhered to until 1988. During the time of Chiang's rule he never wavered from his promise to one day reunify Taiwan and mainland China under his regime. So strong were his beliefs of reunification that it was illegal to pursue thoughts of independence for Taiwan while Chiang was alive. The same was true for Mao Zedong in his bid for reunification. In essence, the "One China Policy" was established long before Richard Nixon and Henry Kissinger proclaimed it in 1972.[3] In 1965, some reports contend that Chiang Kai-shek agreed to establish peace talks with mainland China for the purpose of a peaceful reunification. This agreement was based upon the following six conditions:

1. Chiang Kai-shek can return to mainland China with his subordinates and can settle in any province of China except Zhejiang. Chiang will remain as the top leader of Guomindang (GMD).

2. Chiang Ching-Kuo, Chiang Kai-shek's son, will be governor of Taiwan Province. Taiwan will retain what it has for twenty years except giving up rights over diplomatic and military affairs and agreeing to Beijing's requests that tillers have their own lands. This agreement to be negotiated after twenty years.

3. Taiwan will not receive any aid from the United States. If there is financial difficulties, Beijing will provide the same amount of money as the United States used to provide.

4. Taiwan's naval and air force will be re-organized and reduced to four divisions with one division stationed in the Jinmen and Xiamen areas and three divisions in Taiwan.

5. Xiamen and Jinmen will become one free city standing between Beijing and Taipei as a buffer and liaison zone. The commander of the army division in this area will also be mayor of the city. The commander will have the rank of lieutenant general and should be politically acceptable to Beijing.

6. The official ranks and salaries of all civil officials and military officers in Taiwan remain the same and living standards of people in Taiwan will only go up and will not be allowed to go down.[4]

The Great Proletarian Cultural Revolution in May, 1966, brought a screeching halt to all negotiations for reunification and would remain at a stand still until after Chiang Kai-shek's death.

Prior to 1972, Taiwan enjoyed a close and secure relationship with the United States. However, on October 25, 1971, Taiwan's relationship with the United States and many other prominent Nations changed when under duress by Beijing, these countries were forced to switch official recognition from Taipei to Beijing.[5] It was on this date that the 1971 United Nations Resolution accorded China's seat in the United Nations to the People's Republic of China in Beijing, thus forcing Taiwan out of the United Nations. Additionally, in 1972, when Nixon made his famous trip to China the birth of the Three Communiques began. The first was made by Nixon and simply stated, "The United States acknowledges that all Chinese on either side of the Taiwan Strait maintain there is but one China and that Taiwan is a part of China. The United States Government does not challenge that position."[6] Thus the "One China" policy was born. The second communique came in 1978 when the Carter Administration reaffirmed Nixon's position, fully normalizing diplomatic relations with China. At the same time, Congress passed the Taiwan Relations Act (TRA) which continued unofficially political, military, and cultural ties with Taiwan. The Taiwan Relations Act in essence states the United States will help provide the means for Taiwan to defend itself and will view with **grave concern** any use of force. The final communique was issued in 1982, by Ronald Reagan's Administration when he pledged to limit the quantity and quality of arms sales to Taiwan. However, Reagan did pledge "Six Assurances" to Taiwan:

1. United States agrees not to alter the TRA
2. Not to terminate arms sales
3. Not to consult with China before making decisions on United States arms sales
4. Not to mediate between China and Taiwan
5. Not to pressure Taiwan to enter into negotiations with China
6. Not to formerly recognize Chinese sovereignty over Taiwan

In all three communiques and the Six Assurances, the "One China" policy was maintained.[7] It is during these "Three Communiques" that Chiang Kai-shek's son became the leader of Taiwan.

Chiang Ching-kuo, the new leader of Taiwan, issued a decree in 1980 called the Three Noes: no contact, no negotiations, and no compromise with communist China. This was Chiang Ching-kuo's response to the first two communiques. However, while publicly denouncing China, he also re-opened negotiations secretly with the mainland. Nevertheless, in January 1988, all discussions ceased when Chiang Ching-kuo died.[8]

The new leader of Taiwan, Lee Teng-hui, was first elected to the position of President by the Parliament, thus ending the rule by an authoritarian government. The process of democracy began to be established and a democratic election was set for March 1996, when Lee

Teng-hui was elected President by the voters of Taiwan; making Lee the first directly elected Chinese leader in 5,000 years. President Lee Teng-hui's initial focus for Taiwan's future included the commitment for reunification "under the banner of freedom, democracy, and equitable prosperity."[9] Under his jurisdiction many organizations were established to open negotiations and create think tanks, included among these is the National Unification Council, the Mainland Affairs Council, and the Straits Exchange Foundation.

President Lee Teng-hui has faced a number of confrontations with China since he took office as President. The first one came when Lee visited the United States in June 1995, under the pretense of attending an alumni reunion at his alma mater, Cornell University. Lee's visit marked the first time in United States and Taiwan history that the President of Taiwan was permitted entrance into the United States. Previously, Lee had been allowed to stop in Honolulu to refuel his plane. However, he was not allowed to stay overnight and only permitted to visit a small reception room in the airport. President Lee was so angered by the United States inhospitable attitude that in 1994 he refused to disembark preferring to remain aboard his aircraft.

This visit to the United States just a year later was a well orchestrated plan to force the Clinton Administration to grant him access into the United States. Lee Teng-hui was under no circumstances supposed to make any political statements nor were any ranking dignitaries allowed to meet him. The welcoming committee at Syracuse Airport included the Mayor, the President of Cornell University, and three Republican Senators, including Jesse Helms. Senator Helms was the Senate Foreign Relations Committee Chairman and when he greeted President Lee, he made references to a future visit one-day to Washington, D.C. This visit angered the Chinese officials and the incompetent manner in which the Clinton Administration handled the situation only made matters worse.

In retaliation for allowing President Lee's visit, the Chinese government on July 19 issued a statement that they would be conducting military exercises for the next week in the East Sea, north of Taiwan. As promised, the Chinese launched four M-9 missiles into the East Sea causing the stock market to plummet in Taiwan. This action directed at Taiwan by China caused the United States to acknowledge that China must be treated as a major problem facing American foreign policy.[10] Following the military exercises near Taiwan, the United States government sent several communiques to China expressing their disquiet in the manner in which

China was dealing with Taiwan. Tensions between the United States and China continued to escalate and China made indirect overtures that the conflict between them and Taiwan could lead to nuclear exchange. One People's Liberation Army Leader said, "China was prepared to sacrifice millions of people, even entire cities, in a nuclear exchange to defend its interests in preventing Taiwan's independence. You will not sacrifice Los Angeles to protect Taiwan."[11]

This response by the Chinese was construed as a warning to let the Clinton Administration know that they no longer were afraid of the United States as they had been in the mid-1950's when President Eisenhower's Administration threatened nuclear attacks on China if they interfered with Taiwan. The Clinton Administration could no longer turn a deaf ear to the Chinese and in response sent the American aircraft carrier Nimitz along with a cruiser, destroyer, frigate, and two support ships to the Taiwan Strait. This act would mark the first time since 1979, that any American aircraft carrier had entered the Taiwan Strait. To placate the seriousness of this action, President Clinton informed the Chinese government that these vessels were merely passing through the Strait due to inclement weather.[12]

The second confrontation that President Lee Teng-hui had to deal with came with the approaching democratic elections scheduled for March 23, 1996. This event would mark the first time a President would be elected by the people of Taiwan. In February 1996, the Chinese once again announced that they would be practicing military exercises on the southeast coast of China. This time they amassed 150,000 Chinese troops, a larger number than they had the summer before. The United States dispatched communiques between China and the United States reaffirming the United States position regarding Taiwan, as stated in the Taiwan Relations Act. They reminded the Chinese that "the United States will help provide the means for Taiwan to defend itself and will view with grave concern any use of force."[13] These warnings fell on deaf ears and on March 8, 1996, China fired two M-9 missiles into the waters off Taiwan. These missiles landed thirty miles off Kaohsiung and Keelung, Taiwan's two main ports.

Once again Taiwan's stock market fell and a general underlying panic hit the Taiwan economy. The United States again took the attack serious and this time they decided to send two naval aircraft carriers, the Independence and the Nimitz, along with a frigate, two destroyers and two submarines. The Nimitz included an escort of seven additional warships. This time the United States government did not make any excuses for sending these ships. The message was plain. The tensions subsided and the elections scheduled for March 23 took place. For the most part Taiwan and China settled back down to resume their former relations until 1998.

In 1998, while President Clinton was visiting Shanghai, he made a speech in which he made public his three noes:

1.   No support for Taiwanese independence.
2.   No support for "two Chinas."
3.   No support for Taiwanese membership of international organizations.

At the same time he was making public his Administration's stance with Taiwan, he was also pressuring President Lee Teng-hui to enter into an interim agreement with China for reunification. This pressure tactic by Clinton's Administration was in direct opposition to two points of Ronald Reagan's "Six Assurance." The fifth and sixth Assurances stated that the United States would 1) not mediate between China and Taiwan, and 2) not pressure Taiwan to enter into negotiations with China. This interference by the Clinton Administration generated a sense of insecurity within Lee Teng-hui's Administration. This pressure, coupled with the fact that Hong Kong had reverted back to China in 1997, and Portugal is scheduled to return Macau to China in December, 1999, painted a portrait to Lee that the only "province" that has not been restored to China is Taiwan.[14]

The peace that had settled upon the region was abruptly disrupted on July 9, 1999, when President Lee Teng-hui answered a question posed during an interview by the German Deutsche Welle radio station regarding mainland China's view of Taiwan as a "renegade province." Lee answered the reporter's question by saying "Taiwan sees its relations with China as a "special state-to-state relationship" rather than an "internal" one.[15] Lee felt it was his duty "to defend the sovereign rights and interests of the country and people and he had to give a clearly defined answer to the question."[16] At the time that President Lee made his announcement, he knew China would be outraged about the inference to Taiwan's independence and continue its advancement that Taiwan was a "renegade" province. On July 12, "Su Chi, a Senior Cabinet Official and Taiwan's Chairman of Mainland Affairs Council confirmed that the "One China" policy had been dumped."[17]

Many reasons have been purported as to why President Lee made the announcement at this particular time. Some of these include the need to push the question of Taiwan's independence now because of the upcoming elections in the year 2000 and he is gathering support for his Vice-President and the Nationalist Party. Another is he feels Taiwan's military is more organized and modernized than China's is currently and that if Taiwan waits too long China will rapidly narrow the military balance. President Lee was also disappointed in the vote held in the United Nations this year. The question of Taiwan's admittance was proposed; however, all five of the permanent powers voted against hearing the motion. At the same time, the United States reiterated Clinton's "three noes." Additionally, Taiwan is frustrated because it has met the standards for joining the World Trade Organization, yet Beijing insists that the People's Republic of China must be admitted first. Taiwan supercedes China's imports of U.S. goods by more than one and a half times and is a model for the market reforms that China needs before it can "legitimately" enter the World Trade Organization.[18]

The fact remains that President Lee Teng-hui has a legitimate argument for declaring Taiwan a separate state from China. According to the Montevideo Convention on Rights and Duties of States, that was signed by the United States in 1933, "a state as a juristic person in international law should possess the following four qualifications: (1) a permanent population; (2) a defined territory; (3) a government; and (4) the capacity to enter into relations with other states. The same standards are also stated in the Restatement of the Law of the Foreign Relations of the United States, which represents the general consensus of American lawyers."[19] Taiwan meets those standards proposed by the Montevideo Convention in the following manner:

1.   The requirement for a permanent population. Taiwan has over 22 million inhabitants and since 1949, there has been no significant migration of people in or out of Taiwan; thus creating a stable and permanent population.

2.   The requirement for a defined territory. Taiwan's total territorial area encompasses Taiwan, Penghu, and the offshore islands of Quemoy and Matsu, totaling 14,000 square miles. "Since 1991, Taiwan has acknowledged the People's Republic of China as a political entity effectively controlling Mainland China and itself as a political entity controlling the Taiwan area."[20]

3.   The requirement for a government. The Taipei

government has ruled Taiwan since 1949 and has progressed from an authoritarian government into a democratic one.

4.   The requirement for the capacity to enter into relations with other states. This final requirement is perhaps the most important and controversial one. According to Ian Brownlie in his book *Principles of Public International Law*, "it is clearly established that states cannot by their independent judgement establish any competence of other states which is established by international law and does not depend on agreement or concession."[21] "The determination of the capacity of an entity to have foreign relations is decided by the internal structure and abilities of that entity. Whether other states will or should recognize this state is another matter."[22] Prior to 1972, Taiwan was recognized by half the countries in the world before its departure from the United Nations. Currently Taiwan still has diplomatic relations with 28 states and maintains commercial trade and cultural relations with more than 140 states in the world. These relationships alone clearly prove Taiwan meets the fourth requirement.[23]

By all legal connotations Taiwan clearly meets and exceeds all four of the requirements for statehood. It is no wonder that President Lee Tung-hui felt confident in proclaiming Taiwan's relationship with China as one that is based upon a special state-to-state relationship, rather than an internal one.

Additionally, Lee may have felt that support from the United States is growing because relations with the Taiwanese government are still considered viable by many U.S. Governmental Agencies. On March 24, 1999, Senators Robert Torricelli (Democrat - New Jersey) and Jesse Helms (Republican - North Carolina) introduced their version of the Taiwan Security Enhancement Act to the Senate. This was followed by Representatives Tom Delay (Republican - Texas), Christopher Cox (Republican - California), Peter Deutsch (Democrat - Florida), Robert Andrews (Democrat - New Jersey), and Nita Lowey (Democrat -New York) introducing H.R. 1838 - Taiwan Security Enhancement Act, to the House of Representatives on May 18, 1999.

This Bill reconfirms the U.S. commitment to Taiwan as stipulated in the Taiwan Relations Act (Public Law 96-8) and the Mutual Defense Treaty of 1954. However, this Bill acknowledges the fact that while "most nations in East Asia are reducing military spending, the People's Republic of China continues a major and comprehensive military buildup."[24] It is projected that by "2005, the People's Republic of China will possess an overwhelming advantage in offensive missiles vis-a-vis Taiwan."[25] It is the nature of this bill to provide Taiwan with the capabilities of strengthening its defenses by: a) Maintenance of Sufficient Self-defense Capabilities; b) a Plan; c) Communications Between U.S. and Taiwan Military Commands; d) Missile Defense Equipment; e) Satellite Early Warning Data f) Air Defense Equipment and g) Naval Defense Systems.[26]

It is understood by many within the United States that the U.S. should not let down its guard militarily in East Asia. Taiwan is still a strategic ally and the U.S. needs to maintain this foothold in East Asia as the sleeping dragon in China appears to be waking up.

The question of Taiwan's future is really not one that has any other outcome than reunification with mainland China. Beijing has made its position clear on this matter by offering offensive maneuvers every time Taiwan widens the gap between the two states. The best that Taiwan can hope for is that it can hold out until mainland China itself changes. Beijing wants Taiwan to agree to reunification under the Hong Kong Plan, allowing Taipei to continue to have its own military and local government for a number of years to be agreed upon, (sounds resoundingly similar to the agreement Chiang Kai-shek had been negotiating with Mao Zedong). Taipei contends that since democracy has been instilled on the island that they can never return to the oppressive regime under communism, (exactly the reason Taiwan has such a strong support in the United States). Nor could they trust the mainland in upholding its end of the negotiating bargain. Problems in Hong Kong are already starting to arise that cause serious doubts for Taiwan.

The other factor to contend with is that the new generations emerging in Taiwan no longer look to the mainland for their identity. They have become a society of Taiwanese, not Chinese, and thus have created a culture separate from the mainland. Even with China building up its military along the southeast coast of China and positioning missiles directly at Taipei, the people still seek their freedom. The tensions created by President Teng-hui's statement of state-to-state relations have been put on the back burner since a catastrophic earthquake shook Taiwan in October, 1999. President Lee has had to change his focus from political problems with China to the recovery process for Taiwan. However, even with this disaster, Taiwan has refused all aid from China and contends it can weather this disaster alone. Outside aid from other countries have been channeled to Taiwan through Third World Countries due to China's belligerent stance on aid to Taiwan. The strength that this "state" portrays at least should be acknowledged for its determination and stamina in the face of adversity. One can only wish their dreams are realized.

Endnotes

1. Dryer, June Teufel. China's Political System (New York: Addison Wesley Longman, 1999) 79.

2. Platt, Kevin, "A Push for Unity Widens Gaps," Christian Science Monitor 91 (September 1999): 6.

3. Manning, Robert A., "Straits Jacket," New Republic 221 (September 27, 1999): 13.

4. Yu, Peter Kien-hong, "Negotiating with Beijing: What Should Taipei and a Third Party Know?" East Asia: An International Quarterly, 17 (Summer 1999): 81-82.

5. Teng-hui, Lee, "Understanding Taiwan: Bridging the Perception Gap," Foreign Affairs, November/December 1999.

6. Manning, "Straits Jacket," 82.

7. Ibid., 82.

8. Yu, "Negotiating with Beijing: What Should Taipei and a Third Party Know?" 81-82.

9. Ibid., 82.

10. Mann, James, <u>About Face</u> (New York: Alfred A. Knopf, 1999) 315-329.

11. Ibid., 334. Mark Lagon, "Taiwan Gets Bold," <u>National Review</u>, 51 (August 9, 1999): 25.

12. Mann, <u>About Face</u>, 334-335.

13. Manning, "Straits Jacket," 82.

14. Mann, <u>About Face</u>, 337. "The Truth About Taiwan," <u>Economist</u> 352 (July 24, 1999): 19.

15. Platt, "A Push for Unity Widens Gaps," 6; Manning, "Straits Jacket," 13; Lagon, "Taiwan Gets Bold," 25.

16. "Taiwan President Explains 'Special State-to-State' to U.S. Guests," *China Times,* August 8, 1999.

17. "Taiwan's Unnerving President Does It Again," <u>Economist</u> 352 (July 17, 1999): 36.

18. Lagon, "Taiwan Gets Bold," 25.

19. Yang, Phillip, "Taiwan's Legal Status: Going Beyond the Unification-Independence Dichotomy," paper delivered at the CSIS Seminar on Cross-Strait Relations at the Turn of the Century, September 21-22, 1999, Washington, D.C., 2.

20. Ibid., 3.

21. Brownlie, Ian, <u>Principles of Public International Law</u>, op cit., p.90.

22. Yang, "Taiwan's Legal Status: Going Beyond the Unification-Independence Dichotomy," 3.

23. Ibid., 2-3.

24. The U.S. 106th Congress, 1st session, May 18, 1999, House of Representatives, Washington, D.C.

25. Ibid.

26. Ibid.

Chapter 9

Taiwan's New Party and The Reunification of China

Xiansheng Tian

The unification of China has always been a thorny problem for the governments on both sides of the Taiwan Strait ever since 1949. It is also a big headache for American policy makers almost all the time since then. Getting into the 1990s, the problem has become even more sensitive when Taiwan's Nationalist government is trying to follow a pragmatic diplomacy to obtain more international recognition and the Beijing government is fighting back severely whenever Taipei made a move. The problem is becoming even more complicated when the movement for Taiwan's independence began to pick up momentum in recent years.

With Taiwan as one of the most developed areas in Asia and mainland China becoming a rising economic and political power, the relations between the two have been the focus of many people throughout the world, since the development of such relations has a lot to do with the stability and peace in the neighboring areas as well as in the whole world.

The political arena in Taiwan has experienced great changes since the late 1940s. The most important change, however, took place in the late 1980s when the ruling Nationalist Party (Kuomintang, or KMT) abandoned its censorship on the new media and allowed different political organizations to function again. Many new groups were formed, representing different ideals and interests.[i] The New Party, as one of the newest political organizations, was born in 1993 with its goals clear in mind---political reforms in Taiwan and unification of China, beside others. However, the outside world so far has not known very much about this new political party, its history, its organization, its political agenda, and its perspectives. As the third largest political force, the New Party is playing significant roles in Taiwan politics. Its policies and potentials need our studies if we want to have a realistic understanding of Taiwan today.

In this paper, the author will try to use some of the recent findings in Taiwan to have a brief analysis of this third political force in Taiwan, from the origins of its birth to its current policies, so that our knowledge of the political trends in Taiwan will be improved. By such exploration, the author also hopes that more people will be engaged in studies about the issues and we will become better prepared for the question of China's unification in the future.

Background

Up until July 1987, Taiwan had been under the shadow of the so-called "Temporary Provisions Effective During the Period of National Mobilization for Suppression of the Communist Rebellion," which was amended to the Constitution of the Republic of China by then the KMT-controlled National Assembly in 1948. The "Chieh Yen Fa" (literally translated as "vigilance measures law," or "martial law" as generally referred) that followed gave the ruling Nationalist Party absolute power to run the government without worrying about the terms in the Constitution.[ii] This would continue as the Nationalist government was defeated by the Chinese Communists and had to flee to Taiwan.

However, changes did take place in Taiwan through years. Since the late 1960s, more and more native-born Taiwan representatives began to replace the members in both the National Assembly and the Legislative Yuan who were born on the mainland as the government began to become somewhat more tolerant to different ideas within Taiwan. In 1980, a "genuine competitive national election" was held, with opposition candidates openly criticizing the ruling KMT in a manner that people in Taiwan had never experienced.[iii] In December 1986, some so-called "tang wai" politicians[iv] organized the Democratic Progressive Party (DPP). Thus, for the first time a two-party election was held in Taiwan, or in a larger sense, in China's history.

The next year, President Chiang Ching-guo formally announced that the "Chieh Yen Fa" was abandoned. In early 1991, the National Assembly followed up by officially abolished the Temporary Provisions and adopted ten amendments to the Constitution, which effectively removed the old delegates representing areas on the Mainland. The following year, the second National Assembly, almost exclusively representing the population of Taiwan, further amended the Constitution. The new laws changed many rules for the National Assembly elections, and more importantly, decided that "direct election" would be conducted in choosing the president and vice president of Taiwan, who in turn, would enjoy more power in appointing the members of other branches of the government.[v] It was during the same period, however, that more and more challenges began to face the KMT and the party ranks also began to see more splits.

The Birth of the New Party

Since the beginning of the late 1980s, the Nationalist Party had begun to show the signs of weakening unity among its members. Groups frequently referred as the conservative "hard-liners" against the Communists and for China's reunification began to feel more and more doubtful about their leaders' moving away from the Party's principal lines. Since the late 1980s, they began to charge that the Party leader, Lee Teng-hui, was adopting more and more ideas that were the cores of the Democratic Progressive Party, the opposition party that preferred to have an independent Taiwan instead of unifying with mainland China.

They were also worried that the DPP was increasingly changing into a party that only represented the ethnic Taiwanese who were seeking for the island's independence. In March 1992, these "non-mainstream" KMT factions registered with the government to form the "New Nationalist Party Line" group, with several of their leaders such Wang Chien-hsuen, the Finance Minister and Jaw Shao-kang, the Director of the Environment

Protection Agency resigning from their government offices to run for the Legislative Yuan seats. With heavy pressure from the KMT party machine and strong opposition from the DPP, the new political group persisted. On August 10, seven of its leaders, all members or former members of the Legislative Yuan, declared the birth the New Party.

In its Declaration, the New Party criticized the ruling KMT, charging the KMT leaders with corruption and "refusing to learn from its past failure." The DPP was whipped too. The Declaration labeled the opposition party as "non-responsible," "exclusive," and "becoming the champion of Taiwan's independence," which put the security of Taiwan at risk. The New Party leaders claimed they were the real representatives and spokesmen of the common people, the genuine democratic party that was determined to follow political reforms against government corruption, for stable social orders, and a balancer in Taiwan's two-party political system. Beyond these, the New Party also claimed that it would regard the security of Taiwan as the highest principle and urged the KMT and DPP to do the same. The three parties, the NP leaders argued, "should watch over each other, avoid Taiwan being betrayed, and start the negotiations with mainland China actively."[vi]

From the very beginning, the New Party was under the attacks from both the KMT and the DPP. The KMT party system had never stopped giving its "traitors" a hard time. The DPP went even farther. In both 1993 and 1994, DPP members frequently used violence against the New Party's gatherings and campaign efforts. However, this new organization survived and saw the support among the population increase significantly. For example, during the 1994 election for the Provincial Assembly and the Taipei City Council and Kaohsiung City Council contests, the New Party candidates won 6.09% of the popular votes. For the offices of the Provincial governor and mayor of Taipei, the NP performed better, gaining 7.7% in general votes and more than 30% in Taipei city. Altogether, the NP candidates captured two seats in the Provincial Assembly, eleven seats in Taipei City Council, and two seats in Kaohsiung City Council.[vii]

The New Party's performance in the December 1995 election for the Legislative Yuan was the most impressive, "the main victor in the polls" and "the biggest winner," as the news media commented. Running on a platform of reconciliation and reunification with mainland China, the NP candidates won 12.95% popular votes, sending twenty one of them into the Legislative Yuan (12.8% of the chamber). The ruling KMT, on the other hand, suffered the biggest setback by losing quite a few seats to both the NP and the DPP. The eighty-five KMT representatives in the 164-membered law-making body barely maintained their majority position. Three months later, the New Party once again played a major blow to the ruling KMT by sending 46 of its members into the National Assembly (about 13.8% of the House total seats) and claiming 13.67% of the popular votes.[viii]

Some people attributed the New Party's victories in part to the threats posed by mainland China that it would attack Taiwan if it drops a pledge to reunify and adopts the policy of Taiwan's independence. The New Party leaders agreed. The ruling KMT government efforts to broaden Taiwan's international roles and especially President Lee's personal visit in June 1995 to his Alma Mater Cornell University in the United States had offended Beijing government, who regarded these moves proof of Taiwan leaders' moving toward independence. During the summer, the People's Liberation Army conducted a series of military exercises, including missile launched into the sea around Taiwan, to intimidate the Taipei government. The New Party, at the same time, started its campaign criticizing the KMT for "unnecessarily antagonizing the mainland" and putting the security of the Taiwan people at risk. The NP leaders once again pledged their determination for the reunification with mainland China and to take new initiative in repairing badly-damaged ties with the Mainland. "We will actively play a leading role in the future policy toward China," the New Party secretary-general Jaw Shao-kang stated confidently.[ix]

It seems that China's threat to use force if Taiwan declares independence indeed had a great impact upon Taiwan's politics. The DPP increased its popular votes only by two percentage points, a disappointing show compared with its performances in earlier elections. This is especially true in the frontline areas like Jinmen and Matsu, islands only miles away from the Mainland. The DPP only got 2.8% and 1.1% of the votes respectively while the New Party gained 43%.[x] Several of the DPP's more radical representatives who advocated independence lost their seats. Their behavior in the Legislative Yuan, frequently involved with fistfights, had failed to impressed the increasingly maturing Taiwan voters. The party had to toned down its pro-independence stand, which in turn, caused the party ranks to split.[xi] However, the New Party's progress can also be explained, at least partially, as the result of the party's advocacy of clean government and political reforms in Taiwan, where vote-buying and corruption have been a headache for years. The DPP candidates' image as street fighters probably also alienated many middle-class urban voters

New Party's Political Agenda and Policies

From the first days of the New Party, this third political force in Taiwan made it clear that they were the spokesmen for the common people. As the ruling KMT was actively involved in political games and corruption and the DPP engaged in "dangerous tricks" of Taiwan independence, people in Taiwan were feeling increasingly helpless and hapless, the New Party leaders stated, and the situation was crying for a third political force to balance these two parties so that political reforms in Taiwan would continue and the security of the island would not be at risk. They declared to the public that the New Party was a brand new organization that would have "the National Assembly as its center, public opinion as its direction, general election as its means, and serving the people" as the party's policy and organizational principles.

As a minority party, the NP leaders continued, the New Party would keep the equal distance from either the KMT or the DPP, leaving the cooperation with either of them a possibility so long as these two parties' policies were in the interests of the Taiwan people. The key points were that the KMT must end corruption and the DPP would not cause more crises across the Taiwan Strait. The party's "Three Parties, No Majority" doctrine states that the third political force is the natural product of Taiwan's political situation where the ruling party and the oppositions party are engaged more in political games rather than following a pragmatic policy in dealing with Taiwan's major problems. The new force, then, will serve as a major balancer, watching over the other parties, forcing them to follow the rules of fair play, and help to rebuild people's confidence in Taiwan's democratic reforms.[xii]

The party is also new in terms of its organization. The New Party Constitution does not require its members to pledge in, to pay the organization fees, or to attend regular group meetings as other parties did. There are no chairpersons, the central committee or executive committee and so on. There will be only "coordinators" to call the meeting and all decisions will be based on the results of the democratic procedures. The party even welcomes the so-called "spiritual members," who do not have to register with the party so long as they support the New Party and its agenda.[xiii] The New Party is proud to announce that it has nothing to do with the powerful financial cliques that have long been an active interest group in Taiwan's politics. This probably has reflected the desires of Taiwan's new middle-class urban population. Checking through the party's organization chart, people will notice that almost all the New Party representatives in both the Legislative Yuan and the National Assembly belong to this group and all the party's supporting organizations are made of volunteers. The structure of the party organization is also different from other political parties.[xiv]

The ideals of the New Party have some similarities to that of the KMT at the first glance: both promote the establishment of a democratic, free and equitable prosperous (reunified) China. However, the New Party puts much more emphasis on the reforms in Taiwan and the relations with the Mainland. The highest priority of the party, the Declaration of the New Party states, is the security of Taiwan, which has a lot to do with the relations with mainland China. The New Party pledged that it would cooperate with other parties and initiate negotiations with Beijing government while urging the ruling KMT and the DPP to be more practical. As New Party leader Jaw Shao-kang commented after the party's victory in the 1995 election: "we will actively play a leading role in the future policy toward China."[xv]

The New Party's "Mainland Policy" states that both Taiwan and the Mainland are parts of China and people on both sides of the Taiwan Strait should have this consensus. However, the New Party makes it clear that it does not promote a fast reunification with the Mainland and. "The unification should follow the strengthened communication, mutual trust, system adjustments, and the trial of time across the Strait. It should be achieved through peaceful means, and if necessary, to be accomplished by the future generations." The New Party supports the maintenance of the status quo of the Taiwan-Mainland relations while promoting more exchanges, rather than KMT's "slow down" approach, between the two sides. This, the NP leaders argue, will greatly promote the democratic reforms and economic prosperity on the Mainland. The final reunification with the Mainland should take place after Beijing finally gives up its communist authoritarianism and when the majority of Taiwan people consider that time is ripe.

The two sides should put aside the issue of sovereignty, which both sides are claiming now, and sincerely consider the possibility of a confederate system for a future "Greater China". For the near future, the NP "Mainland Policy" proposes to establish more channels with the Mainland, including cultural, educational, athletic, and journalist exchanges. The Policy also suggests that some special "free economic and trade areas" be established on both sides of the Taiwan Strait so that more economic cooperation between the two sides will be greatly promoted. Taipei should support the Mainland's activities in the international affairs. In return, Beijing should also respect Taiwan's role in the world.[xvi]

These, also show some similarities to the policies of the KMT, actually some people argued there is nothing new from the New Party. The difference, the NP leaders argue, is that the KMT leaders have been trying to use "slow reunification" to hide their real purpose of realizing the independence of Taiwan. Considering the fact that the younger generations who were born and brought up in Taiwan and have little idea about the Mainland, the future of Taiwan's elections probably will bear very different fruits from that of today. The NP leaders worries seem real.[xvii]

Perspectives

The six-year old New Party is playing an important role in today's Taiwan politics. That does not mean it has fewer problems than others. Coordination (or lack of it) of activities, different opinions as well as personalities, short of financial support, and so on, have always been the problems the new third force has to deal with.[1711]

Since the successful 1995 election, the New Party has suffered from these problems and for a while some people even started talking whether it would survive at all. However, since late 1997 the party began to launch new reforms within the party and another wave of "mass mobilization" campaigns aimed at 1998 year-end's election for Taipei mayorship. Besides listing a lot of policy plans regarding Taiwan's education, environment, public safety, finance, welfare and women's issues, the New Party also give some more emphasis on its Mainland policy. In last February, the New Party Congress decided to form a new Mainland Policy Committee to coordinate the party's policies toward the Mainland. The new committee reiterated the Party's "One China" policy and required the party members avoid any confusion by not openly expressing their different opinions. Looking at the new statement by the Committee, we may once again notice the similarities to the ruling KMT's policies, though criticism of the KMT policy is also present. For example, the statement makes it clear that

1. The sovereignty of China cannot be divided; there is only one China.

2. The reality that Beijing's control has never extended to Taiwan and Taipei's control has never reached the Mainland shows that there are actually two governments in China, or two "political entities" ruling two different parts of China. However, only the "one sovereignty shared by two sides" idea will help friendly development of the relations across the Taiwan Strait.

3. Like the KMT, the New Party does not think Beijing's "one country, two systems" model that has been applied to Hong Kong will work in Taiwan. This is especially true that most people in Taiwan believe the only time they are going to agree on the reunification of China is when the Beijing government decides it will give up its Marxist-Leninist dictatorship and allow the ideas like liberty and freedom to develop in China. China will reunify, but there should not be a set schedule or deadline.

4. The only way to solve the confrontation between the two sides, according the New Party, is to promote more exchanges of all kinds across the Strait. With improved communication between the two governments and especially among the people, the crisis will be solved and consensus will be reached.

Obviously, the position of the New Party as Taiwan's third political force is taking roots.

It looks also pretty sure this new minority party will continue to follow its set policy of possible cooperation with either the KMT or the DPP on different domestic issues and watch carefully the other two parties' moves on China's reunification issue. The NP leaders are very confident of the party's future in Taiwan's political reforms as well as in the process of reunification, as Wang Cheih-hsuen, one of the founders of the New Party and the current leader, stated in his declaration for running the Taipei mayorship. "We are optimistic about our future, since our position as a strong minority in both the Legislative Yuan and in the National Assembly will make it hard for the two bigger parties to become dominant. They have to seek for cooperation from us," New Party National Assembly member Sheng Chen added.

However, the results of the 1998 year-end's "Three in One" election (the Legislative Yuan, Taipei and Kaohsiung Mayors' offices, and the tow City Councils' election at the same time) really served the New Party a big blow. The lack unity and coordination continued, making the campaign efforts even more difficult. When the election results came out, the New Party found it had lost about one half of its voters-- only 7.09% of Taiwan voters supported the New Party candidates. The Legislative Yuan seats also dropped from 21 to 11.

Many major NP leaders lost their seats while the KMT won quite a number of seats, regaining its majority control in the Legislative Yuan. The KMT even won the Taipei Mayor's office from the DPP. Facing the disappointing results, the NP members criticized each other for the failure, some of the NP leaders even complained that they would never again work for the Party.

But many people also realized the victory of the KMT in this election had something to do the NP voters, especially in the competition for Taipei Mayor's office. According to some research, about 77% of New Party supporters actually voted for the KMT as a result of the urge by some old anti-Taiwan independence NP supporters. Without the NP votes, the KMT candidate might well lose the election to the DPP candidate, even the KMT winner, Ma Yingjiu, agreed that the key of his victory was the NP votes. It is understandable to see the New Party members voting for the KMT---it is better to have the KMT, rather than the pro-independence DPP, in the office since the KMT is still talking about China's reunification. Besides, Lee Teng-hui's idea of "New Taiwanese" in one way or another also helped to undermine the DPP's ethnic hatred propaganda and improve the KMT image. The DPP's pro-independence stand also caused many people to worry whether it could really take good care of the Mainland-Taiwan relations. The result of the election fully reflected the general trend among majority of the Taiwan people on the issue of China's reunification: No fast unification, no fast independence either.

The New Party did not give up easily. During the year of 1999, the NP members made some serious self-criticism and are now concentrating on the preparation for the 2000 presidential election. It looks like that the New Party will continue to play certain role in Taiwan politics in the future, since the reunification will continue to be the core issue of the Mainland-Taiwan relations and such relations, in turn, will have great impact on the debates over Taiwan's future. Within Taiwan, the existence of such a third party also provides people in Taiwan one more option in dealing with their domestic issues. Scholars have predicted that this three-party system will very probably survive and grow, which will further help Taiwan's democratization and set examples for the Mainland to learn from, if the reunification of China finally comes.

As the third political force in Taiwan, the New Party has existed for six year. The establishment and the development of this new political force reflected, in certain way, the changes that have taken place in Taiwan since 1980s. The New Party's stand on China's reunification is clearly and firmly defined, but careful readers will find that the NP policy actually contains some "not-that-practical" but rather idealistic elements. Many of the NP policies will have a hard time to meet the Beijing government's demands, while the support for the New Party in Taiwan will also see some serious challenges in the future as more and more younger voters, who are born and grow up in Taiwan and have little idea about Mainland China and China's reunification, start going to the poll. However, as long as the problem of unification remains, the surroundings for the New Party's survival will exist. Along with the increasing world attention to the Taiwan issue, the studies on the Taiwan's political forces will also increase. What future roles the New Party will play will also be the focus of attention for many people in the coming years.

Endnotes

i. By August 1997, a total of 84 political parties had registered with the Ministry of the Interior. However, only three of these are considered indeed playing a significant role in Taiwan's politics. These are the Kuomintang (KMT, Nationalist Party), which boasts a membership of 2.1 million; the Democratic Progressive Party (DPP), the largest opposition party, which claims a membership of 152,000 and the New Party (NP) with a registered membership of 72,000. For details, see The Republic of China at a Glance published by the Government Information Office (Taipei, Taiwan, 1997).
ii. For more details, see John F. Copper's Taiwan: Nation State Or Province? (Boulder, CO: Westview, 1996), 85.
iii. Ibid., 107.
iv. "Tang wai," literally translated as "outside the party," are those opposition politicians who used to run in elections as independents and were tolerated by the KMT since the Party began to change its attitude toward the party competition in the 1960s.
v. These officials include the members of the Control Yuan, the Judicial Yuan, and the Examination Yuan. See A Brief Introduction of ROC (Taipei, Taiwan: Government Information Office, 1996).
vi. See "The Chronicle of the New Party" in The List of the New Party's Public Servants (Taipei, Taiwan: The New Party Personnel Department, 1997), 225-226.
vii. Ibid., 227.
viii. Alejandro Reyes, "Now, a Third Force?" (December 15, 1995). The article can be found at www.pathfinder.com/@23SDC2M4LQAAQLq8/asiaweek/95/1215/nat.ht

m1

ix. Ibid., "Thunder Out of China: The Mainland's 'Missile Diplomacy' Jolts Taiwan" (Aug.4, 1995). Also see Reuter Information Service, "Taiwan's Ruling Party in Biggest Ever Election Setback" (Dec. 2, 1995) at www.nando.net/newsroom/ntn/world/ 120295/world642_13. html.

x. Alejandro Reyes, "Now, a Third Force?"

xi. In October 1996, the DPP finally saw its ranks split. Several of its major members declared that they were organizing a new party, the Nation-building Party (NBP, or more accurately translated, Taiwan Independence Party). They regarded the party leaders had betrayed the party's founding principle of pursuing Taiwan independence when they moved to form a "grand reconciliation" with the pro-unification New Party in late 1995 and sought for a coalition government with the KMT in the spring of 1996. See details from the Taiwan Independence Party's website at www.taiwandc.org/taip-idx.htm

xii. "Three Parties, No Majority" in The New Party Policy White Paper (Taipei: New Party Headquarters, 1995), 15-17 and 27.

xiii. "The Declaration of the New Party," ibid., 1-5 and 8.

xiv. For more details, check the New Party website at www.np.org.tw/np11.htm

xv. The Reuter Information Service report, December 2, 1995.

xvi. "The Relations across the Strait and the Mainland Policy" in The New Party Policy White Paper, 105-108.

xvii. Interview with Dr. Sheng Chen, the New Party representative in the National Assembly, Taoyuan, Taiwan, May 24, 1998.

1. In early 1998, a major New Party leader had to resign from the post of the party's "Policy Research Committee" and the Coordinator of New Party delegation in the National Assembly for his taking part in a conference and expressing his ideas on the Mainland policy that were different from that of the Party, and thus causing confusion among the party rank-and-file. In another case, the Party Congress and the General Secretariat failed to coordinate with a group of party members who were trying to organize a speech for one of the party leaders. Disciplinary decisions were also made against some of the party members who were suspected having conducted "inappropriate activities" during the campaigns. See New Party New Releases on March 7 and 25, and August 17, 1998 at the party's website.

111. See Wang's speech on the New Party's website at
www.np.org.tw/np8/news/n108.htm
1111. Interview with Dr. Sheng Chen, May 24, 1998.

Chapter 10

Nationalism vs. Communism in China's Modernization

David Shapard

In recent years, China has been undergoing great changes. While the present leaders of China are the Communists, they are also Chinese. Although they are determined to weed out many social and economic traditions, much of the traditional Chinese culture continues to be preserved. No regime, even if it wished, could sweep away long cherished ideas and customs overnight. Consequently, even though the Chinese society has greatly changed with the Communist rule, many elements of traditional Chinese life remain. The teachings of Confucius, the noted philosopher of ancient China, doubtlessly influenced the thinking and behavior of more people than any other body of spiritual or ethical teaching in man's history.

China experienced a major upheaval and rapid growth during the first half of the twentieth century. Three men played important roles in the birth and development of China during this time. They are Sun Yat-Sen, Chiang Kai-Shek, and Mao Zedong. In addition, Mao played a fundamental role in the transformation of the nation into the People's Republic of China. He was aided in this by Zhou Enlai.

The Russian Revolution of 1917 affected China although no immediate change occurred in China at the time. Lenin, leader of Russia's Communist government had indicated his support for all Asian revolutions against foreign colonization and imperialism. The Chinese saw a promise of revolution in China in the success of the Russian revolution. Socialist groups began to appear in China in December 1919. The Chinese Communist Party (CCP) formally organized in July 1921 in Shanghai. Under the urging of the Soviets, the Chinese Communist Party agreed to cooperate with Sun Yat-Sen and the Chinese Nationalist Government known as Kuomintang (KMT). By working with individual communists, Sun hoped to gain Soviet support for stabilizing the nation and defeating the Chinese warlords. He did not intend to be bound by either the Russians or the Chinese Communists. The KMT and CCP agreement worked well between 1921 and 1927. Some members of the Communist Party thought that they could eventually control and guide the Nationalist Government.

1. Nationalism and Nationalist Government

In 1928 the Nationalist revolutionaries celebrated the creation of a new nationalist government dedicated to the unification and rebirth of China. Now they hoped to be able to show what they could do for their country. When Chiang Kai-Shek founded his government in Nanking, the task of unification was only half achieved. Much of China was still ruled by independent warlords determined to keep for themselves the wealth of the provinces they dominated. These warlords belonged to an older China and had no sympathy for the changes advocated by scholars and businessmen who supported the Nationalist revolution.

Moreover, despite Chiang Kai-Shek's raid against the Communists in 1927, he had not eliminated the Communist movement from China. The Chinese Communists were intent on bringing about a social and economic revolution as well as a nationalist one.

Another menace to China was Japan. Determined to dominate East Asia, the Japanese government was hungry for more conquests at the expense of China. Against these enemies, Chiang Kai-Shek waged almost constant war for twenty years. Increasingly, he came to rely on the

Nationalists army and to postpone seeking solutions to China's domestic problems. Pressing needs for reform were allowed to slip into the background as issues to be dealt with after national unity and security had been achieved. The very existence of a freed China was at stake.

As life became a struggle for survival, the people of China became increasingly disenchanted with the Nationalist government. The Nationalists were not only blamed for the many hardships that the people had to endure, but were also accused of dishonesty and corruption. The Chinese Communists had increased their power and had won much popular support.

It is obvious that Chinese nationalism and Japanese imperialism would eventually clash. In 1931, an incident in Manchuria finally touched off a conflict. Japan had special interests in Manchuria. Many Japanese subjects had settled there. The region had rich natural resources Japanese investments which included a railroad were very heavy and Japan had already been granted special rights in Manchuria by China. Moreover, this northern borderland served as a useful buffer between Japan and Russia.

One night in September, 1931, Japanese soldiers exploded a bomb on the tracks of the Japanese railroad near the Manchurian city of Mukden. Quickly the Japanese officers sent their troops into action against the Manchurian warlord, Chang Hsueh-Liang. He was called the "Young Marshall". Although not hostile to Nationalist government, this warlord had insisted on maintaining his rule in Manchuria. Now his troops had to face the advancing Japanese. Though the warlord's forces fought stubbornly, they were easily swept aside by the Japanese. At the outset the Japanese objective had to been to occupy strategic places in southern Manchuria. Within the next six months the Japanese army swept over all of Manchuria. The Nationalists were infuriated by the Japanese attack but Chiang Kai-Shek knew that his country was no match for Japan on the battlefield. Also he knew that China still needed time to achieve unit. War with powerful Japan might well bring disaster.

China sent a protest to the League of Nations. The League sent a committee of representatives from five nations to investigate the situation in Manchuria. After a careful study, this committee, called The Lytton Commission, drew up a report which held Japan guilty of an unjustified attack on China. The League members were unwilling, however, to take any effective action against Japan. The Chinese were unhappy. The Japanese were also displeased. Calling the decision one-sided and prejudiced, Japan in 1933 withdrew from the League of Nations. The Japanese set up a puppet government in Manchuria and gave it the name of Manchukuo, meaning "land of the Manchus." It was a "puppet" government because it was dependent upon the Japanese. No one was deceived by this make-believe country. In fact, Manchuria was transformed into a vast Japanese military base.

The loss of Manchuria was a serious blow to the National government. In addition to being rich in coal and iron ore, Manchuria was a large and fertile region. It was not densely populated but it had provided an outlet for China's growing population. To show their anger over the invasion of Manchuria, the Chinese began to boycott Japanese goods. Their boycott proved effective and Japanese trade with China dropped off sharply. In early 1932, Japan sent a naval expedition to Shanghai, a center of the boycott. Large parts of Shanghai were destroyed in the attack and China suffered from Japanese thrust into inner Mongolia and northern China. The inability of Chiang Kai-Shek's government to fight off these attacks revealed its military weakness.

The number of Chinese Communists had been reduced in the late 1920's, but the Chinese Communist movement was revived because of the show of the Nationalist government military weakness. The Communists were more determined than ever to destroy the Nationalist government and cease power in China. They realized that their dream of a Communist China would require a long struggle to overthrow the Kuomintang. Communists had always believed that their revolution would have to be spearheaded by oppressed factory workers in the cities.

Supposedly, they alone were desperate enough to rise against the existing society and replace it with a Communist system. Their leader, Mao Zedong, began to stir up the peasants resentment against the government which seemed to be indifferent to their misery. From these peasants Mao recruited members for the Chinese Communist Party and troops of military force were called the Red Army. In the areas under his control, Mao established a Communist-styled government called the Chinese Soviet Republic.

2. The First Civil War between the Nationalists and Communists

In 1931, Chiang Kai-Shek decided to eliminate the Communist threat once and for all. Over the next three years he launched five military expeditions against Mao's base in southeast China. These offensives were called "Bandit Extermination Campaigns." Chiang Kai-Shek made use of warlord armies near Mao's refuge for these operations. He hoped that the

Communists and warlords would destroy each other. When the Red Army easily routed these forces and captured their military equipment, Chiang Kai-Shek sent his Nationalist troops against the Communists and the Communists were caught in a giant squeeze. The Communists were subjected to a blockade. Mao realized that they might be destroyed. The whole Communist community of about 100,000 men, women and children broke through the Nationalists' blockade and fled for their lives. The flight of Mao's revolutionary force from southeastern China in 1934 and 1935 was an agonizing ordeal. The Communists call this episode the "Long March". The route led westward to the edges of eastern Tibet and then turn northward across barren, uninhabited regions. The Communists finally ended their year-long trek in the mountains of northwest China, more than 5,000 miles. Some veterans of the long march became the iron core of both the Chinese Communist Part and the Red Arm To have taken part in the grueling march was considered a mark of distinction and unit The al of destroying the Communists had to wait because Japan which had become a militaristic government began to flex her muscles.

During the late 1930's, aggressive dictators ruled in Germany and Italy and Japan had become a military state. These land-hungry nations posed a threat to their neighbors, including the Soviet Union. Joseph Stalin, the Soviet dictator, ordered the Communist parties in various countries to suspend their efforts to overthrow existing governments, for the time being, they should establish united fronts against the common enemy. This meant that the Communists were to cooperate with any government that opposed the German and Italian dictators and the Japanese militarists. The Chinese Communists and Mao did not overestimate their own power. They knew that only an alliance between the Communists and the Nanking government had any chance for success against Japan and later for uniting China. The opposition to the Chinese Communist movement relaxed and greater freedoms was committed in the regions under their control. China remained weak economically and militarily and political unity was greatly furthered during the early months of 1937.

During this time some attempts at reform was made by the Kuomintang but the country was still politically divided and an honest and efficient government had not yet been achieved. Reforms in agriculture were way overdue. Industrial development was lagging and the transportation net work was totally inadequate. There were few modem schools or hospitals and competent scientists and engineers were in short supply. To start the transformation of China into a modem nation called for the wisdom of a Solomon. Resources that might have improved living conditions were used in the Nationalist's campaigns against the warlords and the Japanese. In mid-1937 Chiang Kai-Shek had created an effective modem army but had been done at the expense of much needed improvements in other areas of Chinese life. The most serious problem that faced the Nationalist government was the extreme poverty that the Chinese people had suffered for centuries. The Chinese peasant was known as the "forgotten man." In a year the average Chinese peasant perhaps earned as much as an American worker made in a week. The Chinese peasant went hungry or even starved. Painful sacrifices were demanded from people who had already had suffered too much. It could have been predicted that the Nationalist government was headed for trouble unless it could provide relief for the peasants.

Land reform was badly needed and with the passing of time the situation had steadily worsened. Peasants were mercifully squeezed for taxes by local governments and warlords. A Nationalist government planned many programs to help the peasants but had little success. While the governments encouraged the formation of cooperative groups for purchasing, these groups encountered opposition from large landlords and the city merchants. The government also established agricultural schools and research laboratories but unfortunately, their programs and findings did not reach the peasants because of corruption. The Nationalist's failure to solve the farm problem had unfortunate results. China urgently needed food stuffs to feed its growing population. The inability of the peasants to increase crop production met hunger throughout the land. Lack of farm surplus to use in trade limited China's ability to purchase machinery abroad. Furthermore, the suffering of the peasants furnished the Communists with a powerful weapon to use against the Nationalist Government which was blamed for all of China's troubles.

The Chinese educational system had been gradually introduced after World War I. Many leaders of the Nationalist government had been educated in modem schools established by foreign missionaries. Hundreds of training schools and textile institutes and universities had been founded. Yet, far greater efforts were necessary to keep up the growing need for education. China had at least 40,000,000 children of elementary school age but schools existed for no more than 15,000,000. Given time the Nationalist government might have used education to lead the people of China into the Twentieth Century but this hope was shattered by the outbreak of war with Japan.

3. The Coalition in WWII and the Communist Development

On July 7, 1937, soldiers of the Nationalists Army clashed with Japanese troops near the Marco Polo Bridge outside Peking where Japanese force had been stationed since the Boxer rebellion. This fighting was called the "China incident." The word "incident" makes it sound unimportant. Yet, this encounter was to lead to a long and cruel war. This second Sino-Japanese war is generally regarded as the beginning of World War 11. The war in Europe did not officially begin until 1939. Germany, Italy and Japan reached agreements which drew them together to become known as the Axis Powers. On December 7, 1941, when the Japanese bombed Pearl Harbor in Hawaii, the day after the attack, China officially declared war on Japan though actually the two countries had been fighting since 1937. The United States also ended up joining the allied powers.

Thousands of Chinese retreated into the interior of China and established Chungking in southwest China as the capitol of free China and it remained so until World War Il was over. To continue this resistance against the Japanese, great numbers of Chinese people made their way westward to Chungking. Whatever material and equipment they could transport was carried away a step ahead of the invaders. Machines and factories were taken apart and carried piece by piece on the backs of volunteers. Hospital equipment and medical supplies were also boom -into free China.

Free China struggled to survive. Teachers and students were determined to keep their classes going despite the war. The Chinese moved many schools to Nationalist held regions. Educational supplies, entire libraries, and precious laboratory equipment were packed to transport it to their destination by every available means. Japanese military authorities seized the crops of helpless peasants. The Japanese airplanes bombed towns and cities in the Nationalist held areas, yet free China miraculously managed to hold out. While the American government was concerned that the Chinese Nationalists might collapse before Japan could be defeated, the United States managed to send supplies into free China over two routes, the more famous of these-the Burma Road-tied southwest China with the outside world. The second supply line was over what they called "the Hump" as the mountains along the China-Burma frontier were called.

The United States took steps to strengthen the morale of the Chinese. One such action concerned special rights in China which had been granted to the United States. In 1943, the United States voluntarily surrendered its special rights in China and this was quickly followed by Great Britain. Nationalist China was treated as an equal by the leading allied powers.

More significant when the United Nations was organized in 1945, after the defeat of the Japanese, Nationalist China was included in the Security Council as one of its five members, but some American officials and generals criticized certain conditions in free China. The Nationalist regime had many corrupt leaders and dishonest officials. Living conditions in China were miserable and the plight of food and other basic commodities increased almost daily. Soaring inflation threatened to make Chinese money worthless. For these reasons the Nationalist government became increasingly unpopular with the war-weary Chinese people. Many of the conditions stemmed from China's poverty which was made worse by the war. The Nationalist government was responsible for part of the trouble. The Nationalist movement had never lost sight of the threat presented by the Chinese Communist Party and its Red Army.

The Chinese Communists and Nationalists cooperated in fighting the enemy during wartime. This joint action continued until 1940 when the alliance began to crack. During the last half of the war both Nationalists and Communists acted more to advance their own interests than to fight the common enemy-Japan. As a result, China was torn by "triangular war" among Nationalists, Communists and Japanese, until the end of the war in 1945. During the war with Japan, Mao Tse-Tung did not abandon his main goal to establish Communist control over all of China. He made use of the war to further his aim. He knew that the success or failure of his Red Army would determine the future of the Communist movement in China. So, Mao concentrated on strengthening the Chinese Communist army with a show down that lay ahead with the Nationalist regime.

4. Mao's Military and Political Triumph

The Communists sought to win popular support. They now posed as champions of reform. Improvements were carried out under the areas of their control. As a result, Mao's followers were welcomed wherever they went. Mao's Red Army soldiers also gained many recruits among the peasants. By the end of the war the ranks of the Red Army had swelled to a million men. In August, 1945, after the United States had dropped two atomic bombs on Japanese cities, the Emperor of Japan accepted the terms of surrender. China was utterly exhausted.

The Nationalist government was more than ever held responsible for the nation's plight and so was extremely unpopular. Mao and the Communist movement on the other hand, stronger and bolder than ever before. At the war's end China was a gutted land. Food and other essentials were scarce and prices sky-rocketed. Not even in the worst of the pre-war years had China been so close to disaster. The United States and United Nations tried to provide relief for China. This aid prevented a complete breakdown but an even greater problem was widespread cheating, corruption and dishonest government officials. Both the Nationalists and the Communists were eager to win control of the areas in eastern and northern China, the ones that the Japanese had held for so long. As clashes between the rival Chinese forces increased, the shattered country was plunged into even greater chaos.

In an effort to prevent war between the Nationalists and the Communists, President Harry Truman of the United States sent General George C. Marshall to China in late 1945. Marshall's mission was to close the breach between Chiang Kai-Shek and Mao Tse-Tung. The United States believed that cooperation between the two leaders was urgently needed if China were to have a chance to heal the wounds of eight years of war. The Marshall mission ended in failure. It was like trying to mix oil and water. The struggle between the Nationalists and the Communists came to a head in Manchuria. Nationalist's efforts were also obstructed by the Russians who had invaded Manchuria in the closing week of the war. Before withdrawing in 1946, the Russians stripped the area of its industrial equipment.

A fierce struggle for Manchuria broke out in 1947. The Nationalists' garrisons in the cities were gradually surrounded and finally isolated by the Red Army. The Red Army seized valuable military equipment that the United States had famished to the Nationalists troops. There was no stopping the Communist tidal wave. With Manchuria securely in its grasps, Mao opened a gigantic offensive for the conquest of China. Striking power and combat efficiency of the Red Army amazed the Nationalist troops and the world. The on-rushing Red Army occupied Peking and scarcely a shot was fired in defense. The conquest of the rest of mainland China was largely a mopping up operation. Unable to check the Red Army advance, Chiang Kai-Shek and the Nationalist government retreated to an island off the China coast by the name of Taiwan. On the mainland, the Communists proclaimed a new government–the People's Republic of China, on October 1, 1949.

The lack of manpower or inferior weapons did not cause the

Nationalist's defeat. A crucial factor was the spirit and the morale; tired of the wars and misery which had filled their lives for more than a decade, the Chinese people also had lost confidence in the Nationalist leadership. In the struggle between the Nationalists and the Communists, the great majority of Chinese were probably neutral, desiring nothing but peace. Most of them did not actively support the Communists, neither did they rally behind the sagging regime of the Nationalists. In the eyes of many Chinese, it seemed that the Communists might represent an improvement over the Nationalist government. China's destiny was decided in the years immediately following World War II. The efforts to reach a political settlement between the Nationalists and the Communists failed. With his victory in China, Mao Tse-Tung established himself as the foremost Communist revolutionary of the times.

The challenge of present-day China also emphasizes the need to learn more about its land and people. In recent years, however, China's Communist leaders have insisted on playing a major role in world affairs. They are determined to recapture the position of leadership in Asia long held by their ancestors . They have also proclaimed their views on the crucial issues affecting all mankind, such as world disarmament, nuclear testing, war and peace and the future of newly independent countries in Asia and Africa. To reinforce its claims to the status of a major power, Communist China has engaged in a mighty drive to build up its industry and military capabilities.

Great sacrifices have been demanded of the Chinese people and impressive advances have been made. Communist China today has the largest standing army in the world and has also developed nuclear power. Although industrially it is still dwarfed by the United States, Great Britain and Russia, the time may not be far off when this Asian colossus will achieve a productive capable of that of the leading industrial nations. Communist China no longer can be dismissed as merely one of the leading nations of Asia. It has become a major world power. The internal turmoil that has recently shaken China, however, may seriously handicap the country in its economic development.

Even though our lands have been drawn nearer to each other in terms of travel and time, Americans and Chinese remain separated by gulfs of ignorance and misunderstanding. The average American today knows little more about the Chinese people than his ancestors did a country or two ago. The main in the street in China is just as poorly informed about the American people. If Americans and Chinese knew more about each other, this alone would guarantee that we would get along better. But one thing is certain, mutual ignorance only increases the likelihood of tension and conflict. China is a sleeping giant that is half awakened.

5. Ideology and Modernization in China

China's destiny was decided in the years immediately following the second world war. A full-scale struggle for control of China broke out. The triumph of Mao Tse-Tung in China was the most important victory for communism since the Bolshevik Revolution in Russia. The Chinese communists lost little time in making clear what they hoped to achieve in relation with the rest of the world. They announced that the humiliation of China at the hands of foreign powers was to be ended once and for all. Mao and his followers demanded that China be treated with full respect by other governments. The leaders of communist China took it for granted that their country ranked first among the nations of Asia. They also set forth their qualifications for providing leadership to the world communist movement.

From the day the new regime was proclaimed Mao and his comrades made known their determination to forge a new life for their country. Captivated by the dream of building a better life for their children and grandchildren they regarded no price too high to pay in working for this goal. Never before in China's long history had such great changes been made in that country's way of life. An all-out drive to transform China into an industrial nation got under way. The agricultural system was shaken up more drastically than at any time during the past forty centuries. Government, schools, families, relations and culture all felt the impact revolutionary change.

The Chinese communists met many of the goals of their revolution. But there were also notable failures. Mao and his comrades had to turn from one crisis to another. Moreover, after years of political unity, they, themselves, were drawn into a vicious rivalry for leadership. No doubt crises will continue to arise within communist China and the affects of these crises will be felt throughout the world. In 1949, the Red Army easily wiped out the last resistance of the Nationalist force. Only those of Chiang Kai-Shek's troop who escaped to Taiwan survived these mopping up operations. Soldiers of the Red Army also eliminated the last of the war lords and other marauders who had held out in isolated areas. With these missions accomplished the wars that had wracked China for four decades came to an end.

The communists then hunted down supporters of the Kuomintang which meant anyone who had been associated with the ousted regime was a suspect. In the cities and the villages former officials of the Kuomintang government and officers of its army were imprisoned for their crimes. Landlords in the countryside and city merchants were accused, rightly or wrongly, of being spies, saboteurs or counter-revolutionaries. Many hundreds of thousands--some say millions-fell victim to the communist blood baths, but the true numbers will never be known.

The new rulers of China made special efforts to re-educate and win over intellectuals and technicians. People who would be useful in the party's programs for rebuilding a new China. Some years later Mao ordered a relaxation of state controls in speech, press and thought. He had that b allowing scholars and thinkers greater freedom, they would serve the state more effectively. Mao wanted to replace the old nationalist government with a new political structure. From 1949 to 1954, the system of government which the communists ruled China was regarded as temporary. In theory, the Nationalist's People's Congress had been the supreme organ of government in China. Its members are created by regional congresses in the provinces. These bodies, in turn, are elected by political assemblies operating in smaller geographical units. Actual power in China has been wielded by the communist party.

This is the largest communist party in he world. By the mid-1960's its membership stood at about 20 million. This figure, however, is less than 3 percent of the total Chinese population. Even if allowances are made for the high proportion of children and young people in China, the percentage is still very low. The party has obviously been a very select organization. Its members have been strategically situated to dominate the life of the country. By holding a monopoly of important positions they have controlled the government, the army and the police. They have also dominated the schools the trade unions, community organizations and cultural associations.

The Chinese communists saw rapid industrialization as the key to greater power for China. They were determined to change the basic pattern of the country's economy. In a communist country, the government can formulate and carry out an overall plan or economic development. China was to be transformed as quickly as possible from an agricultural country into an industrial giant. Day after day the speeches and writings of communist leaders was sprinkled with statistics of production. The country's progress was to be measured in terms of its annual industrial output. Mao and the party directors boasted that they intended to overtake the western industrial nations. Their ultimate I was to rank first among the industrial powers of the world. The communist leaders also had plans for modernizing agriculture and reforming the land-holding system. The first task facing the Chinese communist party was to clear away the rubble and make repairs. Then, they could begin their new programs.

An inadequate transportation system was a major handicap in the Chinese drive toward industrialization. Railroads and highways were expensive to build and could not be constructed overnight. But, they are necessary if goods and raw materials are to be moved quickly.

Soon after the communist came to power they made an inventory of the country's known resources and began a search for new locations of raw materials. China possesses many of the natural resources necessary for modem industry. Coal comprises China's principal mineral wealth. Excellent deposits are located in central Manchuria and other valuable beds of coal are found between the Yellow and Yangtze Rivers. Iron ore, copper and tin and there are some deposits of aluminum, magnesium and gold. One of the serious mineral weaknesses is the scarcity of crude oil but exploration has started and will continue to try to find new oil fields. One of China's biggest handicaps has been the lack of money to exploit natural resources. It often was said that differences among the people were not based on the differences in wealth but rather on different degrees of poverty.

The Chinese launched a fresh program of industrialization and it was called "First Five Year Plan." This was an all-out effort at industrialization and heavy industry was given priority. The country's slim resources were committed to the expansion of steel mills and the building of machinery. Railroad construction, power plants and tractor assemblies were also emphasized. Light industry received little attention. Everyone was expected to make sacrifices for the success of the Five-Year Plan. A strict rationing system-price controls, and the elimination of profiteering put an end to many abuses that had been common under the Kuomintang.

The hard work of the Chinese people caused the production of iron and steel to triple between 1952 and 1957. During the same time period the output of coal soared from 65 million tons to 130 million tons. Railroad mileage increased from 15,000 to 18,000 miles. A beginning was made in the construction of dams and power plants and the Chinese were proud of their achievement. Confident that they were on the right track, the communist party announced plans for a still more ambitious economic offensive--one in which the entire country was called on to make a great leap forward. This first Five Year Plan went from 1953 to 1957.

Communist China overreached itself In the second Five Year Plan, from 1958 to 1962, emphasis was placed on heavy industry, again, the peasants were expected to pay the price. An all-out effort was made to boost the production of iron and steel. A government encouraged its citizens to build small blast furnaces near their homes and to turn out crude iron. It was estimated that if each of these small furnaces could produce a few hundred pounds, China's total iron production would amount to a million tons by the end the year. But the backward furnaces were a failure.

Glowing reports of success had been announced at the end of the first Five Year Plan and at the end of the first year and the second Five Year Plan. The claims of the communist government were not believed in many parts of the world. It was discovered that China had been falsifying their production reports. Many problems contributed to the failure of the second five Year Plan. The transportation system bogged down. Factory managers tolerated low quality and waste in their zeal to meet production quotas. Perhaps the major factor in the nationwide slow down was the Chinese people, themselves. Driven by factory foremen and party officials they buckled under the heavy strain. While working long hours in factories and mines, people received very little in return. The second Five Year Plan proved to be a tremendous disappointment to the communist party.

Agriculture was a big concern. The concern was how to feed the people and to increase production of food to meet the needs of a growing population and also for export. When the Communists came to power in 1949, they had confiscated farm land and turned it over to the peasants. A few years later the party organized the peasants into small cooperative farms of 30 or 40 families each but the production of these small fanning groups did not keep pace with the needs of the industrial population. The Chinese communist government was disturbed by the lagging production of the farms. To realize its goals, the government decided to overhaul the agricultural system. The cooperatives were united into large communes.

In about a year 25,000 of these communes were established. The peasants not only lost their remaining rights in the land but also had to turn over their work animals and farm equipment to the communes. communist leaders assumed that agriculture would become more efficient under the communes. They had hoped that better use would be made of labor, machines and capital. But these hopes were not realized and before lo the communes were in trouble. Long periods of drought, floods and severe storms dangerously reduced farm output. Some areas were plagued by swarms of locust that ate crops before they could be harvested. As a result, serious shortages of food developed. The setbacks of the second Five Year Plan slowed down the pace of the drive to industrialize China. In succeeding years exacting demands were made on the people and much more attention was given to the problems of agriculture because the people had to eat. It appeared that the Chinese leaders had realized that more time would be needed to reach their economic goals. They did not change these goals, but were more cautious in planning for them.

In 1964, it became apparent that China's economic planners were given top priority to the development of atomic power. In the same year, with the successful explosion of its first atomic bomb, China became the fifth nation to possess nuclear energy. Over the next two years the Chinese set off four more test explosions at their nuclear installation at Lop Nor.

In order to build a strong state, Mao's regime sought to win the complete allegiance of the people, but the teachings of Confucius which had influenced Chinese thinking and behavior for centuries were an obstacle to this goal. Consequently, the party made a persistent effort to up root Confucian ideals. Eve means of persuasion was used to transform men, women and children into loyal subjects of the communist state. In the process many time-honored custom and traditions were trampled under foot. The party regarded education as the key to rearing loyal and obedient citizens. The classroom was also the obvious place in which to tackle the old-Age problem of illiteracy. China's education needs, however, were staggering. Since more than half of the population is under the age of 20, merely to provide for the requirements of the younger generation makes a tremendous demand on the state's limited resources. Certainly, there will not be enough schools, teachers and classrooms supplies for years to come, but the communists are also eager to provide educational opportunities for the adults. They realize that a modem, industrial nation must have workers who can read and write.

Furthermore, literate adults can be more efficiently drilled in the ideals of communism. Undoubtedly, opinions about communism vary among the Chinese, themselves. The older generation can vividly recall the agonies of life in China during the first half of the century. The young Chinese on the other hand have never known another way of life. They may have grievances and disappointments but they have been instilled with patriotic fervor. Until communist China stepped into the stage of international affairs, it was commonly assumed that the communists everywhere followed the Soviet Union's leadership. But, as we have seen, the rise to power in China of Mao Tse-Tung and his comrades was the greatest prize won by communism. China has a question to be settled, but only by the Chinese, themselves. The turmoil within communist China today makes it impossible to predict what the future will hold for this giant of a nation.

References

Barnett, Doak. China on the Eve of Communist Takeover. New York: Praeger, 1964.

Bianco, Lucien. The Origins of the Chinese Revolution: 1915 to 1949. Translation by Muriel Bell. Stanford, California: Stanford University Press, 1971.

Brothwick, Mark. Pacific Century. Second Edition. CO: Westview Press, 1992.

Creel, Herrlee. Confucianism the Chinese Way. New York: Harper.

Crubb, Edmond. Twentieth Century China. New York: Columbia University Press, 1963.

Dawson, Raymond. Chinese Chameleon.. New York: Oxford University Press, 1967.

Franke, Wolfgang. A Century of Chinese Revolution; 1851-1949. Translation by Stanley Rudman. New York: Harper and Row, 1971.

Gasster, Michael. China's Struggle to Modernize. New York: Knopf, 1972.

Hahn, Emily. Chiang Kai-Shek, an Unauthorized Bibliography. Doubleday, 1955.

Harrer, Heinrich. Seven Years in Tibet. Dutton, 1954.

Hu, C. T. China, Its People, Its Society, Its Culture. Human Relations Press, 1960.

Isaacs, Harold R. Scratches on Our Minds, American Image of China. John Day, 1958.

Karol, K. S. China the Other Communism. Hill & Wang, 1967.

North, Robert C. Moscow and the Chinese Communists. Stanford University Press, 1963.

Payne, Robert. Portrait of a Revolutionary; Mao Zedong. Schuman, 1961.

Portisch, Hugo. Red China Today. Quadrangle Books, 1991.

Snow, Edgar. The Other Side of the River; Red China Today. Random House, 1989.

Spence, Jonathan D. Search for Modern China. New York: W. W. Norton and Company, Inc., 1990.

Wu, Ch'eng-En. Monkey. Translated by Arthur Waley. Grove Press, 1965.

Chapter 11

Language, Identity and the Asian Crisis: Is English Causing an Identity Crisis?

Joan McConnell

When economic turmoil dragged the Asian markets to record lows, financial experts watched and waited for the worst. They hoped that the dreaded but often predictable **ripple effect** would not produce an economic tsunami which would shake, maybe even shatter, global markets. As they watched and waited, they devised strategies to avoid an economic and financial catastrophe.

The Asian countries too watched and waited as they gazed beyond the national borders of their economic crisis. They looked outward, and worried about the global repercussions of the internal crisis which had, in some cases, all but paralyzed their economies. At the same time, they also looked inward, and in a deep moment of painful introspection, tried to define – perhaps even redefine – their identity. They wanted and needed to understand the unique blend of characteristics that defined them both as individuals and as members of a particular national group.

At this point, some of you may be wondering what identity has to do with language. The answer is quite simple. Language shapes our identity. As babies, we learn to interpret reality through language, because language is the key which opens the secrets of the world around us. Although it frees us from personal solitude, it locks us in the cultural constrictions of our language. Most people do not understand how language conditions their perception of reality until they begin studying a foreign language. Then they suddenly discover that their vision of reality does not always make sense in another language. They must learn to look at the world around them through the "eyes" of the language that they are studying.

Let's look at a few simple examples which illustrate how the perception of reality changes from language to language. In English, for instance, gender follows the natural division between animate and inanimate nouns. Thus, men and male animals are masculine, women and female animals are feminine, and everything else is neuter (1). In Italian, by contrast, gender is simply a grammatical category that depends on the final vowel of each noun. Nouns that end in –a are feminine, while nouns that end in –o are masculine. Speakers must memorize the gender of nouns ending in –e, because there is no rule for this category (2).

English speakers often feel confused as they study Italian or, for that matter, the other Romance languages, because there is no **neuter** gender. They find it difficult to think of words such as **meat, pencil, stockings, television,** or **economy** (3) as feminine, but words such as **bread, felt-tip pen, socks, computer** or **money** (4) as masculine. In their frustration, they forget that native Italian speakers experience the same difficulties but in reverse. Unaccustomed to the neuter gender, Italians who are learning English may refer to a dishwasher as **he** (5) or a washing machine as **she** (6).

Family relationships are another area which offers interesting examples of how language conditions our perception of reality. Japanese has separate words to distinguish an **older sibling** from a **younger one** (7). Native-English speakers find this distinction superfluous, because their culture does not consider age as an important factor in the social hierarchy. In Japanese, there are special words which express the traditional respect for age. When English speakers simply make these distinctions, they simply add descriptive adjectives such as **younger** or **older**.

Language creates our personal identity and, at the same time, strengthens our national identity, especially in monolingual nations. For example, if you are Japanese, you are supposed to speak Japanese. In the past, Americans were expected to speak English. In view of the recent waves of immigration to the US, however, one can no longer make this assumption. Today many Americans do not speak English, and some simply do not want to learn the language. They live in their ethnic communities where they follow the cultural customs and linguistic traditions of their homeland. It is not surprising that more and more Americans worry that this multilingualism may weaken the strong yet invisible links between language and identity.

In multilingual societies such as Singapore or the Philippines, the relationship between **language and culture** is more complex. For instance, Singapore has four official languages: Malay which is considered the "national" language, English which is the language of administration, Chinese which is the language of over two million speakers, and Tamil which is used by approximately 100,000 speakers. The official languages of the Philippines are Tagalog which is considered a "national" language (8) and English which is the predominant language in administration, education, and mass media (9). Since children in these countries often study two or three languages at school, their perception of reality is multilingual. The speakers' identity is generally safe as long as members of the various linguistic communities respect or, at least, tolerate this diversity. When problems erupt, the underlying causes are usually political, religious, social, or economic rather than linguistic. In many cases, language becomes the vehicle for expressing these tensions.

If speakers in Asian countries can express their identity in more than one language, why is English creating an **identity crisis** in Asia? More specifically, why does English pose more of a threat to the speakers' identity than the local languages of Asia? Today English is a very powerful, international language which sends a mixed message. It awakens disturbing memories of the past, encourages optimism in the present, and stimulates dramatic dreams for the future. Depending on the speakers' perspective, English can make their blood boil with anger or fill their hearts with joy. It can open or close the doors of communication. It can heal old wounds or create new ones. No matter what Asians may think about English, they cannot ignore its power and its potential as a communication tool. Whether they approve or disapprove, English affects their identity, because this language has spread its linguistic nets around the world.

Although English is the unofficial international language, many people forget that the global role of English is **not** a new phenomenon. The globalization of English started about three hundred years ago when Great Britain expanded trade routes and established colonies first in North American and then in Australia, Asia, and Africa. The British brought their language to every corner of the world, and made it the prestige language in their overseas colonies. English was the medium of elite education, and **Received Pronunciation** (10) - **RP**, as linguists often call it – was the socially correct model. English speakers who did not know or use RP were victims of linguistic discrimination. The snob appeal of RP did not, however, stifle the emergence of new, local varieties. Many of these speakers were proud of their "non-British" English, and even flaunted it as a sign of their "non-British" identity. While they recognized the importance of English as a **communication language**, they considered British English as the symbol of linguistic imperialism. Today many Asians accept the role of English – in particular, the American variety – as the international language, but often they resent the economic domination of the US, especially in the area of technology, and thus the subsequent exportation of American culture by the media.

Until the middle of the 20th century, British English was the standard version at the international level. At the end of the Second World War, Great Britain lost her primacy when her huge Empire was dismantled. In the post-war years, the US quickly assumed Britain's role as the undisputed leader of the so-called Free World. Not surprisingly, American English replaced her British "cousin" as the dominant international variety. The US has dominated global markets, especially since the dramatic expansion of the communications technology. It is no wonder that people all around the world are now eager to learn American English.

The popularity of American English has spread American values, which often clash with local customs. Much to the dismay of politicians, educators, and parents, many young Asians are imitating the American lifestyle that they see on TV, videos, and movies. They equate these American values with progress, power, and profit. In order to "protect" local languages and cultures, some governments – in particular, Singapore and Malaysia – have implemented policies aimed at curtailing what they define as the linguistic and cultural imperialism of the English-speaking world, especially the US.

Today English is the most popular foreign language in the world.

Students want to learn English, because it opens career possibilities, especially in trade, tourism, and technology. They insist that a knowledge of English is their passport to success. With English, they can travel around the world, communicate with people from different cultures, and access information on the Internet. They can use English as a lingua franca among speakers of different languages. They can negotiate business deals in English, publish scientific papers in English, or attend scholarly seminars in English.

The popularity of English has produced negative consequences that have surprised students and worried educators in Asia. In many countries, the increase in the number of students learning English has produced a decrease in quality of instruction. In Japan, for example, educators agree that the English language program has not been successful. High school students study English so that they can pass the required English section on the dreaded University Entrance Examinations. Unfortunately the results of the long hours of study at home (11) and at the famous **jukus** (12) are unimpressive, particularly in the area of speaking and listening. Compared to other countries, Japanese students score poorly on the TOEFL examination. The lackluster skills of Japanese students have reduced their linguistic self-esteem. In order to correct these problems, the Ministry of Education is currently developing a new program aimed at integrating the four skills – reading, writing, speaking, and listening – in English language instruction. One of the most important proposals is the introduction of English instruction in elementary schools.

Unfortunately English has created an identity crisis in many Asian nations, because some students judge their self-worth in terms of their English skills. Those who do well feel confident and proud. Those who do poorly feel ashamed and insecure. These individuals are rejecting the identity that they have built in their own language, and are trying to replace it with a new, English identity. Subconsciously they measure their individual worth in relation to their performance in English. They do not realize that a "foreign" language, even a prestigious one like English, can never replace the identity shaped by the language of their childhood. The most effective way to avoid an identity crisis is to take pride in one's language. After all, languages are like people. Whether they are international stars or everyday dialects, they all deserve respect.

Asians feel uncomfortable when they speak English, because they know what the individual words mean but not what they mean in **cultural**

context. Far too often, language study focuses on mechanics rather than on meaning. It stresses form over content. As a result, the speakers interpret the words according to the definitions of their native language. They forget that the perception of reality varies according to the language that they are speaking. Thus, if Japanese students think in Japanese as they speak English, their message will be unclear or maybe incomprehensible to the native speaker. Likewise, if Japanese students use their native frame of reference to interpret spoken messages, they may not understand what the native speaker is saying.   To avoid mis-communication or non-communication, they must learn culture along with the language. The incorporation of culture in language instruction is a challenge for educators and communication specialists everywhere.

The linguistic identity crisis in Asia has been exacerbated by the attitude of some native speakers. In many cases, Asians are victims of linguistic discrimination. Please let me explain. Linguistic discrimination has a powerful potential for creating social inequality and intensifying prejudice. It undermines individual self-esteem, because it encourages people to judge other individuals by the way that they speak. The British used linguistic discrimination to strengthen the social hierarchy of their empire. In a less dramatic but equally effective manner, the Americans use linguistic discrimination to divide the insiders from the outsiders. In both cases, these native speakers behave as if English belongs to them.

The relation between language and identity will, in my opinion, be a key issue in the new millennium. As globalization propels us into the international track, more people worry about losing their identity. They want to be individuals, not numbers on a computer screen. They take pride in their local or national customs, they like to speak their native language, they insist that an international identity can never replace a local or national identity. In their opinion, an international language is, by definition, an auxiliary language which facilitates communication among speakers of different language but which never replaces native languages. Many feel that the role of English will change dramatically in the coming years, precisely because people do not want to give up their identity in the name of globalization.

In order to understand this seemingly contradictory comment, we must examine the reality of the English language.   Today English has approximately one and three-quarter billion speakers (13). Of this huge number, only about 350 million are native speakers, most of whom live in the US. All the other speakers use English as a second language or a foreign language. Some of these people speak fluent English, some use a mixture of English and their local language, while others have a very limited command of the language. But in one way or another, all these speakers can communicate in English.

Once upon a time, English was primarily a national language. As it gained international status, however, the language has adopted foreign words to describe things that did not exist back home. It created new words to express ideas that were born in distant places. Today English is more than a national language. Some linguists refer to it as an international language. I prefer to describe it as a democratic language which belongs to everyone. If we look around, we can see the tremendous vitality of the language. English is changing so rapidly that even the most current, online dictionaries cannot keep pace with the changes.

Linguists use the term **New Englishes** to describe the varieties of English that have developed in Asia and Africa. Today many non-native speakers blend the vocabulary, syntax, and intonation of their languages into English. They are proud of the English that they speak, although not everyone shares their enthusiasm. For example, Singapore English is the local version that speakers use in daily life. For international or official situations, they switch to standard British English. Many experts insist that the New Englishes threaten the future of English. They predict that English will split into separate languages. Some of their fears may be justified, because the varieties of English often cause communication breakdowns between native and non-native speakers. At times, it seems as if they are speaking different language – not English!

Many Asians insist that English belongs to all its speakers. They reject the idea that the standard varieties such as British, American, Canadian, or Australian are the only correct models. In their opinion, English must reflect the reality of **their** world. In this way, English fits into the pattern of multilingual societies like Singapore or the Philippines. These New Englishes are helping Asians to forget the unpleasant associations of English as the language of colonial oppression and cultural imperialism.

International observers have measured the economic, political, and social repercussions of the Asian crisis, but they have generally ignored the causes for the linguistic identity crisis. The economic crisis will pass as the Asian nations rebuild their economies, restructure their societies, and once again reaffirm their strong position in the global community. But the identity crisis will not pass until Asians stop feeling like second-class citizens in an English-dominated world. They must remember that the English-speaking world includes both native and non-native speakers. After all, English belongs to everyone.

Identity crises are a natural part of life. The crises involving language identity are perhaps more complex, because many people do not recognize the insidious power of language. It can undermine an individual's self-esteem. Those of us who are native-English speakers may find it difficult to appreciate the frustration and inferiority complex of many non-native speakers. The power of this international language threatens their native language and thus erodes their identity. Unfortunately the aggressive enthusiasm with which many English speakers promote the international benefits of English as a global language often offends the linguistic and cultural sensitivities of other speakers, especially in moments of economic volatility. It is not surprising that many people – both at the political and personal level – criticize the lack of linguistic and cultural sensitivity among many native-English speakers who sometimes act as if their linguistic birthrights make them superior individuals.

Although native-English speakers are not responsible for the linguistic identity crisis among people in other parts of the world, they can and should think about the issue of linguistic sensitivity. At this particular historical moment, English happens to be the most powerful language in the world, but there is no guarantee that the situation will continue. An aggressive linguistic newcomer may try to replace English. As a matter of fact, some linguists already point to signs that English is losing some of its international characteristics. As the number of non-native speakers increases, the language is subdividing into more and more local varieties. If these speakers insist on expressing their individuality at any cost, English will become more local and less international.

I wish that I could look into a crystal ball and predict the future. Unfortunately I cannot. The best that I can do is share with you the precious lesson that I learned from my professor at Columbia University many years ago. In his words, respect is the key to solving many problems. If we respect language – our own as well as others – we will respect ourselves and, by extension, others too. Then when we experience an identity crisis, this respect will help preserve our self-esteem. Although my professor's advice may not solve the problem, it can certainly help people everywhere cope with identity crises.

Endnotes

(1)   In daily conversation, there are some exceptions to this rule. For instance, English speakers might talk about their car or boat as **she.**

(2)   Most Italian nouns come from Latin. Although Latin had three genders (masculine, feminine, and neuter). Italian only uses two. Nouns that were neuter have become masculine or feminine according to their final vowel.

(3)   These words are translated as follows: la carne (meat), la matita (pencil), le calze (stockings), la televisione (television), l'economia (economy).

(4)   These words are translated as follows: il pane (bread), il pennarello (felt-tip pen), i calzini (socks), il computer (computer), and il denaro (money).

(5)   The Italian word for dishwasher is **il lavapiatti.**

(6)   The Italian word for washing machine is **la lavatrice.**

(7)   The Japanese words for these family relations are as follows: **imoto-san** (younger sister), **one-san** (older sister), **ototo-san** (younger brother), **onii-san** (older brother).

(8)   **Filipino** is a modified version of Tagalog and is used as the national language of the Philippines

(9)   Although English is the predominant language of education, mass media, and administration, it has lost some of its popularity after the revolution of 1986.

(10) **Received Pronunciation** (often abbreviated as **RP)** is a term used by linguists to refer to the pronunciation model for educated British English. Today many non-native speakers prefer the pronunciation of American English.

(11) Japanese mothers are particularly energetic in supervising their children's study habits.

(12) A **juku** is a cram school which helps students prepare for the entrance examinations to high school or college. English jukus are popular.

(13) For more information on this topic, please see **Countries, Peoples and Their Languages,** edited by Erik V. Gunnemark (Gothenburg, Sweden, 1992).

Chapter 12

China's Reform and The "New Silk Road"

Charles H. Winwood

Since the visit of Marco Polo, China and its economic potential has fascinated westerners. Author Adam Smith, for example, devoted some coverage of China in The Wealth of Nations, published in 1776. Views about the economy of China and its prospects for modern economic development have varied considerably. Prior to World War II, western powers and Japan saw China as a large potential market for their own economic productions and, possibly to a lesser extent, as an important source of raw materials for their industry and economic expansion.

In today's world, new policies provide opportunities for enterprises from foreign countries to trade and invest in China. Japan, the United States, and numerous other countries have taken advantage of these opportunities. These new policies also provide scope for mutual economic gain by China and other foreign countries. In the Asian–Pacific region these policies provide new prospects of economic development and increase the likelihood that China will emulate the economic growth achieved by its near neighbors (Hong Kong, Japan, South Korea, Singapore and Taiwan). It is also hoped that China's economic development will benefit these neighboring countries. It is possible that the type of greater East Asian co-prosperity which Japan hoped for before World War II may be established without resorting to territorial imperialism.

With the growing fear that the world may become locked into major trading blocks, the European Market block, the North American Block, and countries outside of these blocks, such as Japan and Australia, are likely to look increasingly to trade and investment within their own region, providing some alternative economic outlets. Within this context, Northeastern China (Manchuria) will become an important region. The Northeast is sitting on many raw materials, has a large population, and is close to key transportation points; the Trans-Siberian railroad to the east and the Port of Vladivostok to the west. The development of China becomes increasingly significant to the economic future of the Asian-Pacific region.

I

In 1949 the Communist Party (CPC) became the effective government of China after victory in its civil war against the Guomindang (Nationalist Party).[i] The CPC faced the immediate problem of rebuilding a society and economy that since the 1920s had suffered civil war. There were also more fundamental problems rooted in the inherited exploitative system fostered under China's emperors. Whatever achievements under that imperial past, China's economy had failed to make the technological and organizational breakthrough to "modernity" achieved by the West and Japan. The CPC achieved its victory on the basis of mass support for its struggle against the Japanese invasion, and the land reform implemented in areas it controlled in the previous decade. However, the CPC inherited fundamental problems and there were few guidelines for resolving them.

China's population was increasing and the fertile land was limited. The modern sector of China's economy was restricted to its support cities, largely fashioned by western imperialism and a Japanese developed 1949, Mao Zedong, chairman of the CPC, proclaimed that China had "stood up" and that the party would build a "prosperous and flourishing country." Forty years later this remains to be achieved, and the argument remains as to whether Mao's own methods have delayed this goal or made it more possible. Certainly the politics which followed him have negated his ideas as to what are proper socialist policies. The growth in prosperity evident for many Chinese in the 1980s under Deng's leadership has created its own problems. These problems are turning out to be as hard to resolve as those created under Mao's leadership. The Communist Party can be seen as but one group of Chinese reformers of the last century who wanted China to withstand outside aggression and achieve modernity. Although there are disputes about how the party interpreted socialism and communism, and the extent from which it departed from Marxism or Soviet thinking and practice, there can be no doubt that the CPC believed that economic growth and modernity was to be achieved through building socialism. In practice this meant that the Communist Party of China controlled political power and made the central decisions on economic and social policy.

The Soviet Union initially became the model for the organization of government and society. In the post-1949 economy, there were three key areas which can be identified as China's declared socialist elements. These are: (1) In rural affairs, the collective ownership of land and other means of production and a state-directed plan for the procurement of foodstuffs and industrial crops, (2) centralized control over the accumulation and reinvestment of capital, in combination with state ownership of major industries and financial institutions (and in effect, local state ownership of smaller scale enterprises), (3) restrictions on the impact of foreign capital and external economic factors while pursuing self reliance). Looking at each of these elements and their implementation in the period 1949-1976, each has been effected drastically by the policy changes pursued by the post-Mao leadership under Deng Xiaoping. In a sense, it is clear that the policy has been reversed rather than reformed.

II

After 1949, the new government completed the land reform already begun in areas it had controlled in the civil war. This massive redistribution of land away from landlords and the richest peasants was welcomed by the majority. For the leadership however, this greater equalization of landholdings was a temporary objective. Private and family farm holdings were not regarded as socialist policy and many in the party argued that allocation of land would not remain equitable for long. New divisions, exploitation, and uneven land ownership quickly showed signs of reemerging. The land reform did not generate much capital for family or state investment. From the mid-1950s the CPC enforced the collectivization of rural land, equipment and animals. The new collectives were given production targets to supply the state with part of their output of grain and industrial crops like cotton, at state-defined prices. This tied them into the national plan through the local administrative structure. Targets and prices were transmitted downward through the provincial structure to the individual commune and then to the team.

Collectives offered the means of pooling labor-power and capital to transform rural China. Communal labor facilitated the improvement of land, the construction of dams to conserve limited rainfall, and irrigation systems. It enabled surplus to be generated to pay for schools and health centers; often the first ever available to ordinary people in many rural areas. The introduction of the people's communes was linked with the Great Leap Forward (GLF) of 1958-1960 (a bad attempt to achieve full communism virtually overnight).[ii] Free collective kitchens, communal childcare and universal industrialization were promoted by Mao Zedong throughout the countryside. The idea was mass growth. The reality was that China plunged into disaster.

The years 1959-1961 witnessed a famine across a large part of China. Authorities are still reluctant to discuss it openly. The evidence from the 1982 Chinese census reveals the worst disaster in the world during the century. It appears that during these three years between 14 and 26 million plus deaths[iii] were attributed to hunger and associated illness. A revised form of commune, which was intended to extract China from the famine disaster, became the basic building block of rural economy and government until the post-Mao changes. On average, a commune had about 15,000 members but numbers varied from around 80,000 in the densely settled fertile areas of eastern China to 8,000 or less in sparsely populated mountainous or arid areas. Peasant life was largely organized around the collective, in which the basic unit was the production team.

This organized labor and capital and distributed rewards. This was like a dividend. Work points represented a claim on the collective output of the team, supposedly proportionate to individual effort. Rural electrification and small scale rural industries such as brick works, irrigation schemes, clinics and schools could be built by mobilizing labor which did not have to be immediately paid in cash. The work would be done in return for work points, since this increased people's eventual claim to the produce of the team. The team would distribute produce and income to the families on the basis of the work points the family had earned and the income the team had gained through selling its produce on the state controlled markets. Whereas in other third world countries, surplus rural labor migrated to the cities, this did not occur in China.

Geographically, one of the most important aspects of Maoistic policy was the emphasis on regional and local self-sufficiency. A common slogan was "take grain as the key link and promote all-round development." This signaled the regime's awareness that adequate grain output (especially wheat and rice) was vital to preventing both famine and urban unrest. It also indicated the importance of local self-reliance; the idea that local areas should pull themselves upwards—out of poverty. Maoist policy created a particular kind of organization and a particular geography in rural China. If the team and the commune were organizational units of rural life, their activities were shaped by the decisions of central and provincial governments.

Decisions on priorities between investment in agriculture, industry, transport and other infrastructures, welfare and the location of investments were made by the bureaucratic organization of government and party. In agriculture, decisions on priorities between different crops were largely made by central and then provincial governments setting output targets and determining prices. In theory, the lower level of the hierarchy could communicate their views upward. Chinese now insist that, in practice, the system was essentially a "top-down" model and that local officials were under immense pressure to fulfill central directives which were often insensitive to   local conditions   Despite Maoist emphasis on rural development, most of the effort was expected to come from collectivized resources and local self-reliance.   There was little direct government investment in agriculture.

The Communist Party in 1949 had scant experience in managing either cities or large-scale industrial enterprise. The revolution had been fought largely in rural areas, based amongst peasants rather than workers, and most of the leaders had little idea how to run the cities. For a period, existing industrialists were permitted to operate more or less on their own. Then, from the mid-195s, major changes in ownership were begun; involving nationalization. There were few industries available to a new socialistic government and it is understandable that the Soviet Union became China's mentor. Not only did the Soviet Union appear to be successful industrially, it was willing to lend capital to China to provide technical assistance. Communist wisdom implied that socialism was virtually to be equated with large-scale enterprise, and that the promotion of heavy industry was a model which the Soviets had pioneered.

In 1953, China launched the first "Five Year Plan" (FYP)[iv] modeled upon Soviet lines, with state control of most urban industry. Profits from industrial production, incorporating the profits made from cheap purchases from the agricultural sector, were directed into what were seen as key sectors that would make China prosperous and strong. Steel, iron and textile industries were among those particularly developed. Chinese economic planners shared Soviet thinking that western capitalism before 1949 had produced unequal regional development in China. The first FYP involved the construction of new inland industrial based in cities. In 1956, Mao was signaling the pragmatic advantages of development in the established coastal region, betraying a belief in the virtues of regional inequality.

The close relations between China and the Soviet Union and the basic similarity of models of economic development were both short-lived. A variety of issues, including Mao's question of the Soviet model, led to conflict between the two communist giants. From 1958, a section of the Chinese leadership under Mao's domination was able to promote an entirely new economic development strategy – the "Great Leap Forward" (GLF). The Great Leap Forward ended in 1960, a disastrous failure; so did the special relationship with the Soviet Union. Soviet aid was cut off and is technicians abruptly withdrew. Mao was forced into the background of economic policy as a result of the failure of the GLF and the associated famine tragedy. However, the GLF did produce the valuable new concept of rural industrialization.

Ironically, this provided a legacy without which today's dynamic rural enterprises would probably not exist. Little was altered in the urban sector and the concentration on heavy and large-scale industry continued as in the first FYP. Emphasis on predominately urban and large enterprise was accompanied by a respectable rate of industrial growth, even during most of the cultural revolution. Capital was being used wastefully, allocated by the state to be used by enterprises without any charge.

This meant that more capital was needed, compared with the goods produced for the people's consumption. Living standards were therefore relatively stagnant; a victim of the high proportion of funds used for productive investment compared with the amount left available for the people's consumption. Consumer goods were not given priority and there were shortages of many ordinary products. Luxury products, such as bicycles, radios, and varied clothing materials were impossible for the people to purchase. The industry fetish also meant a low level of investment in urban infrastructure and welfare. Living standards were affected through the inadequacy of housing, public transport, sewage networks, and electric supply.

Limited investment in basic infrastructure affected the productivity of industry itself. Too little capital was directed to power generation and to transport. The Chinese media today now emphasizes the shortcomings of the pre-1979 communist industrial planning system. Still, we should remember that a respectable rate of industrial growth did occur. The modern sector of the economy was increased in geographical extension and in terms of absolute production.

China's industrial planning system was criticized in the 1980s for its highly centralized, bureaucratic nature. Factories were constrained by shortages of components of raw materials, owing to the intricacies of the quota target system which determined the production of the state-run sector. At the other extreme, the quota might be reached but the product be of unusable quality, or no longer needed. This strategy was perhaps more suited to the initiation of industrial growth but less appropriate for long-term development. Criticism has also been directed at the system's reliance on production and prices being determined by bureaucratic decision rather than by the market.

In this discussion of industrial China, we should mention the changing attitude to foreign trade and the role of foreign investment and technology. In the 1950s China did use Soviet technology, capital and expertise to help modernize its industrial sector. From 1960, China largely had to go it alone, and until the 1980s foreign trade was a very small component of the economy. In the 1960s and 1970s, Maoist development policy emphasized the benefits to China of self-reliance.

A statement from the 1960s encapsulates the thinking "a country should manufacture by itself all the products it needs whenever and wherever possible". Self-reliance also means that a country should carry on its general economic construction on the basis of its own human, material, and financial resources. Such statements of principle may have been shaped by pragmatic necessity, since trade and access to capital and modern technology were limited. China was in conflict with either or both the Soviet Union and the United States for most of this period. China's post-Mao leadership has taken a very different view of the role of foreign trade and technology.

III

In the period 1949-1976, there were three elements considered crucial to Socialist development in China. These elements were: (1) the collectivization of land and state directed agricultural planning, (2) central control over the accumulation and re-investment of capital, coupled with state ownership of major industries, and (3) a policy of self-reliance and the exclusion of foreign capital. The description has only touched on the policy conflicts and choices in China's post-1949 development strategy. These issues need to become central to explain what happens after Mao's death.

Communist ideology was capable of generating conflicting strategies in China's post-1949 development. The problems facing the Chinese leaders were horrendous; including a large and poor population, limited fertile land, a vast territory with immense transport difficulties, and limited capital. While mush has changed in the forty years since, these and other problems remain. In 1949 there was broad agreement in the Party that socialism, involving the three key components, was the way to deal with these problems. In the 1980s, many of the self-same leaders presided over policies which admit to the limitations of those three aspects of socialism.

Soon after Mao Zedong's death in 1976, there was a coup d'etat which overthrew a small group of party leaders whose power depended on Mao's patronage. A section of the party, combined with groups in the security forces, installed a new CPC chairman, Hua Guofeng. A number of the "ultra-leftist" political leaders associated with the policies of the Cultural Revolution of 1966-1076 were imprisoned; chief among these was the "Gang of Four", which included Mao's widow Jiang Qing. In 1980, they were tried and convicted of undermining the revolution and using illegal means to defeat their opponents (including imprisonment, torture, and persecution to death).

The changeover of power was peaceful, but not uncontested, and there was conflict over the role of Hua Guofeng and others who supported a continuation of Maoist economic policies. The two years following Mao's death were marked by intense political in-fighting, and exponents of contradictory economic policies tried to gain the upper hand.   By increasingly blaming Maoist strategy for the country's economic problems, section of the CPC favored economic reforms brought together by so-called pragmatists.

By 1978 a party grouping around Deng Xiaoping has coalesced, established a clear power-base, and begun a new direction for economic development. At an important CPC meeting in December of that year, Deng was victorious in establishing his policies for economic reform as the official line. The leadership has called for the people to achieve the four modernization's; agriculture, industry, education, and science and defense. The Four Modernization's became the watchword and politics and class struggle were subordinated to economic progress. This slogan is revived from a speech given by Premier Zhou Enlai in 1964.

The attitude it embodies was curtailed in the cultural revolution of 1966-76, but at the 1978 Third Plenary of the CPC the policy shifted and emphasized the achievement of the Four Modernization's through readjustment, reform, consolidation, and improvement. Readjustment meant shifting priorities from industry to agriculture, from heavy industry to light industry, and focusing attention on bottleneck sectors.

Reform came to mean moving away from the Stalinist style economy and embarking on the types of economic reform already implemented in eastern Europe. Consolidation and improvement meant essentially trying to upgrade the level of management and efficiency. The key aspects of development policy under Deng's leadership in the decade indicated how they have altered those central features of China's policies which previously were considered vital components of its socialist principles: the collectivization of land and state-directed agricultural planning, central control over capital with state ownership of industry, and self reliance.

IV

In the countryside the changes form Mao's policies came early and took effect quickly. The impact of the reforms have been extensive and fundamental, and the collectivized landscape is now gone. The new policies for rural China are rooted in the "responsibility system," which represents a return to family farming. The communes were criticized on the basis that the work-point system meant that personal incomes were not sufficiently sensitive to the amount of individual effort put in, so that allegedly those who did not work hard were rewarded with not much less than those who did. There was a basic ration of grain allocated to all before work-points were assessed.

The diagnosis of the rural problem, low incomes and slow growth, was of a failure of incentives. Under the reforms, families have been allocated land leases of up to thirty years; in return for they contract to sell to the state at a fixed low price an agreed quota of grain or other industrial crop. The remainder of their output is used or sold for consumption, and any surplus can be sold at higher prices to the state or on the private markets; which grew rapidly during the 1980s. The new rural strategy was based on the assumption that increased productivity would occur through releasing individual and family effort in the responsibility system.

Alongside this private farming, a tremendous growth in rural business initiative has occurred in commercial and manufacturing as well as agricultural enterprises. Some of the older collective workshops and sidelines developed under the commune system such as piggeries, fish ponds and small factories, have been dispersed while others have been leased out to groups or private individuals. More crucially, completely new enterprises have sprung up entirely in private hands. Such economic growth in villages and small towns, is central to the development of post-1979 China. China estimates that about 30% ᵛ of rural population is deemed to be surplus to the needs of agriculture.

One of the issues is the nature and extent of urbanization permitted and even encouraged during the last decade. Under rural reforms farmers have been producing more and the leadership considers this to be a response to the incentives inherent in the responsibility system. Extra income can be earned by individuals and families, once the state quota and personal consumption needs have been met. Peasants are free to dispose of any surplus to earn extra cash. Near the larger towns and cities, the policies have also led to the development of rural industry, and the higher personal incomes have produced a boom in new rural housing. However, these development are eating away at China's limited arable land and posing severe problems of pollution and environmental management.

This raise the issue of population growth, and the reform leadership's conviction is that the country is overpopulated. Increased production represents one way of solving China's problem of the relationship between people, land and production. Under Deng's leadership, the country has also sought to limit population growth much more extensively than in the previous decade, through policies such as the one-child only families; this has been more effective in urban China.

The building and maintenance of rural infrastructure, of water conservation projects, and schools and clinics is being neglected under the new system. Without communal efforts, the people's new prosperity may be short-lived and current wealth earned at the expense of running down local facilities. There is a dangerous combination of labor productivity which cannot be further increased and the lack of any system in place to promote the regeneration of agricultural investment and infrastructure development. The market is increasingly replacing government and party as a mechanism for stimulating what is produced locally. Regional self-sufficiency and the Maoist emphasis on grain is criticized for creating a situation of shared poverty; rather than the preferred differential growth.

Market forces are to be used to encourage regional specialization and regional inequalities are accepted as necessary to building socialist modernization. The slogan, "readjustment and reform" [vi] reveals two different policy directions. Readjustment suggests that the pre-existing system was basically fine and only needed adjusting. Reform suggests that something more fundamental was required. During Deng's decade, rural China had certainly been reformed. Supporters of the commune system might say that a more accurate term be "counter revolution."

Changes to urban China have taken longer and proven more difficult to implement. It has been difficult for some party leaders to accept the ideology of a reduction in the state's role in directing the industrial economy. Large-scale, state-owned enterprises, employ many people and represent much of the state's capital investment. Changes is how these should be owned and managed, and in who decides what is to be produced and sold at what price, created extreme controversy. Significant changes to the urban industrial sector did not take effect until after 1984.

In October of 1984, the Twelfth Central Committee of the CPC stated that "defects in the urban economic sector seriously hinder the expansion of the forces of production." This meeting set out the outlines for reform. Its key features included a cutting back of party control over the rigid economic structure; with government withdrawing from management and taking a more regulatory role. There was still to be an emphasis on state planning, but mandatory planning was only to cover key commodities like steel and large scale infrastructure such as railway construction. Urban enterprises were to become more independent and be responsible for their own profit and loss, with managers having more power. The price system should be reformed and reflect economic laws.

Editorials in the "People's Daily," said that the prices of goods would be determined by their production costs; that the law of value would become "a special feature of Chinese socialism." That wages should reflect productivity, egalitarianism, and worker's belief in a secure job for life, regardless of effort, and the "iron" rice bowl, was attacked. Regional industrial specialization was to be encouraged, and this has been linked with a consistent policy to promote the more rapid development of the coastal region, which is seen to have an initial advantage and lower production costs. This has not been accepted without dispute from other parts of the country.

Foreign investment and an expansion in trade, were central to Deng's modernization strategy, and self-reliance is a policy of the past to promote China's new role in the international scene. Very early in the reform period, the leadership declared and "open door" policy which was designed to improve business confidence among potential traders and investors. The process of reduced tax liabilities and other concessions was begun, to entice investment from outside sources.

The rationale for breaking from the previously defined socialist policy was, that if the Four Modernization's were to succeed, new technology had to be brought into the country. Initially, the idea was to focus developments in the four Special Economic Zones (SEZ) on the southeast coast; partly to isolate the decadence of capitalist influences. In fact, over the reform decade, many coastal cities and areas were opened up to encourage foreign investment and there is acceptance of such involvement anywhere. The decision to use foreign technology in much larger amounts than before has serious consequences throughout the economy. Some technology could be introduced by foreign firms locating in the SEZs and taken over by the Chinese at the end of the contract but this route has not been very successful. The SEZ policy has been criticized for this shortcoming.

To buy expensive imports of equipment involves increasing China's exports, and this entails using scarce resources which can also be of use within the country. The 'cost versus benefits" analysis that is entailed in this cannot be economic. Considerable political opposition has arisen (i.e., the massive exports of oil to Japan used to pay for technology) from that country. The severe energy shortages in China make it fairly easy to guess the arguments.

It has been difficult for government to control the level of imports to China. While the manufacture of goods for export has increased enormously since the 1980s, the total value of all exports has often failed to keep up with imports; resulting in a very large balance of payment deficits. Instead of earning money through exports in order to buy technology, China has broken from one of the strictest aspects of Maoist policy and borrowed money from foreign banks and governments. In the early 1980s, it confirmed its new role in the international economy by joining the World Bank and other institutions previously regarded as tools of the imperialist system. The events of May and June 1989, involving the violent crushing of popular demands that the party end corru0ption which the reforms of the 1980s engendered, throw into doubt the continuation of the reform policies in their existing form.

The political instability which the reforms generated led to conflict in the Party leadership over how to deal with it. After several weeks of confusion, in May supporters of Deng Xiaoping and Premier Li Peng (the Army and Party) came together to crush demonstrations and remove from leadership those who would have granted some political reforms. Zhao Ziyang, the General Secretary of the CPC and the man responsible for the implementation of the economic reforms, was removed from office and accused of splitting the Party. In his place, Jiang Zemin was installed.

In mid-1989, the conservative wing of the CPC was strengthened. It is not only firmly against political reform and democracy, but it also includes elements who are opposed to the more extensive role for market forces and commercialism which the reform leadership (especially Zhao Ziyang) had pushed. This group of leaders is also more likely to try to deal with the issue of corruption and cleaning up the party, one of the demands of mass demonstrations, because they see it as a by-product of the over-commercialization of economy and a reduction of central direction.

A "two-track" pricing system of some goods, especially raw materials and producer goods, led to the corrupt manipulation of the price differences between fixed state prices and free market prices of the same goods, but those in leadership or management positions in party or enterprise. A strengthening of party direction of economy is likely to try to deal with this, although the power of the Beijing leadership to control matters effectively in the provinces is more doubtful. The leadership seems keen to reassure foreign groups that the country is still open for business. In spite of some trade sanctions immediately after the student uprising and massacre at Tiananmen Square, it is unlikely that western and Japanese investors will be put off for long. If the are, the delaying factor will likely be their concern about the political stability affecting their investments rather than sensibilities.

V

China has suffered severe environmental problems in urban industrial and rural areas and has pursued an environmental policy which has remained surprisingly consistent despite significant changes in the political situation. Unfortunately, it was also consistent in its inability to fulfil all of the environmental measures. The developmental approach must be, at least to a degree, as an eco-development approach held to the conviction that environmental consideration is an integral part of development policy and economic and ecological issues could not be reasonably separated. This conviction was obvious in important aspects of rural development.

It is less obvious in urban industrial policy during the earlier stages of which environmentally sound strategies, such as waste recycling and energy saving, are strongly promoted for economic reasons. As public health deteriorated and working conditions steadily worsened, and as environmental hazards and effects of environmental damage in rural and urban settings made themselves felt, it became clear to the leadership that neglect factors also had serious implications. Environmental policy has never been fully implemented despite intention, consistency, and bureaucratic institutionalization.

The country lacks the financial resources to install expensive technology on a large scale. There is little incentive at factory level to implement costly policies. There is insufficient enforcement of pollution fines, because this would involve the state, as property owner, taking money out of pocket and putting it into another. Bureaucracies are not usually made to implement novel strategies. Successive failure of economic reforms suggest that not more can be expected of environmental policy.

A well planned and sophisticated environmental protection policy is useless if, at the same time, economic reform abolishes the very institutions needed to implement policy measures. Counter-productive effects will have to be eliminated if Chinese environmental policy in its eco-development approach is to be implemented successfully. Aware of this, the Director of the Environmental Protection Bureau, Qu Geping, argues for stronger environmental management at all levels of administration. This should include an environmental protection responsibility system designed to motivate provincial governors, mayors and other leaders, down to factory heads, to take action. Over a longer term, the basic social, economic, and political trends that have been identified, will come into play to carry forward a process of socio-economic pluralization and political democratization which will be reinforced by changes in the international political environment.

VI

It needs to be understood that getting exact information on China is difficult. To get information on a particular region in China is almost impossible because China its self publishes information for the entire state as one factual report, after passing strict censorship. Policies and principles that are true for one region should also be true for the others, in general.

As China goes through change and more countries depend on trade, the northeast will become especially important because of the Trans-Siberian railroad to Europe and the Port of Vladivostok ensuring easier access to the United States. Growth brings change.

In politics, as in economics, liberalism will likely be the guiding force for change; though this will be grafted on to elements of the previous system. Whatever the result, it will be distinctly Chinese. The most likely scenario is a form of state capitalism along East Asian lines, comparable to Japan and South Korea, and Taiwan since the mid-80s, with a competitive political system and a capitalist economy, combined with a high degree of state involvement. While such a combination promises to be economically dynamic, it may well be socially exploitive, and politically unequal, if politics and economics operate according to the intersecting logics of class structure and market dynamics.

While some basic elements of Chinese state socialism (i.e., subsidies, basic welfare services, job security, and relatively equalitarian distribution) might have reflected the actions of a quasi-patriarchal, totalism state and pose problems from the point of view of economic efficiency, they are also valued attributes of a humane society. While Russia and some of the post-socialist eastern European nations seem prepared to throw out the social baby with the socialist bath water, there are elements of the "old" which can be made complementary with the "new" in the form of some kind of social democracy along western European lines. Some contemporary Chinese, political theorists (such as Su Shaozhi) believe that China may evolve, in both economy and politics, towards a form of social democracy which steers a middle course between and away from the Seylla of authoritarian state socialism and the Charbidis of unfettered capitalism. The belief is, of course, a long way from their original goal of market socialism, though outcome may go some ways towards meeting the aspirations of Chinese reformers who set out in the post-Mao era to build a society which combined the virtues of state and market, equity and growth, individual incentives and collective responsibility, socialism and capitalism.

Endnotes

1. United States Government, China, A Country Study, Secretary of the Army, 4th Edition, 1st Printing, 1988, 30.

2. Dorothy J. Solinger, China's Transition from Socialism, M. E. Sharp Inc., 1993, 18-20, 167.

3. United States Government, China, A Country Study, Secretary of the Army, 4th Edition, 1st Printing, 1988, 218.

4. Dorothy J. Solinger, China's Transition from Socialism, M. E. Sharp Inc., 1993, 19, 21, 159.

5. Ken Griffin and Zhao Renwei, The Distribution of Income in China, St. Martins Press, 1993, 60.

6. Dorothy J. Solinger, China's Transition from Socialism, M. E. Sharp Inc., 1993, 39.

Chapter 13

The Taiwan Straits Crisis

James A. Robertson

The loud piercing screams of several M-9 missiles startled people on Taiwan's western coast, as several M-9 missiles slammed into the waters of the Taiwan Strait. The time? It was the spring of 1996, immediately prior to that nation's first ever free presidential election. This incident occurred during the fourth major crisis in the strait since the end of the Chinese Civil War in 1949. Communist China had flexed its muscle and attempted to intimidate its island neighbor with the new found might and technology of the People's Liberation Army. Taiwan, under the leadership of its president, Lee Teng-hui, refused to accept status as a Chinese province. Instead, she sought independence. Beijing's actions aimed at both influencing the Taiwan election and frightening the island into falling in line.

The roots of this crisis lay in the years immediately following the end of World War II, particularly 1949. Once the Japanese threat ended, civil war between Mao Zedong's Communists and Chiang Kai-shek's Kuomintang (Nationalists) erupted once again. By latter 1949 the

Nationalist picture looked bleak, as the bulk of American equipment had fallen into Communist hands and almost half of the Kuomintang army had joined the enemy. (1) Mao's military successes forced Chiang and his Nationalists to abandon the Chinese mainland for the island of Formosa. Analysis indicated Mao would most likely seize that island sometime the following year, thus rendering further aid to Chiang pointless. (2)

There matters remained until the following year. On June 25, 1950, over 100,000 North Korean soldiers invaded South Korea. (3) Five days later Chiang Kai-shek offered the assistance of 33,000 "seasoned troops," 20 C-46 air transports, air cover, and naval escorts. He guaranteed their arrival inside of five days. (4) Washington declined Chiang's offer, noting concern over Taiwan's own defense requirements. Therefore, President Truman ordered reconnaissance flights over the Chinese mainland to investigate potential danger from attacks on Taiwan (Formosa). He also requested his Far East Commander, General Douglas MacArthur, to submit an assessment of Nationalist defense needs on Formosa. (5)

MacArthur flew to the island, shortly thereafter, presumably to provide Truman with the requested evaluation. He met for two days with Chiang. Later, from Tokyo, MacArthur dispatched three fighter squadrons to Formosa. (6) Soon Chiang issued public statements implying that he and MacArthur had allied themselves against the mainland. Furthermore, pictures of MacArthur kissing Madame Chiang hit the world press. (7) The implication seemed clear: Nationalist troops would be used in Korea and perhaps to invade the Chinese mainland.

Beijing became livid. That anger did not soon subside, for at the end of August MacArthur sent a message to the VFW (Veterans of Foreign Wars) Convention at Chicago. To these veterans the Far East Commander promoted Formosa's strategic value to American defense. Without that island the United States would have to defend itself from its own western coast. In other words, the Pacific Ocean was an American moat and Formosa an outlying fortress. (8) MacArthur compared Formosa to "an unsinkable aircraft carrier and submarine tender...." (9) To Beijing it must have seemed as though MacArthur sought Formosa as a center for operations against the mainland.

Although early in 1950 Truman had expected China to capture Formosa, the North Korean invasion forced his hand. He quickly adopted a Formosa "neutralization" policy and positioned the Seventh Fleet between the island and the mainland. The President wanted to eliminate the potential for conflict originating from either location, believing Korea conflict enough. Naturally this action earned no accolades from the Chinese Communists. (10) In the words of historian Walter LaFeber, "Mao Zedong was shocked at the sudden U.S. move into China's Civil War." (11)

The Taiwan Strait once again became the focus of attention, merely one year after the Korean armistice. On September 3, 1954, the PROC or People's Republic of China (Communist China) commenced artillery barrages on islands in the Taiwan Strait. Numerous islands in that strait are possessions of the Nationalist government on the island of Formosa, now known as the Republic of China (ROC), though mainland China is less than two miles distant. By comparison, Formosa lies over one hundred miles away. Among the islands of the Taiwan Strait are Jinmen, Mazu, the Dachens, Yijiangshan, and the Pescadores. Collectively they are known as the offshore islands.

The People's Liberation Army's artillery assault initially targeted Jinmen and Mazu, earning retaliatory shelling from Nationalist batteries. Thus began an artillery war that lasted until normalization of relations between the United States and the People's Republic of China in 1979. America sprang to the ROC's defense. Two days later elements of the Seventh Fleet, including three carriers, three destroyer divisions, and a cruiser division plied the waters of the Taiwan Strait. (12)

Three major crises over the offshore islands erupted during the Cold War. Both the United States and Communist China developed their offshore islands policy during the 1954-55 crisis. They reacted similarly in later crises. In the words of one historian, "The Eisenhower Administration drifted into a commitment to defend Jinmen and Mazu during the 1954-55 crisis." (13)

Washington feared that the September shellings of the offshore islands constituted a prelude to a full-scale invasion of Taiwan by the People's Liberation Army. The loss of Taiwan could have had damaging international consequences, especially vis-a-vis SEATO (South East Asia Treaty Organization). (14) Then, in January 1955 the PROC nabbed Yijiangshan Island. These actions fit the American view of aggressive Chinese intentions. However, Chinese Premier Zhou Enlai's April 23 declaration that China did not desire war with the United States defied the mold. Why then did China take these actions?

Five different explanations have generally been offered. First, the attacks represented probing actions, designed to test American dedication to defending Taiwan. (15) Secondly, they could have been responses to the apparent comradeship between Taipei and Washington, as well as retaliations for Nationalist raids on the Chinese mainland. (16) Furthermore, some historians pictured a PROC sensitive to Chinese territorial sovereignty: Beijing considered Taiwan a province of China. (17) Some observers linked the attacks with Beijing's need for promoting domestic political and economic mobilization. (18)

Lastly, one view insisted "that the PRC intended to question and undermine the legal status of the Nationalist government in the international community through its military activities against the Nationalist offshore islands." (19)

More recent analyses, based on newer documentation, suggested that the crisis resulted from Chinese efforts to get American attention!

The Chinese leaders intended to talk to the Americans in order to get full acceptance of the world community through breaking out the isolation created by the United States since the Korean War.

Beijing signaled its willingness of a negotiation with Washington through its shellings of Jinmen and other offshore islands in the Taiwan Strait. The bombardment, as military means to serve political purpose, was designed to draw American attention and bring world opinion to put pressure on the Eisenhower Administration. (20)

Eisenhower finally agreed to Sino-American ambassador level meetings. These began on August 1, 1955 at Geneva. Soon thereafter the PROC eased its military operations in the Taiwan Strait, including PLA landings on the offshore islands. Artillery barrages against Jinmen and Mazu occurred now only as responses to Nationalist artillery fire. Zhou Enlai continued insisting that China wanted only peaceful reunification with Taiwan. (21)

American resolve to defend Taiwan and the intricately linked offshore islands underwent another test three years later. The People's Liberation Army resumed regular shelling of the offshore islands, including Jinmen, on August 4, 1958. It is doubtful the PROC had invasion on its mind. Most likely Mao had observed that the United States sat embroiled in a Middle East crisis, thus making conditions ideal for striking in the Taiwan Strait. Probably he anticipated one of two results. Either the Americans would bomb the mainland, thus bringing Russia to China's aid, or Jinmen's garrison would soon capitulate. Instead, Beijing found the Seventh Fleet once again in the Strait, providing armed escort for ROC troops and supplies. Washington sent U.S. Marines and eight-inch howitzers to Jinmen, the latter possessing atomic shell capacity. (22)

PROC shore batteries, situated along China's eastern coast in Fujian

Province, initiated heavy shelling of the offshore islands on August 23. The Chinese air force lost ten Mig-17's during a fiery air battle over the Taiwan Strait. One month later Beijing announced a reduction in artillery barrages, limiting them to every other day. (23) Relations between the United States, the ROC, and the PROC over the offshore islands sizzled once again in 1962. (24)

Taiwan, officially the Republic of China or ROC, is America's seventh largest trading partner, while the People's Republic of China is our sixth largest trading partner. This, however, is misleading, as the People's Republic is 250 times the size of Taiwan. Its population is 60 times that of Taiwan. Her larger volume of trade with the United States is due to her large trade deficit. Moreover, as Beijing intensified its military intimidation of Taiwan just prior to her March 23 presidential election, some Congressional leaders saw the Washington-Beijing economic relationship less important. Representative Cox of California made a powerful observation on that matter. (25)

In just two weeks Taiwan will have its first direct presidential election, the first fully free and democratic election of a head of state in nearly 5,000 years, in 4,700 years of Chinese civilization. This is a remarkable achievement, and Americans should be enormously proud of Taiwan's democracy. The thriving democracy on Taiwan stands in marked contrast to the continuation of communism across the Taiwan Strait and the People's Republic of China. (26)

On December 15, 1978, the United States announced a normalization of relations with the PROC through establishment of full diplomatic relations, effective January 1, 1979. (27) But in April 1979 Congress passed the Taiwan Relations Act, legislation containing certain provisions which badly upset the Carter Administration. It established not dejure, but defacto relations with Taiwan. It called for arms sales to Taiwan in quantities sufficient for her to maintain her own defense. (28) These provisions seemed at variance with the Administration's gestures towards the People's Republic of China.

One carefully worded passage declared that the United States would view any embargo or military moves against Taiwan as a direct threat to US interests. This act angered Beijing. (29) Essentially, American relations with Taiwan took on a largely unofficial character, conducted through a private organization called the American Institute of Taiwan. Taiwan's relations towards the United States passed through another private organization, The Taipei Economic and Cultural Office of the United

States. (30)

In addition to the Taiwan Relations Act, American security policy is regulated by three US-PROC communiques. The Shanghai Communique, issued in 1972 during Nixon's China visit, announced a one China policy.

The United States acknowledges that all Chinese on either side of the Taiwan Strait maintain there is but one China and Taiwan is part of China. The United States Government does not challenge that position. (31)

Early 1979 witnessed the Normalization Communique. Made public on December 15, 1978 by President Jimmy Carter over national television, this communique, as its name suggests, called for resumption of full diplomatic relations, effective January 1, 1979. Under its provisions the United States recognized Beijing as the only government in China. It also ended a Mutual Defense Treaty, as well as diplomatic relations, with the Republic of China. (32)

Most controversial, however, had been the US-China Joint Communique of 17 August 1982. Ambiguously worded, this document appeared to contradict parts of the Taiwan Relations Act. It provided that American arms sales to Taiwan should not surpass, either in quantity or quality, those levels in existence concurrent with the establishment of diplomatic relations with the PROC. In addition, the United States promised a gradual reduction in those sales. For its part, the PROC agreed to pursue only peaceful solutions to the Taiwan dispute. The entire policy seemed ambiguous, as Washington did not commit itself to Taiwan's defense, yet somehow guaranteed its security! (33)

Although Mao Zedong originally sought Taiwan's acquisition through military force, modifications in that policy had developed by the time of third generation leader Jiang Zemin. On January 30, 1995, Jiang announced his Eight Points. In essence, he aimed at preventing Taiwan from acquiring dejure independence. He would use military force only to counter independence moves by Taipei. If Taipei merely maintained the status quo, then all would be well. (34)

In the spring of 1994 Taiwanese President Lee Teng-hui's plane landed at Honolulu for refueling. He and his party had been granted permission to land in the United States, en route to both Central America and the inauguration of South Africa's new President, Nelson Mandela. Offended by the third rate reception prepared for him at the air force base, Lee refused to disembark. News of this insult soon reached Congress, infuriating many of Taiwan's supporters. Because the United States had recognized the PROC as the sole legitimate government in China for fifteen years, administration officials had provided Lee only a Spartan reception, hoping to avoid upsetting Beijing. (35)

But conditions had changed since the 1970's. Not only did the United States no longer need China's cooperation in holding the Soviet menace in check, but Americans had become less sympathetic towards her. The Tiananmen Square Massacre made Beijing's poor record on human rights painfully obvious. Although American businessmen regularly favored MFN (Most Favored Nation) trading status for China, they also viewed her as markets for the future, not the here and now. Conversely, they recognized Taiwan as the source of profits for the present. Taiwan imported $16 billion worth of goods in 1993, while the value of China's purchases stood at less than eight billion dollars. American firms engaged in heated bidding for contracts tied to Taipei's $300 billion public works projects. (36)

Taipei soon understood that it could gain more from lobbying Congress than it could from dealing with the Clinton administration. With that in mind, a close Lee associate founded the Taiwan Research Institute, essentially an arm of the wealthy Kuomintang or Nationalist Party. This institute soon invested over four billion dollars in Cassidy & Associates, a Washington lobbyist, in an effort to liberalize American Taiwan policy. The 1994 Republican Congressional sweep couldn't have pleased Taipei more or come at a better time. Meanwhile, Cornell University received donations totaling nearly $2.5 million from Taiwanese seeking to establish a professorship in Lee's name.

Requests besieged Washington for a visa permitting Lee to make a "private visit" to the United States. Although Secretary of State Warren Christopher assured Chinese Foreign Minister Qian Qichen that the Clinton administration would not grant Lee a visa, pressure continued to build in Congress. During May of 1995 the House of Representatives passed a non-binding resolution urging the White House to issue Lee a visa, 396-0. The Senate soon did the same, 97-1.

Concern arose within the administration that Congress might eventually pass binding laws allowing Lee to visit. Furthermore, Clinton had granted MFN status to China in 1994 based on Beijing's promise to improve its record on human rights, a promise gone unfulfilled. As a result, of both domestic political realities and his irritation with China, Clinton authorized a visa for Lee. (37)

Jiang's rather accommodating attitude changed dramatically, following Taiwanese President Lee Teng-hui's June 1995 visit to the United States. (38) Lee came to the United States to visit his alma mater, Cornell

University, where he made a speech considered inflammatory by Beijing.

Today, we are entering a new post-Cold War era, where the world is full of many uncertainties. Communism is dead or dying, and the peoples of many nations are anxious to try new methods of governing their societies. Democracy is thriving in my country. No speech or act allowed by law will be subject to any restriction or interference. Different and opposing views are heard every day in the news media, including harsh criticism of the president. The people of the Republic of China on Taiwan are determined to play a peaceful and constructive role among the family of nations. We are here to stay. (39)

An angry China first responded in the diplomatic sphere, canceling or delaying scheduled meetings between various officials of the two governments. For example, Beijing postponed Defense Minister Chi Haotian's trip to Washington and recalled a Chinese air force group on business in Washington. James Sasser, recently appointed as the new American ambassador to China, learned he could not yet assume his post in Beijing, as his formal acceptance by the Chinese had been postponed. Furthermore, China recalled her ambassador to the United States, Li Daoyu, on June 17! (40)

Beijing now initiated a military response by conducting maneuvers along the coastal areas opposite Taiwan, as well as missile tests in the Taiwan Strait.(41) On July 19 the People's Liberation Army broadcast plans for a week of maneuvers in the East China Sea just north of Taiwan. These would involve warplanes and warships, along with live ammo. The latter included missiles targeted to land near Taiwan's coastal waters. The announcement proved accurate. Within a few days four of China's solid fuel M-9 missiles plunged into the East China Sea, too close to Taiwan for comfort. In a matter of weeks Taipei's stock market declined 33%, while the Taiwan Dollar reached the lowest level in four years. (42)

The Clinton administration responded with concessions to placate Beijing. That August Clinton extended an invitation to Chinese President Jiang Zemin to visit Washington. He also issued guarantees which became known as the "three noes." First, the United States would oppose any independence move by Taiwan. Secondly, she would not support a policy of two Chinas, or one China and one Taiwan, as did Lee Teng-hui. And lastly, she would not back Taiwan in her efforts to gain admission to the United Nations. Shortly Ambassador Li Daoyu returned to Washington and James Sasser gained Beijing's acceptance as the United States Ambassador. (43)

During late 1995 Beijing sent indirect threats to Washington, implying that friction between the United States and China over Taiwan could result in nuclear confrontation. However, just as Beijing lacked tolerance for lectures on Taiwan from Washington, so did the United States rue threats from Beijing. Consequently, the American aircraft carrier Nimitz plied the waters of the Taiwan Strait during December 1995. Her escort consisted of two support ships, a frigate, a cruiser, and a destroyer. (44)

Only weeks before the ROC's March 23, 1996 presidential election, the Chinese news agency Xinhua announced a continuation and intensification of the tests and maneuvers begun the previous July. The PLA, or People's Liberation Army, would conduct missile launch tests in both the East and South China Seas during the week of March 8-15. (45) A series of M-9 missiles landed less than thirty miles from the Taiwanese ports of Kaohsiung and Keelung. These are Taiwan's biggest ports, handling approximately 70% of her trade. (46)

Meanwhile, Chinese Vice-Premier and Foreign Minister Qian Qichen held a press conference on March 11. A CNN correspondent asked him about the Chinese government's attitude concerning the United States government's decision to dispatch the USS Independence to the Taiwan Strait. The Chinese Vice-Premier responded in a firm manner. (47)

It is common for the US Fleet to operate in the high seas. But it is preposterous for some people in the US to call openly for interference on the Taiwan issue by the Seventh Fleet, or even for protecting Taiwan. Maybe they have forgotten that Taiwan is part of China's territory, not a protectorate of the United States. (48)

China's news agency Xinhua made another announcement concerning the Taiwan Strait, a mere three days after its first. Naval and Air Force units would conduct maneuvers off the coast of Fujian Province from March 12 through March 20. (49) Here the navy employed its most recent frigates and destroyers. The Air Force used its most advanced technology, including Su-27 aircraft and S-300 anti-air missiles. (50) These maneuvers clearly represented an attempt to intimidate Taiwanese voters immediately prior to the March 23 presidential election. A third announcement reported maneuvers scheduled for the week of March 18-25. Therefore, while Taiwanese cast their ballots the PLA assembled 150,000 troops along the Fujian Province coast. Concurrently, naval and air forces operated in the Taiwan Strait. Hostility between Beijing and Taipei soared. Taipei's stock and gold markets plummeted. (51)

As mentioned earlier, during December 1995 the United States sent the aircraft carrier USS Nimitz cruising through the Taiwan Strait, accompanied by supporting naval forces. (52) Now the navy once again dispatched the USS Nimitz and the USS Independence, mainstays of the US Seventh Fleet, to the Strait. One stationed itself 200 miles northeast of Taiwan and the other 150 miles south, where the two carrier groups observed events. (53) Why the excursion? First, the United States Government wanted Beijing to understand that America had strong interests in the region. Secondly, other Asian countries needed to know that the United States would continue to provide security in Pacific Asia. Furthermore, President Clinton needed to appear strong in his handling of foreign policy during an election year. (54)

Beijing declared the enhancement of its armed forces' effectiveness as the sole purpose of the maneuvers. But in fact, she was highly concerned about certain groups within Taiwan that wanted to detach the island from China. (55) These groups became known as the Tai Du factions. And she hardly trusted Taiwanese President Lee Teng-hui and his diplomatic methods. Under the "silver bullet method" Lee sent financial aid to third world countries. In another scenario, known as the "vacation method," top level Taiwanese leaders "vacationed" in countries with which Taiwan had no diplomatic relations. These methods had one purpose: to remove the ROC from the status of a mere Chinese province and make her a serious player on the international scene. (56)

As noted earlier, Lee Teng-hui's visit to Cornell University aroused suspicions concerning his intentions. Furthermore, Beijing became upset over his declared China policy: two Chinas, or one China, one Taiwan. (57) During the crisis Beijing issued statements to "calm" Taiwanese citizens.

The residents in Taiwan should not worry about the on-going military exercises of the mainland. What they should worry about most is that some people in Taiwan are attempting to make use of foreign forces for Taiwan independence and separation of the motherland....If foreign forces invade Taiwan, or the Taiwan authorities attempt to declare Taiwan independence, we will not sit idly and remain indifferent. (58)

Taiwan held its first ever presidential election on March 23, 1996. The four major candidates represented three main parties. The Democratic Progressive Party stood radically for "Tai Du" and nominated Peng Ming-min. Peng received 21.3% of the vote, a figure lower than his party's candidate customarily received. Beijing liked the Chinese New Party because of its radically anti-Tai Du stance. Its candidates, Lin Yang-Kung and Chen Li-an, received 14.9% and 9.98% of the vote, respectively. Although Beijing realized that the Chinese New Party could not capture the Presidency, it hoped the party could capture enough seats in the Yuan and the National Assembly to undermine the independence efforts of the Democratic Progressive Party and the Kuomintang. President Lee Teng-hui of the Kuomintang easily won reelection by capturing 54% of the vote. (59)

Two days later Beijing's military exercises ended. The crisis was over. Wen Wei Po, a PROC publication, claimed that the United States lied about desiring the peaceful reunification of China and wished instead for an independent Taiwan. As evidence, the publication cited the use of aircraft carrier groups in the Taiwan Strait and the sale of missiles, as well as aircraft navigation equipment and electronic controlled aircraft, to Taiwan. (60)

On March 29, 1996, the China Daily insisted that if Taiwan wanted to ease tensions in the strait it must abandon attempts to gain admission to the United Nations and its pursuit of dual recognition. (61) Meanwhile, polls taken at intervals from 1994 through 1996 indicated a remarkable change in Taiwanese attitudes towards immediate independence versus immediate unification. In January 1994, 4.2% desired immediate unification versus 2.9% in April 1996. But 4.3% desired immediate independence versus 11.8% in the same period. (62) The purpose of Beijing's military maneuvering?

While the long term objective of the military exercises is to deter Taiwan's future disturbing actions in the cross-strait relations, Beijing's short term objectives were aiming at Taiwan's presidential election. To most Western commentators, however, the war game was a counterproductive action conducted at the wrong time and for wrong objectives. It got the Taiwan issue internationalized. (63)

One question easily arises. What differences existed between the 1996 Taiwan Strait crisis and earlier crises? For one thing, communist leaders in earlier crises largely viewed them as continuations of the Chinese Civil War. Also, Chiang Kai-Shek, his son, and the Kuomintang all looked forward to regaining control of the mainland, not to sailing an independent course. Finally, the Kuomintang actually had a certain military superiority over the PROC. The latter lacked skilled and technologically developed naval and air forces. They also had no nuclear weapon capabilities. (64)

The earlier description of America's Taiwan policy as rather vague became known during the 1996 crisis as "strategic ambiguity." Howard Lange, Director of the Taiwan Division of the State Department, confirmed that the Taiwan Relations Act does not constitute a guarantee of assistance to Taiwan in case of an attack. (65) Parris Chang, a Representative in Taiwan's Legislature, the Yuan, insisted that a policy such as "strategic ambiguity" constituted folly. (66)

There are valuable lessons to be drawn by the U.S., Taiwan, and China following the Persian Gulf Crisis and the Taiwan Strait Crisis of 1996. When one nation fails to unambiguously articulate its security interests and foreign policy goals, the results can be devastating. (67)

Senator Bob Dole, 1996 Republican Presidential candidate, has also criticized this policy. He felt that American policy should be crystal clear: any attack on Taiwan would bring swift reprisals from the United States. (68) But Beijing believed its action absolutely necessary, as it viewed both Taiwan and Hong Kong as integral parts of China. The imminent return of Hong Kong to China could have been jeopardized by an independent Taiwan. (69)

This raises an important question: did the Taiwan Strait crisis of 1996 constitute an international crisis, thus making U.S. involvement imperative? Usually an international crisis is considered as having three main characteristics. First, one nation must feel its interests clearly threatened. Secondly, the nation's leaders must sense a need to bypass normal decision making methods in order to make hurried decisions. Lastly, not only must the likely outcome appear unclear, but the crisis could easily spread into a general conflict. (70)

This would appear to have been an international crisis. Chiang Kai-Shek and his son Chiang Ching-Kuo always dreamed of returning to the mainland. However, Lee Teng-hui is native Taiwanese. (71) While he has never openly embraced a goal of independence for Taiwan, it seems most likely that he wished to see her assume a place among the family of nations. Beijing could never tolerate that! On the other hand, the Democratic Progressive Party, the Kuomintang's chief rival in the March 23 election, did openly advocate an independent Taiwan. Lee's desire to appropriate the Tai Du issue undoubtedly played a part in his decision to attend his 1995 Cornell University reunion.

By abandoning the Chinese mainland for a refuge on Formosa, Chiang Kai-Shek established the confrontational arrangements that made the Taiwan Strait crises inevitable. The Korean War, along with a series of major showdowns in the Strait, brought both world attention to this regional conflict and the Cold War to East Asia. Following the opening of diplomatic relations between Beijing and Washington in 1979, the Taiwan

Strait ceased to be such a "hot spot." Unfortunately, the situation changed in 1995.

At just that moment when Beijing began fearing that Lee's activities would clearly place Taiwan on the international scene, a regional problem erupted into an international crisis. Beijing feared Tai Du.

Endnotes

1. Walter LaFeber, <u>America, Russia, and the Cold War, 1945-1996</u>, 8th ed. (New York: The McGraw-Hill Companies, Inc., 1997), 87.

2. Ibid., 88.

3. Burton I. Kaufman, <u>The Korean War: Challenges in Crisis, Credibility, and Command</u>, 2nd ed. (New York: The McGraw-Hill Companies, Inc., 1997), 18.

4. Richard H. Rovere and Arthur M. Schlesinger, Jr., <u>The General and the President</u> (New York: Farrar, Straus and Young, 1951), 125-26.

5. Harry S. Truman, <u>Memoirs</u>, vol. 2, <u>Years of Trial and Hope</u> (Garden City, New York: Doubleday & Company, Inc., 1956), 349.

6. Kaufman, 46.

7. Rovere, 125-26.

8. Trumbull Higgins, <u>Korea and the Fall of MacArthur</u> (New York: Oxford University Press, 1960), 39.

9. Arthur M. Schlesinger, Jr., ed., <u>The Dynamics of World Power: A Documentary History of United States Foreign Policy, 1945-1973</u>, vol. 4, <u>The Far East</u>, "MacArthur's Message to VFW," (New York: Chelsea House Publishers, 1973), 385.

10. LaFeber, 106.

11. Ibid., 107.

12. Xiao-bing Li, <u>Diplomacy Through Militancy in the Taiwan Straits: Crisis Politics and Sino-American Relations in the 1950's</u> (China Education Press, 1993), 1.

13. Ibid., 6.

14. Ibid., 7.

15. Ibid., 8.

16. Ibid., 10.

17. Ibid., 11.

18. Ibid., 12.

19. Ibid., 13.

20. Ibid., 202.

21. Ibid., 203.

22. LaFeber, 197.

23. <u>The New Funk & Wagnalls Encyclopedia Yearbook, Events of 1958,</u> 1959 Deluxe ed., s.v. "Taiwan (Formosa)."

24. Li, 6.

25. Congress, House of Representatives, Representatives speaking on calling on the People's Republic of China to conduct its relations with Taiwan by peaceful means, <u>Congressional Record</u> (7 March 1996): H1971

26. Ibid.

27. Dennis Van Vranken Hickey, "The Taiwan Strait Crisis of 1996:

Implications For US Security Policy," Journal of Contemporary China 7 (Nov 1998): 405.

28. James Mann, About Face: A History of America's Curious Relationship With China, From Nixon to Clinton (New York: Alfred A. Knopf, 1999), 95.

29. Ibid.

30. Harvey Sicherman, "An Interview With President Lee Teng-hui of the Republic of China on Taiwan," Orbis 39 (Fall 95): 583.

31. Mann, 48.

32. Sicherman, 583.

33. Hickey, 406.

34. Gang Lin, "The Changing Relations Across the Taiwan Strait," Interpreting U.S.-China-Taiwan Relations: China In The Post-Cold War Era, Xiaobing Li, Xiabo Hu, Yang Zhong, eds. (New York: University Press of America, Inc., 1998), 128.

35. Mann, 315-18.

36. Ibid.

37. Ibid., 320-25.

38. Lin, 129.

39. Mann, 326.

40. Ibid., 328.

41. Lin, 129.

42. Mann, 328.

43. Ibid., 330.

44. Ibid., 334-35.

45. Yue Ren, "China's Dilemma in Cross-Strait Crisis Management," Asian Affairs: An American Review 24 (Fall97): 132.

46. Mann, 335.

47. "Qian On World and Regional Issues," Beijing Review 39 (March 1996): 8.

48. Ibid.

49. Ren, 132.

50. Weixing Hu, "Beijing's Military Exercises and the Changing Cross-Strait Relationship," Interpreting U.S.-China-Taiwan Relations: China in the Post-Cold War Era, Xiaobing Li, Xiabo Hu, Yang Zhong, eds., (New York: University Press of America, 1998), 153.

51. Ren, 132.

52. Hickey, 406.

53. Hu, 158.

54. Ibid.

55. Ren, 132.

56. Ibid., 133.

57. Ibid.

58. "Qian on World and Regional Issues, 7.

59. Lin, 131.

60. "China and Taiwan: Near A Flash Point?," World and I 11 (June 96): 41.

61. Ibid, 40.

62. Ren, 19.

63. Hu, 155.

64. Ren,134.

65. Hickey, 407.

66. Ibid., 408.

67. Ibid.

68. Ibid.

69. Ren, 133.

70. Ibid.

71. Ibid

References

"China and Taiwan: Near A Flash Point?." World and I 11 (June 96): 40-45.

Hickey, Dennis Van Vranken. "The Taiwan Strait Crisis of 1996: Implications for US Security Policy." Journal of Contemporary China 7 (Nov 1998): 405-19.

Trumbull, Higgins. Korea and the Fall of MacArthur. New York: Oxford University Press, 1960.

Hu, Weixing. "Beijing's Military Exercises and the Changing Cross-Strait Relationship." Interpreting U.S.-China-Taiwan Relations: China in the Post-Cold War Era. Edited by Xiao-bing Li, Xiabo Hu, and Yang Zhong. New York: University Press of America, 1998.

Kaufman, Burton I. The Korean War: Challenges in Crisis, Credibility, and Command, 2nd ed. New York: The McGraw-Hill Companies, Inc., 1997.

LaFeber, Walter. America, Russia, and the Cold War, 1945-1996, 8th ed. New York: The McGraw-Hill Companies, Inc., 1997.

Li, Xiao-bing. Diplomacy Through Militancy in the Taiwan Straits: Crisis Politics and Sino-American Relations in the 1950's. China Education Press, 1993.

Lin, Gang. "The Changing Relations Across the Taiwan Strait," Interpreting U.S.-China-Taiwan Relations: China In The Post Cold-War Era. Edited by Xiao-bing Li, Xiabo Hu, and Yang Zhong. New York: University Press of America, 1998.

Mann, James. About Face: A History of America's Curious Relationship With China, From Nixon to Clinton. New York: Alfred A. Knopf, 1999.

"Qian On World and Regional Issues." Beijing Review 39 (March 1996): 7-9.

Ren, Yue. "China's Dilemma in Cross-Strait Crisis Management." Asian Affairs: An American Review 24 (Fall 97): 131-51.

Rovere, Richard H., and Arthur M. Schlesinger, Jr. The General and the President. New York: Farrar, Straus and Young, 1951.

Schlesinger, Arthur M., Jr., ed., The Dynamics of World Power: A Documentary History of United States Foreign Policy, 1945-1973. vol. 4, The Far East. "MacArthur's Message to VFW," 385. New York: Chelsea House Publishers, 1973.

Sicherman, Harvey. "An Interview With President Lee Teng-hui of the Republic of China on Taiwan." Orbis 39 (Fall 95): 583-94.

Truman, Harry S. Memoirs. vol. 2, Years of Trial and Hope. Garden City, New York: Doubleday & Company, Inc., 1956.

United States Congress. House of Representatives. Representatives speaking on calling on the People's Republic of China to conduct its relations with Taiwan by peaceful means. Congressional Record (7 March 1996): H1971.

Chapter 14

The Cinema, Racism, and America's Three Asian Wars

Richard Lee Matthews

America's history is replete with episodes where mistreatment of one group of people by another, based on race or culture, played a large role in domestic and foreign policy.

The people of the great American "melting pot" have, enslaved Africans, subdued the Native Americans, displaced other peoples, and their cultures, for reasons including the national interest, economic interest, or some other social necessity.

Racism toward peoples of other nations has been significant, especially during wars or other conflicts with those peoples. In the three major Asian wars which America has been involved in the twentieth century, racism was rampant, and during World War Two, it was partially United States Government sponsored.

Along with the government, "Hollywood" film factories created and reinforced negative stereotypes of Asians in motion pictures. Perhaps it was this Hollywood effort during World War Two that left long lasting anti-Asian feelings among the American people. This negative view of the Japanese, as well as that of other Asians, was created by the government, the film industry, and the general media during World War Two and carried over into the Korean and Vietnam wars as well. The racism that evolved out of World War Two was modified to fit new enemies such as the North Vietnamese, the Viet Cong, and also the Chinese Communists in the Vietnam War.

Anti-Asian feelings by Americans were, and are, directed most strongly toward East Asians rather than those people on the rest of the continent. For instance, the people of West and Southwest Asia, including Turks, Persians, and those of Arab stock, are portrayed in films as being infidels, treacherous, and inhuman, but not inferior or subhuman in biological terms.

Moving east to the subcontinent, including India and Pakistan, the people are portrayed as deeply religious, stoic, sometimes violent, but not generally inferior.

However, the regions of deep Southeast Asia, also China, Japan, and the Philippines are shown in film as being populated by subhuman, sinister, and inferior racial stock. Curiously, the Pacific islanders, farther east, are viewed merely as childlike, peaceful, and innocent. Admittedly, this is a racial stereotype in itself, but it lacks the deep-seated hatred reserved at various times for the Japanese, Chinese, Koreans, and Southeast Asian people. Why is the region of East Asia viewed by Americans with such disdain and mistrust?

Certainly, the racial prejudice towards Asians goes way back in American history. The Chinese immigrants of the middle nineteenth century felt the sting of discrimination and were generally unwelcome by a people who themselves were immigrants just a generation or two before. The racism that the first Asian immigrants were subjected to was actually more ethnocentric in cultural terms than racial ones. In reality, there is a great difference between cultural and racial hatred.

Full-fledged anti-Asian sentiments, both racial and cultural, exploded in the years just before World War Two as the Japanese began their conquest of East Asia in 1931. Of course as early as the teens, "Yellow Peril" short films were being made such as the anti-Japanese *Patria* (1917) and *Pearl of the Army* (1916), in which "fearless" Pearl White saves the

Panama Canal from Oriental spies.[1] It is obvious that latent racist tendencies of Americans were being exposed in film even early in the century.

Japanese ruthless behavior in China in the late 1930s was made to order for these seeking to portray them as evil, and at the same time inferior. The Japanese capture of Nanking on December 12, 1937, and the atrocities they committed afterwards, lent credence to the existing suspicions that the Japanese were ruthless subhuman. The "Rape of Nanking," as the episode was to be called, was a six-week orgy of "...widespread execution, rape, and random murder of Chinese men and women both in the captured city and outlying communities."[2] Atrocities by the Japanese were commonplace in the captured areas. Toward the end of the war in 1945, Japanese atrocities in Manchuria were performed on a large scale by a murderous contingent of scientists known as "Unit 731."[3] When the Japanese attacked the United States at Pearl Harbor on December 7, 1941, they, themselves laid the groundwork for the propaganda and racist campaign which was to be waged against them in the following four years, and lingering for decades thereafter.

In the days following Pearl Harbor, United States military chief of staff, George C. Marshall sent for the prominent Hollywood film director Frank Capra and outlined a plan to produce a series of films for Americans "...which would show the man in uniform why he was fighting, the objectives and aims of why America had gone into the War, the nature and type of our enemies, and in general what were the reasons and causes of this War...."[4]

The series of films was called *Why We Fight,* with each installment dealing with separate aspects of the war and each having its own title; seven films were made between 1942 and 1945. The project was the ultimate in wartime propaganda. It was intended to indoctrinate the fighting men and the public against the enemy, that being the German-Japanese-Italian coalition. All three powers were lumped together and portrayed in a purposefully evil light.

Hollywood film makers began to churn out movies full of anti-Japanese stereotypes, much to the delight of American leaders. The circumstances which surrounded the Japanese "sneak" attack on Pearl Harbor, and the stories of Japanese atrocities in China, made it easy and quite believable to portray the Japanese as evil, subhuman, and inferior.

Motion pictures seem to have a great influence on public opinion and emotions. Director Cecil B. DeMille believed that Hollywood cinema was an excellent vehicle for disseminating information about American thought and the American way of life.[5] Clearly, the cinema was also seen to be an excellent vehicle for inflaming the emotions of fighting men and the public against a treacherous foe.

One of the early efforts by Hollywood to portray an actual wartime event on screen and add some of the anti-Japanese racial propaganda was in the movie *Wake Island,* released September 2, 1942. It was a stirring account of American efforts to hold on to a Pacific island at the outbreak of World War Two. The movie was one of the first to present Japan in clearly propagandistic terms.[6] It is clear that the film sought to stir up viewer hatred for the enemy, "...by presenting him as a frightening figure who would shoot a radioman in the back, and who would gun down a brave pilot who had to parachute out of a burning plane."[7] This same image was also presented in the movie *Air Force* (1943).

Of course history shows that the Wake Islanders lost their battle to defend the island. Opening words in the movie equate the island's defense as a heroic "last stand" much like Valley Forge, Custer's Last Stand, and the Alamo.[8]

By the spring of 1942, anti-Japanese racial epithets were gushing from Hollywood productions. The slur "monkey" was the most common, along with its variants "monkey people" and "ringtail."[9] The word "rat" is often used, and is usually prefixed by "yellow" or "slant-eyed."[10]

The term "Jap" is presented in nearly all of the Pacific Theater World War Two movies, especially those made during the war. "The Jap" is viewed as a subhuman, lethal object, that when incinerated, becomes "fried Jap," such as downed Japanese pilots in the movie *Air Force* (1943), and *God Is My Co-Pilot* (1945).[11] In the movie *The Sullivans* (1944), one of the Sullivan brothers says of Japanese soldiers: "They can't fight, they close their eyes when they fire off a gun."[12] In the movie *Flying Tigers* (1942), one person exclaims: "I hear those Japs glow in the night like bugs."[13]

The most blatant and memorable stereotype of the "evil" Japanese used during the war was that of a sinister smiling man with more than a mouth full of teeth, slight of build, and most importantly, a wearer of horn-rim glasses that created a saucer-eyed look.[14] Plainly, the most evil Japanese in the movies were depicted to look a great deal like the hated Japanese General Tojo.

In the December 22, 1941 issue of *Life* magazine, an article appeared which attempted to explain "how to tell Japs from the Chinese."[15] Because America's allies, the Chinese, were being confused with the Japanese in physical appearance, and thus persecuted, *Life* felt duty-bound to offer "...a rule of thumb from the anthropocentric conformations that distinguish friendly Chinese from enemy alien Japs.[16] The article showed the differences between Chinese public servant Ong Wen-hao and Japanese General Tojo in physical terms.

General Hideki Tojo, then Japan's Premier is described as: ...a Samurai, closer to type of humble Jap than highbred relatives of Imperial Household. Typical are his heavy beard, massive cheek and jawbones. Peasant Jap is squat Mongoloid, with flat, blob nose. An often-sounder clue is facial expression shaped by cultural, not anthropological factors. Chinese wear rational calm of tolerant realists. Japs, like General Tojo, show humorless intensity of ruthless mystics.[17] *Life* describes Ong Wen-hao as "...representative of North Chinese anthropological group with long, fine-boned face and scant beard."[18] The article clearly shows what are acceptable Asian traits and what are not.

In the August 7, 1944 issue of *Time* magazine, Yale University anthropological researcher Geoffrey Gorer, doing secret research for the British, put forth a study answering the question: "Why Are Japs, Japs?"

Gorer alleged that the violent toilet training which Japanese children undergo at the age of four months effected their later life thinking, and actions. He claimed that Japanese children in infancy faced many other restrictions and frustrations. At six months the infant is forcibly taught how to bow respectfully. From birth to age two, the infant spends most of its waking hours slung on its mother's back, cramped and uncomfortable. Before the end of its first year, the babies are forced to sit stiffly on their haunches. Also, boys while growing up are allowed some practice in aggression and the domination of females. Girls on the other hand had to learn to survive by using the defenses of "cajolery and bribery."[19]

Gorer believed that this infant training, and the repressed rebellion against it, were the roots of Japanese character, that is devotion to ritual, neatness and order, horror of dirt, unrestrained savagery against helpless peoples, and the Japanese preoccupation with saving "face."[20]

If Gorer's conclusions weren't so tragic and dangerous, they would be comic. His study was just one of many which were commissioned to explain the war in racial terms.

The January, 1945 edition of *Reader's Digest,* contained an article entitled: "To Understand Japan Consider Toyama," which depicted the life of Mitsuru Toyama, a publicly powerful militarist and assassin. His influence was so great in pre-war and wartime Japan that he was called the country's "Unofficial Emperor." His ability to remove by assassination contrary thinking public officials solidified his power. According to the article, Toyama was responsible to a great degree for Japanese aggression and violence. The article was concluded with this racial epithet:

There, then, is the story of Mitsuru Toyama: A lifetime given over to cowardly, cold-blooded murder. And yet he was the best-loved and most revered man in all Japan. What more terrible indictment of a people? What more convincing proof that they are still creatures of the jungle?[21]

Looking upon the Japanese as animals or a different species was common on official levels in the government of both the United States and Great Britain even before the Japanese attacked Pearl Harbor. A year and a half before the war, British Prime Minister Winston Churchill told President Franklin D. Roosevelt that he was counting on the American president "to keep that Japanese dog quiet in the Pacific."[22]

Former U.S. Ambassador to Japan, Joseph Grew, while a great admirer of moderate Japanese, never the less often referred to all Japanese in non-human terms. Grew described Japan as a busy "hive of bees all servicing the queen," in reality, the emperor.[23]

Sir Alexander Cadogan, undersecretary of the British Foreign Office, often referred to the Japanese in his diary as "beastly little monkeys" even before the war began. He also routinely depicted the Japanese as "yellow dwarf slaves."[24]

American Admiral William Halsey was notorious for his racist remarks regarding the Japanese. His favorite phrase for the Japanese was "yellow bastards." He also referred to them as "stupid animals," "monkey men" and "yellow monkeys." He once declared that he was anxious to go on a new naval operation "to get some more monkey meat."[25] He also told a news conference in early 1945 that he believed the old "Chinese proverb" about the origination of the Japanese race as being the product of mating between female apes and the worst Chinese criminals that had previously been banished from China.[26]

All of this "official racism" lent credence to film and press racial propaganda. In Frank Capra's film, ***Know Your Enemy-Japan,*** Capra enlisted animators from the Walt Disney studios to make animated maps and other characterizations.[27]   The cartoonists showed Japan as an octopus grasping Asia in its tentacles. The buck-toothed Japanese had became such a standard animated figure that it prompted a comparison to Looney Tune's character, Bugs Bunny. Warner Brothers' studio followed up on this characterization with a short animated cartoon called ***Bugs Bunny Nips the Nips.***[28] So even at the cartoon level, the Japanese were transformed into animal-like creatures. Of course, all ages of Americans watched these characterizations, and possibly formed many deep-seated prejudices about the Japanese and also other Asians.

After the war ended, the release of "new" blatant racist propaganda ceased. But, the existence of thousands of movies, film clips, articles, and books already produced, kept anti-Japanese/Asian racism in the public eye.

With the invention of television and its widespread use after 1950, World War Two movies were played over and over for entertainment purposes. Even though the war with Japan had ended; racial stereotypes infested television screens for many decades, and still do for that matter.

We must ask several important questions regarding World War Two anti-Japanese racism: Did it effect future American policy involving Asia, and did it change forms to accommodate a hatred of other Asian peoples, namely the North Koreans, North Vietnamese, and the mainland Chinese? Could we say that the mind altering racism which deluged the American people during World War Two, also played a large role in U.S. involvement in the Korean and Vietnamese Wars?

The Korean War began on June 25, 1950 as Communist North Korean forces invaded the Republic of South Korea. In the early stages of the Korean War, the "American superiority complex" appeared in full bloom. American general Douglas MacArthur, commander of United Nation's troops in Korea, assured President Harry S. 'Truman at a meeting on Wake Island just four months after the war began, that the victory was already won in Korea.[29] MacArthur also informed Truman that the Chinese Communists would not enter the war and attack South Korea.[30] MacArthur apparently promised Truman that all fighting would end in North and South Korea by Thanksgiving Day, 1950.[31]

MacArthur's attitude was an example of the view that no Asian country could defeat the most powerful nation in the world---the United States. It was a view that not only underestimated Asian capabilities, but also inferred that they were not capable due to their race and culture.

And of course, Hollywood film makers resurrected the racist propaganda of World War Two days, and began to adjust it in a form that would apply to the North Koreans and Chinese Communists. In film, the U.S. forces were portrayed as outnumbered good guys, who were brave and fearless, while the Communists were either emotionally disturbed innocents or ruthless schemers and killers.[32]

The 1951 film *The Steel Helmet* gave rise to the term "gook" in film to describe Koreans, both friendly and non-friendly. The film also went to great lengths to portray the Communists in terms of extreme bestiality and savagery. This reinforced the view that Asians were not capable of understanding the Aryan values which were put on life and humanity.

Even after the Korean War, films continued to depict the Koreans and Chinese in inhuman and inferior terms. The 1959 movie *Pork Chop Hill* is an excellent example of this, as the film shows outnumbered Americans holding out against scores of faceless, screaming, almost delirious Asian automatons.

In most ways, the films about the Korean War followed the same racist script as the anti-Japanese World War Two films. One difference is that the blind patriotic propaganda of World War Two films was missing, but the racism still remained.

We should remember, that at the time the Korean War movies were appearing, the new device called television was replaying old World War Two movies with great regularity. The Korean War movies merely added to and perpetuated anti-Asian views. To be sure, the racist verbiage of the Korean War films was not as blatant as the World War Two versions. While the Asians were depicted as inferior and ruthless in Korean War films, the accusations that they were really more genetically akin to animals, as was shown in World War Two films, was mostly missing.

After the Korean War, the American people were still being indoctrinated by anti-Asian propaganda, not through some conspiratorial plot, but by happenstance, through anti-Asian portrayals in old and new war movies. Not only were the movie channels on television running racist World War Two movies, but the theaters were playing first-run anti-Asian Korean War movies at the same time. Also, and most importantly, thousands of Americans had just been killed again in the Pacific region---by Asians of course.

Korean War films followed the World War Two practices of depicting friendly Asians as not being equal to Americans. They were almost always shown as ignorant and tied to the land for life, mere pawns amidst the conflict. Those who were not given the agricultural stereotype were most always shown as corrupt government officials, robbing the country while the Americans allowed them to do it.

Hardly had the Korean War ended, than the U.S. became entangled in the Southeast Asian nation of Vietnam. The cost of waging wars in Asia was not lost on all prominent Americans. On his deathbed, General Douglas MacArthur vainly advised President Lyndon Johnson to stay out of Vietnam, just as he had advised presidents Truman and Kennedy. He made clear to Johnson that American soldiers should no more be made to fight on Asian soil.[33] Perhaps the Korean War, and the French debacle in Vietnam had shown MacArthur that Asian inferiority was myth rather than fact.

MacArthur's warnings fell on deaf ears, and America plunged head-long into the Vietnam conflict. American Secretary of Defense, Robert S. McNamara, reflecting back in 1995 on the 1964 situation in Vietnam, stated that the administration was "[e]ager to get moving, we never stopped to explore fully whether there were other routes to our destination."[34]

A great deal of information has surfaced over the years which shows that American involvement in Vietnam was perpetuated by five different American administrations who engaged in a deliberate policy to deceive the public about the conflict. Much of the proof of deception was contained in *The Pentagon Papers,* which were leaked to the *New York Times* by a former Pentagon official, Daniel Ellsberg in 1969. War correspondents sent to Saigon to cover the war discovered only euphemisms, half-truths, and outright lies there. They were told repeatedly that military victory was in sight, when in fact the Viet Cong and North Vietnamese could, and did, match every step the U S. took.[35]

Perhaps this deceit and the lies, were evidence that America and its leaders were in a stage of self-denial, since they could not believe that an Asian people could stymie the American war machine. During the Vietnam conflict, America was still under the influence of the same superiority complex which affected it in World War Two and the Korean War.

Pro-war propaganda is apparent in the first major Hollywood film about the Vietnam War---*The Green Berets* (1968). The making of *The Green Berets* parallels the production and reasons for Frank Capra's *Why We Fight* series of World War Two. In fact, *The Green Berets* is pure propaganda, with the racist aspects of the film being more subtle than World War Two films. The *Why We Fight* series had been U.S. Government sponsored, and in a way, so was the movie *The Green Berets.*

The star and director of *The Green Berets,* was American film icon, John Wayne. Wayne, a well-known right-wing Republican, was assisted, ironically, by President Lyndon Johnson, a Democrat. Johnson offered government assistance in making the film after a personal request from Wayne. Wayne wrote to Johnson that it was "...extremely important that not only the people of the United States but those all over the world should know why it is necessary for us to be there [Vietnam]." And that "the most effective way to accomplish this is through the motion picture medium." Wayne argued that the aim of the film was to "inspire a patriotic attitude on the part of fellow Americans."[36] Certainly, the same reasons were given for the production of the *Why We Fight* series in 1942.

In *The Green Berets,* along with the films, *Go Tell The Spartans* (1978), *The Boys In Company C* (1978), and *The Deer Hunter* (1978), the Vietnamese enemy was portrayed as the "psychic other," a menace and threat to the American heroic masculinity myth.[37] The film *Go Tell The Spartans,* offers three distinct Vietnamese groups: the South Vietnamese corrupt political leadership, a friendly, but childlike, and trusting Vietnamese people, and the Viet Cong, a deadly faceless mass.[38]

Of course these films offer an "agricultural stereotype" of the common people much as the Korean War movies did. The enemy is often clothed in dark attire, without faces being shown. In *The Green Berets* particularly, the idea is presented that the poor, helpless, backward people of South Vietnam are not capable of defending themselves against the ruthless, inhuman Viet Cong and North Vietnamese without American help.

Ironically, as public opinion turned against the Vietnam War, new movies appeared which portrayed <u>Americans</u> in a sinister, inhuman and even ridiculous light. Examples of these were: *Apocalypse Now* (1979), *Full Metal Jacket* (1987), and *Good Morning Vietnam* (1987).

Can we draw any conclusions from the American war films produced in the years after 1940? To be sure, many were blatantly racist towards Asians. But more than that, the films, along with their racism, were a continuing source for the reinforcement of anti-Asian feelings among the American people for decades.

Historians and political scientists will no doubt discount any relationship between the anti-Japanese World War Two propaganda films, and later American involvement in Korea and Vietnam. But are we to believe that the anti-Asian feelings that were so carefully crafted during World War Two miraculously disappeared with the surrender of Japan in

1945? The American people were indoctrinated for over five years, to hate, despise, and see the Japanese as inferior. And it worked; with a nationalistic and racial superiority fervor, the United States mobilized, and rode the back of racial hatred to crush the evil, treacherous, and inferior Japanese.

One of the great failings of humans is that they tend to lump peoples of the same race together, regardless of the differences in cultures. For instance, Americans had great difficulty in distinguishing between Asian peoples during World War Two. Consequently, there was an obvious need for articles such as the one in *Life,* "How To Tell Japs From the Chinese...," discussed earlier, which sought to direct the natural prejudice against Asians, toward the Japanese, and away from the Chinese.

The end of World War Two brought about the occupation of Japan by U. S. forces. The Japanese realized that the Americans were not the demons that their own government's anti-American propaganda had told them they were. The Japanese people found themselves ruled by a basically benevolent occupier.

On the other hand, the American people did not have the benefit of really "knowing" the Japanese. At the end of the war, Americans still saw the Japanese in the same way that they were depicted in the World War Two films and other propaganda. And the films especially, were re-run over and over for decades thereafter.

No coherent scholarly person would claim that World War Two racist propaganda towards Japanese, and hence other East Asians as well, was the main reason for American involvement in Korea and Vietnam. Economic and political matters were both factors in America becoming involved in those conflicts.

We might surmise however, that the racist propaganda of the World War Two years created an "attitude," and an atmosphere, which distorted reality regarding Korea and Vietnam. American arrogance, military and otherwise, was constantly reinforced by old World War Two racism. So, could we dare propose that the methods by which America won World War Two, in large measure through racist propaganda and orgasmic nationalism, actually contributed greatly to the near American failure in Korea, and the actual defeat in Vietnam?

Endnotes

[1]Bernard F. Dick, *The Star Spangled Screen: The American World War II Film* (Lexington, Kentucky: University Press of Kentucky, 1985), 230.

[2]John W. Dover, *War Without Mercy: Race and Power in the Pacific War* (New York: Pantheon Books, 1986), 43.

[3]Morimura Seiichi, *Akuma no Hoshoku* [The Devil's Gluttony] (Kobunsha, 1981), in Ibid., 42.

[4]Frank Capra, interview by A. B. Friedman (date not given), for the Oral History Research Office of Columbia University, (transcript, 1974), page 49.

[5]Leif Furhammar and Folke Isaksson, *Politics and Film,* trans. Kersti French (New York: Praeger Publishers, 1971), 243.

[6]Jeanine Basinger, *The World War II Combat Film: Anatomy of a Genre* (New York: Columbia University Press, 1986), 31.

[7]Ibid.

[8]Ibid., 34.

[9]*The Star Spangled Screen...*, 230.

[10]Ibid.

[11]Ibid.

[12]Ibid.

[13]Ibid.

[14]Ibid., 231.

[15]"How to Tell Japs From The Chinese: Angry Citizens Victimize Allies With Emotional Outburst At Enemy." *Life*, 22 December 1941, 81-82.

[16]Ibid., 81.

[17]Ibid.

[18]Ibid.

[19]"Why Are Japs, Japs" *Time,* 7 August 1944, 66.

[20]Ibid.

[21]"To Understand Japan Consider Toyama," *Reader's Digest,* January, 1945, 87-88.

[22]Churchill to Roosevelt in Dower, *War Without Mercy...,* 82.

[23]Ibid., 83.

[24]Sir Alexander Cadogan in, David Dilks, ed., *The Diaries of Sir Alexander Cadogan, 1938-1945* (Cassell and Co., 1971), 353,358,392,416,445, cited in, Dower, *War Without Mercy...,* 83.

[25]William F. Halsey in, William F. Halsey and Joseph Bryan III, *Admiral Halsey's Story,*(McGraw-Hill, 1947), 141-142,206, cited in Dower, *War Without Mercy...,* 85.

[26]Ibid.

[27]Frank Capra, *The Name Above The Title: An Autobiography* (New York: The Macmillan Company, 1971), 340.

[28]Dower, *War Without Mercy...,* 84.

[29]Harry S. Truman, *Memoirs: Years of Trial and Hope* (Garden City, New York: Doubleday, 1956), 365.
[30]Ibid.

[31]Ibid., 365-366.

[32]Nora Sayre, *Running Time: Films of the Cold War* (New York: The Dial Press, 1982), 79-99; cited in Albert Auster and Leonard Quart, *How the War Was Remembered: Hollywood and Vietnam* (New York: Praeger, 1988), 9.

[33]Douglas MacArthur in, William Manchester, *American Caesar: Douglas MacArthur 1880-1964* (Boston: Little, Brown and Co., 1978), 698.

[34]Robert S. McNamara, *In retrospect: The Tragedy and Lessons of Vietnam* (New York: Times Books, 1995), 108, also in, H. R. McMaster, *Dereliction of Duty* (New York: Harper Collins, 1997), 155.

[35]James C. Wilson, *Vietnam In Prose and Film* (Jefferson, M.C.: McFarland and Co., 1982), 26.

[36]Lawrence H. Suid, *Guts and Glory: Great American War Movies* (Reading, Mass.: Addison-Wesley, 1978), 222:cited in Andrew Martin, *Receptions of War* (Norman, Oklahoma: University of Oklahoma Press, 1993), 107.

[37]*Receptions of War,* 99.

[38]Ibid., 100.

Chapter 15

The American Soldier in Vietnam: Life of a Combat Infantryman

Ryan Paul Jones

"We were in sad shape now. I know that at one point, my feet about to crack open, my back feeling like a mirror made of nerves shattered in a million pieces by my flak jacket, pack, and extra mortars and machine-gun ammo, my hands a mass of hamburger from thorn cuts, and my face a mass of welts from mosquitoes, 1 desired greatly to throw down everything, slump into the water of the paddy, and sob. I remember a captain, an aviator, who, observing a group of grunts toasting the infantry in a bar, said, "You damned infantry think you're the only people who exist." You're damned right we do." (1)

So wrote First Lieutenant Victor David Westphal III, a rifle platoon leader with Company B, 1st Battalion, 4th Regiment, 3rd Marine Division in Vietnam. His words expressed a near universal sentiment among ground troops. The infantryman in Vietnam, better known as a grunt, faced not only a different form of war than his predecessor of World War II and Korea but a changing system as well. New technology, combined with new policy, changed the soldiers experience. In spite of this technology, however, the grunt on the ground still faced the task of defeating a determined enemy. As the saying went, war is hell, but Vietnam had a hell all of its own. Despite the influx of books, articles, movies, and documentaries the public at large failed to understand the combat soldier in Vietnam. Even the numerous memoirs published failed to give an overview of the average soldiers combat experience.

The intent of this paper is to view the life of the grunt in Vietnam. To examine the common aspects shared by all who served. Thus, incidents of fragging (killing ones superior) and drug use, though prolific in Vietnam, will not be covered. Though they reached unprecedented proportions during the war, they did not affect every soldier. The combat infantryman in Vietnam faced an oppressive environment of intense heat and humidity set amid nearly impassable jungle terrain; in addition to intense boredom the soldier lived with constant fear and fatigue as he patrolled areas laced with booby traps, mines, and the elusive Viet Cong (VC) or North Vietnamese Army Regular (NVA) while he completed his one year tour of duty.

For the infantryman, whether a soldier of ancient Rome or a grunt in Vietnam, terrain dictated much of their experience. The environment provided the first obstacle for a newly arrived soldier in Vietnam. Letters and diaries abounded with references to the oppressive heat. Dominick Yezzo served during the height of the conflict and simply wrote in his diary upon arrival, "The heat hit me hard in the face". (2) Leaving the air conditioned comfort of a commercial airliner quickly exposed the G.I. to the harsh realities of Vietnam. The average monthly temperature of 90 degrees often soared into the triple digits. (3) In the winter months, Vietnam's dry season, troops often operated in temperatures between 100-110 degrees. During the summer and fall the endless monsoon rains arrived, ensuring the soldier stayed constantly wet. Exposure alone produced casualties.

The terrain itself provided a formidable obstacle. With over half of South Vietnam composed of mountains and plateaus and the remaining a mixture of rice paddy fields and valleys, all set amid nearly impenetrable jungle, "humping the boonies", as the troops called it, proved difficult. (4) Movement through fifteen feet high elephant grass, knee deep in mud, not only slowed a soldiers progress, but produced considerable fatigue as well.

The troops spent a large amount of time, up to sixty days, patrolling the South Vietnamese countryside. (5) Due to the weight each soldier carried, movement became a debilitating task. Combined with the heat, the situation produced numerous non-combat related casualties. For the American infantryman terrain presented the first among many problems.

Exposure to the jungles of Vietnam proved as harsh and deadly as the Viet Cong. Infested with snakes, mosquitoes, ants, and leeches the soldier dealt with discomfort, pain and even death from the environment. Common afflictions included bacterial and fungal infections, referred to as jungle rot, malaria, hepatitis, and ringworms (from bad water). In addition, prolonged exposure to the wet conditions produced immersion foot in nearly 98% of soldiers exposed and rendered some unfit for duty. (6)

Thus, simple exposure and lack of proper hygiene removed soldiers from the war. Jungle rot and immersion foot often combined to worsen an individuals experience. Willie Booth, a typical grunt, faced this horrible combination. He stated, "From my feet to where I hung my pistol belt was nothing but sores. I had jungle rot. I was all f--- up. My feet would turn white" (immersion foot). (7) In addition, insect bites constantly plagued the grunt. Ants and leeches provided endless irritation, so much so that troops often held more contempt for the creatures than the enemy. (8) Though proportionately few deaths or permanent disabilities resulted from these ailments, the soldier lived with them daily in a constant state of discomfort.

As Vietnam's terrain differed from previous wars, so did the soldier. In the early years of the war the U.S. Army fielded the best trained and equipped force in its history. Units initially deployed together. Having trained stateside they possessed the cohesion needed in combat. As the war escalated, however, it became an army of replacements. This resulted from one of the wars most controversial legacies, the rotation system. Unlike the soldier of World War II who only went home upon death, maiming, or the end of the war, the grunt in Vietnam served a one year tour of duty.

The rotation policy resulted from a desire to limit U.S. casualties. Though sound in theory, the effect of the policy proved damaging. First, it destroyed unit cohesion. An infantry company conceivably underwent a complete change in a ten month time span. (9) With the constant rotation of troops in and out of Vietnam, combined with injury and death, a different group of soldiers fought each year of the war. One consistent complaint among veterans concerned the lack of esprit de corps. Pride and a sense of belonging are key components of effective military units. Without sustained membership in the units, however, this proved impossible.

A newcomer to the war felt anything but welcome. As a replacement, a new soldier wore the brand of an FNG (F----- New Guy). Shunned by his fellow soldiers, the new man fended for himself. Few individuals took the newcomer under their wing to "show them the ropes." Thus, a grunts first 90 days often proved the toughest. Conventional wisdom held that if one survived the first 90 days they would survive the 'Nam. Statistics supported this theory. Forty percent of infantrymen killed in action died in their first three months, only six percent in the last three months. (10) Lack of experience accounted for many of the casualties.

A new soldier lacked the knowledge of how to survive in Vietnam. He did not even know the basics of packing his gear for jungle fighting. Thus, he often carried such needless items as underwear, shaving kits, and undershirts. (11) In addition, they did not know how to move through the jungle. When placed on point, the lead position in a squad, they either tripped a booby trap or failed to spot an ambush. (12) Since they were new they received the most difficult or unwanted tasks. Inexperienced and afraid, the FNG lacked the knowledge and stamina to endure Vietnam. Duane Cornellla commented on his experience as a new troop:

I had been in Vietnam two days. In the middle of the night they woke us up and said, 'the company got hit. Get your gear and get out to the chopper pad, because you're going out as soon as its light.' The next morning we're on the choppers, flying out. No one's talking.

It's like, "hug? what?"...There you are in the middle of this grass and you can't see anywhere around you. You can't see any of the guys you're with. Oh my God, here I am, what do I do now? (13)

The rotation policy eroded a unit of one essential element, experience. On average it took a soldier 3-6 months to become an effective fighting man. (14) As soon as a soldier gained competency in the field he rotated out of Vietnam. As experience departed a platoon inexperience flowed in. This included the leadership as well. Whereas an enlisted man spent twelve months in Vietnam(thirteen for Marines), an officers tour lasted only six. Naturally this seemed unfair. A leader, by definition, sacrificed more than his men. In Vietnam the Army dictated otherwise.

The rationalization for the policy rested on the burden of command. A combat officer supposedly reached his psychological limit in a six month time span. (15) In reality, by the time an officer learned the rudiments of command in combat he moved on to another assignment, taking with him all knowledge gained. The unofficial view maintained that officers had their "tickets punched". In order to build an army with combat experienced officers a shorter tour allowed more to serve and consequently survive. Thus, combat service enhanced an officers career. When non-commissioned officers (NCOs) and officers rotated out, it often left a unit with no veteran leadership. This resulted in the development of the "Shake N' Bake" NCO.

The "Shake N' Bake" NCO gained prominence as the war escalated. These instant sergeants comprised soldiers fresh out of basic training who demonstrated some form of potential. Upon completion of advanced infantry training the troop attended a 21 week NCO course. (16) After graduation he received his stripes and shipped off to Vietnam. Thus, at times a platoon lacked not only veteran leadership at the officer level, but at the critical NCO rank as well. Robert Conner, a former instant NCO, commented on his experience: "I took out sergeants just into Vietnam who had been in the service for fifteen years. I don't want that kind of responsibility again. When I look back, God, I was scared. I was so stupid and naive I could hate myself." (17)

The final problem sprung by the rotation system became known as short timers syndrome. (18) A soldier went through three stages in Vietnam. They started as the outcast FNG. By the mid point of their year long tour, however, they learned the arts of survival. (19) Veterans often commented on "getting hard", being able to deal with the horror and terror by not feeling it. (20) This proved a soldiers most effective period. The last three months of a soldiers tour changed his outlook. Once a soldier neared his departure date he became, in their language, "short". Just as a prisoner counted the days until release so did the grunt in the field. The closer a soldier got to that "freedom bird home" the less reliable he became. He generally desired to not take chances when so close to leaving Vietnam. Enter the FNG. When possible, short timers avoided the more dangerous duties, such as walking point. (21) After all, the veteran paid his dues in the jungle, now the new troop had to pay his. This cycle constantly repeated itself.

As the battlefields of Vietnam differed from previous conflicts, so did the nature of combat. Essentially, combat in Vietnam consisted of long patrols searching for the enemy. When engagement was made it occurred in the form of the firefight, often in the form of an ambush. More often than not they failed to encounter the enemy. Generally, firefights were brief and produced only a few casualties. Every firefight, ambush, or booby trap produced a small number of dead and wounded. The pitched battles of World War II did not exist in Vietnam. Firefights and there aftermath became everyday operations. (22) For Angel Quintana it became normal procedure. In his time in Vietnam he fought in numerous firefights and described it rather matter of fact as he stated, "it's a normal thing, you fight and kill people and wound people, and it seems normal." (23) Though sizeable actions occurred, such as the Battle of the Ia Drang and the siege of Khe Sanh, the average grunt experienced combat in brief chaotic moments of terror.

General William Westmoreland, commander of U.S. ground forces until 1968, proposed a war of attrition. For the American soldier this translated into search and destroy missions. Essentially, U.S. troops became bait. (24) They patrolled dense jungle for months at a time looking for the enemy. Exhausted from carrying up to 70lbs of equipment a tree-line could suddenly erupt into small arms fire. A short, chaotic battle ensued. The leader in charge quickly called in fire support and leveled the area. (25) With extraction provided by helicopter the troops left the area, mission accomplished. Generally upon contact one side decided to quit and the firefight ended. Pierre Schoendoffer, who produced the award winning documentary "The Anderson Platoon," caught such a chaotic engagement on film in 1966. After an insertion the platoon, under the command of Lieutenant Anderson, engaged in small arms fire with an unseen enemy. Shortly thereafter, helicopter gunships arrived. Short and chaotic, it typified the Vietnam firefight.

The idea behind the strategy focused on bleeding the enemy to death. After enough damage the enemy would desire peace. Thus, firepower became doctrine. (26) It dictated a grunts life in the jungle. They operated as walking ammo dumps. (27) A grunts typical load consisted of the following: 4-6 ammo pouches with loaded magazines, 1-2 bandoliers (more ammunition), first aid pack, 2 canteens, fragmentation and smoke grenades and a knife. In the rucksack (army style backpack) a troop often carried a claymore mine, trip flares, more grenades and ammunition, Canned rations (C-rats), extra canteen, socks, a rifle cleaning kit, a poncho and poncho liner and an entrenching tool (military slang for shovel). (28) The average weight varied between 40-70lbs and at times even heavier. (29)

The intent behind such a packing list focused on the firefight itself. U.S. troops became reliant on fire support. (30) The first few moments in an encounter before fire support arrived were critical. (31) VC tactics often focused on achieving overwhelming numbers once engaged. (32) In order to combat the superior American firepower the enemy employed the technique of "hugging." They moved in as close as possible to the American position in order to deter fire support.

Once close it proved suicidal to call in fire as the artillery killed friendly troops as well. (33) To deter such actions the grunt ensured he had enough ammunition. U.S. forces often exercised a "mad minute". During such a moment all soldiers fired continuously for one minute. This produced a wall of lead to hold the enemy back. Though effective, it required a large amount of ammunition, hence the grunts packing list. Often, however, there appeared no need to call in fire support. As in the case of the Anderson platoon, they faced no threat of being overrun. Instead of assaulting through, they called for fire. Doctrine became so firmly established that it was used in nearly all encounters.

To better understand the experience of combat in Vietnam the following recollection of Robert Conner, an infantryman with the 25th Infantry Division, is provided:

We were on a search and destroy mission. I was fire team leader. We were going through this wood line. I was third or fourth man back. We went into this jungle. Things sound strange in the jungle; there's an echo. Next thing you know, rounds go off, and we had a guy hit ... Rounds were going off everywhere, people were screaming and hollering, directing mortars in and everything else...I stopped and fired a few rounds. I called for help. The "wait-a-minute bushes" were grabbing me, and they were hugging, and the ants were all over the place.

My Adrenalin was flowing, and I didn't know what to do...And I remember our machine gunner; he moved up as close as he could to me and he was over the top of me. He was firing his M-60 for everything it was worth...The noise blew my eardrums out, and they started bleeding. I heard our lieutenant, who was our forward observer, in the background hollering, "Drop five zero: fire for effect; Drop five zero: fire for effect!" And he kept walking the rounds in and finally, he told us to pull back, pull back...I have never been in a situation where I was so scared in all my life... The whole thing, from the initial attack to almost being burned up by napalm, took less than 30 minutes. But it felt like an eternity. (34)

For the soldier frustration mounted when they fought over an area and later returned to it to fight again. The search and destroy strategy sought to eliminate enemy units rather than occupy territory. (35) The ground troop, however, found this logic flawed. They recognized the futility of such operations. One soldier stated, "We weren't taking over any land, we were just trying to beat the enemy from it. From that aspect, we weren't doing a damn thing if we had to come back to the same place a week later. Even if we had been in contact we'd be back there again. It was stupid" (36) Units operated within an assigned area of operations (AO). Within that area a platoon often traveled the same route on a patrol and set an ambush in the same location as before. The enemy quickly realized this and countered with his own ambush.

Aside from direct contact with the enemy, booby traps and mines offered the most fear. Strewn throughout the jungle, they proved psychologically devastating. (37) Eleven percent of deaths in Vietnam and sixteen percent of wounds resulted from booby traps and mines. (38) Of the wars survivors 10,000 lost at least one limb, more than World War II and Korea combined. (39) The traps proved simple and effective. A tripwire connected to a grenade easily disabled a squad of men. Sharpened bamboo stakes or nails placed in the ground formed the punji stake. Covered in human excrement the stakes worked like a bear trap. Either a soldier stepped into a hole impaling his foot or fell into a pit impaling himself. The human waste smeared on the stakes promoted the possibility of blood poisoning. The bamboo whip provided a variation on the punji stake. When a soldier tripped a wire a whip of sharpened bamboo stakes impaled him. The numerous mines, however, though less inventive, proved more devastating. Aside from the physical damage, booby traps plagued a soldiers mind. In spite of experience and careful movement a well hidden trap proved unavoidable.

The perpetrators of these traps, the VC and NVA, earned the respect of the U.S. infantryman. Commonly referred to as "Charlie", "Victor Charles", or "Chuck", they provided the U.S. military with one of its most formidable foes. Distinct and different organizations, the VC and NVA operated differently. The VC operated as guerilla units whereas the NVA functioned as a regular army. Under the direction of Hanoi General Vo Nguyen Giap they worked together to defeat the Americans. (40) Though often portrayed as expert jungle fighters they felt no more at home among the snakes and leeches than did the American grunt. (41) In fact, snakes and malaria took a heavy toll as they accounted for more enemy deaths than combat. (42)

Both organizations provided a form of basic training to their recruits. Whereas the NVA recruit attended a 2-3 month long induction the Vcs program lasted only 8 days. (43) The focus of the training centered on basic infantry tactics. Camouflage, movement under fire, weapons familiarization, and ambush techniques were common topics. (44) Due to manpower shortages as the war progressed many new recruits received no training but instead went directly into combat. (45) Despite the lack of resources and training both proved capable in battle. The average VC operated in a three man cell. Within this cell remained a veteran to guide the new soldiers. This unit stayed together until death or the end of the war. (46) In contrast to the grunts experience as an FNG, the squads formed from these three man cells provided a disciplined and cohesive group.

In terms of fighting, the VC avoided long battles and occupation of territory. (47) They used the tried and true guerilla method of hit and run tactics. With the aid of the massive underground tunnel complexes stretched throughout South Vietnam, they often operated as "ghosts". The claim many U.S. troops made of rarely seeing the enemy resulted from use of these tunnels. In addition they blended in with the general population. The phrase farmer by day, fighter by night often applied to the VC. They used the villages to hide weapons and escape U.S. capture. For the grunt this proved frustrating. After losing men to a booby trap outside of a village they knew VC operated in the area. Rarely, however, did the local population assist U.S. forces in avoiding booby traps or finding the VC. (48)

With the NVA the situation differed. They wore uniforms and fought like regular infantry. One marine at Khe Sanh noted the difference in a letter home, "It's a lot different up here fighting NVA instead of VC. Up here anyone who isn't an American is an enemy, and they are as well equipped as we, with helmets and new assault rifles and body armor." (49) The NVA often mounted full scale frontal assaults with fixed bayonets as at the Battle of the Ia Drang. Though they suffered massive casualties the assaults had a lasting effect on U.S. troops. Their determination equalled the VC if not more so. Despite their differences both organizations proved capable combatants and earned the universal praise and respect of the American soldier.

Arguably no image personified the Vietnam War more than the helicopter. Vietnam witnessed the birth of a new dimension in war, the airmobile infantry. Tested in Korea, the "chopper" proved itself on the battlefields of Vietnam.   Though troops moved by aid of Armored Personnel Carriers (APC) and often on foot alone, the UH-1 Bell Huey (and its later versions) provided the main transport. Next to the soldier it proved the wars true workhorse.   In addition to insertion and extraction of personnel, they provided logistical support as transports, and fire support as gunships. The role it played as an air ambulance, however, proved most important. Commonly referred to as a medevac, the wounded soldier often arrived at an evacuation hospital within 30 minutes. Due to the success of the medevac concept 81% of wounded soldiers survived. (50)

The use of the helicopter proved a double edged sword, however. Some soldiers viewed them as a hinderance. They provided the enemy an easy target and often gave away the ground troops position. (51) Even efforts to ease the soldiers burden backfired. Often, for the sake of morale, commanders sent hot meals and ice cream to troops in the field. (52) Though welcomed, the enemy easily learned a units location after such a "courtesy call". After sitting in an ambush site for hours or even days one visit from a chopper compromised the operation. In addition, the VC realized that by shooting down one helicopter they seriously delayed any American operation.   Despite the negative drawbacks, the helicopter significantly enhanced Americas mobility in all aspects of the war. The lives saved validated its use.

The combat infantryman in Vietnam faced a different war than those before him. The firefights and endless patrols proved as harrowing and demanding as any previous war. Yet, the grunt endured intense boredom as well. Proportionately, combat occupied the minority of his time. The exhaustive, yet mind numbing tasks of digging foxholes, filling sandbags, cleaning weapons, and burning the human waste from the latrines, forced the grunt to face a daily regime of dread. Amid the terror, however, he enjoyed more creature comforts than any soldier before. At base camp, TV, music, ice cream and beer were available. Though never out of sight of enemy fire the base camp provided some security. In addition, midway through his tour, each soldier received 5 days of Rest and Relaxation (R&R) outside of Vietnam, a luxury not felt by his predecessors.

The soldier in Vietnam lived in an inhospitable environment of intense heat, biting insects, and impassable terrain laced with booby traps. Upon arrival, a new soldier feared not only the enemy, but dealt with the condemnation of being an FNG. From there the grunt patrolled the jungle endlessly in search of an enemy not readily known. They sought not to seize territory, but simply obliterate the enemy.   With numerous engagements fought in the same general area,   the soldier naturally questioned his role. Yet, the grunt of Vietnam, like the Doughboy of World War I and the Dogface of World War II, fought the war in spite of the numerous burdens.

Endnotes

1. Bernard Edelman, ed., <u>Dear America: Letters Home From Vietnam</u>. (New York: Pocket Books, 1986), 85.

2. Dominick Yezzo, <u>A G.I.'s Vietnam Diary: 1968-1969</u> (New York: Franklin Watts, Inc., 1974).

3. Lieutenant General Julian J. Ewell and Major General Ira A. Hung Jr., <u>Sharpening the Combat Edge: The Use of Analysis to Reinforce military judgment</u> (Washington D.C.: Department of the Army, 1974), 13.

4. Mooney, 163.

5. Maurer, 9.

6. Ewell, 31.

7. Maurer, 213.

8. Tim Page and John Pimlott eds., <u>Nam: The Vietnam Experience 1965-1975</u> (London: Hamlyn Publishing, 1988), 18.

9. Andrew J. Rotter, <u>Light at the End of the Tunnel: A Vietnam War Anthology</u> (New York: St. Martin's Press, 1991), 327.

10. James F. Dunnigan and Albert A. Nofi, <u>Dirty Little Secrets of the Vietnam War</u> (New York: St. Martin's Press, 1999), 77.

11. Maurer, 176.

12. Dunnigan, 77.

13. Maurer, 224.

14. Ronald H. Spector, <u>After Tet: The Bloodiest Year in Vietnam</u> (New York: The Free Press, 1993), 65.

15. Spector, 66.

16. Dunnigan, 201.

17. Eric M. Bergerud, <u>Red Thunder, Tropic Lightning: The World of a Combat Division in Vietnam</u> (Boulder: Westview Press, 1993), 97.

18. Page, 396.

19. Maurer, 176.

20. Ibid.

21. Maurer, 174.

22. Ibid, 9.

23. Ibid, 175.

24. Page, 69.

25. Fire support generally consisted of either artillery, helicopter gunships, or mortars. In addition, a leader could request an air strike, usually to drop napalm. Often the troops were at the mercy of whatever support was available.

26. Bergerud, 133.

27. Page, 396.

28. Edelman, 35.

29. Ibid, 398.

30. Ibid.

31. Spector, 54.

32. Page, 147.

33. Despite the danger of calling for fire on ones own position, leaders often did when faced with being overrun.

34. Bergerud, 128-29

35. Charles B. MacDonald, <u>The U.S. Army in Vietnam</u> (Washington D.C.: Office of the Chief of Military History, U.S. Army, 1972), 633.

36. Bergerud, 110.

37. Ibid, 123.

38. Page, 77.

39. Ibid.

40. Page, 73.

41. Page, 109.

42. Ibid.

43. Michael Lee Lanning and Don Cragg, <u>Inside the VC and NVA: The Real Story of North Vietnam's Armed Forces</u> (New York: Fawcett Columbine, 1992),41, 53.

44. Ibid, 54.

45. Ibid, 63.

46. Page, 107.

47. Ibid, 146.

48. In fairness to the villager, many faced a bad situation. Desiring to help neither the VC or U.S. they faced punishment from both sides for their unwillingness. If they aided one side they faced reprisal from the other. If they aided neither they faced pressure from both. A classic Catch-22.

49. Edelman, 64.

50. Spector, 56.

51. Graham, 135.

52. Ibid.

About the Contributors

Walter Jung is a professor of Geography in the Department of History and Geography, the director of Western Pacific Institute, and editor of *Western Pacific Journal* at the University of Central Oklahoma. He has published numerous articles about regional development and city planning and conducted consulting projects in Korea. His books include *Nation Building: A Geopolitical History of Korea* (1998), *Korea and Regional Geopolitics* (1998), and *Koreans in Manchuria* (1989). His major research interests are economic-political developments in Northeast Asia.

Haoruo Zhang is one of China's national leaders. Among Minister Zhang's current national positions are the member of the Standing Committee of the PRC National People's Congress, executive vice chairman of China's Congress' Environment and Resources Committee, honorary chairman of All China Commerce Federation (China's Chamber of Commerce), chairman of China's Petroleum Engineering Association, and senior advisor of China Society of Strategy and Management Research. In 1995-98, Zhang served as the executive vice minister of the State Economic Reconstructing Committee. In 1993-95, he was the Minister of Trade. In 1987-92, he was the Governor of Sichuan Province, the largest province in China with a total provincial population of more than 100 million people. In 1985-87, he served as the vice minister of Foreign Trade Ministry. In 1982-86, he was the vice president of China Petro-Chemical Corporation.

Yong U. Glasure is an associate professor of Economics at Wayland Baptist University and adjunct associate professor of Political Science at Texas Tech University. His recent works have appeared in *Journal of Northeast Asian Studies, Asian Survey, Resource and Energy Economics, Southwestern Economics Review,* and *Journal of Energy and Development.* He is also an economic and policy consultant.

Aie-Rie Lee is an associate professor of Political Science and former acting director of the Asian Pacific Rim Areas Program at Texas Tech University. She has recently published articles in *Comparative Political Studies, International Journal of Political Economy, International Journal of Public Opinion Research, Social Science Quarterly, Policy Studies Journal, Asian Survey,* and *Asian Affairs.*

Yajie Wang is an associate professor of International Finance, International Credit, and International Settlement at Harbin Finance College, Harbin, China. She has published more than 10 research papers, and two of them have been awarded. Her research interests include international finance, financial reforms in China, and financial crisis in Asia.

Xiaoxiao Li is a research fellow at the Western Pacific Institute (UCO), associate editor of *American Review of China Studies,* and business consultant of Phoenician Import, Inc. in Miami. In his 16 years' experience in international trade, he has been traveling to more than 30 countries in Asia, Africa, Europe, and North America for business negotiations and promotions.

Yue Yang is an associate professor of Economics, director of the Department of Social Sciences at Harbin Senior Finance College, Harbin, China, and director of Chinese International Personage Association. She has published 10 academic papers and three of them received awards. She is the co-editor of *Political Economics* (in Chinese, 1996) and *Opening China to the World* (in Chinese, 1994). Her research interests include state enterprise reforms, financial reforms, and security investment in China.

Anthony Song is a reporter and associate editor of *Asian American News* (Boston, MA) and reporter of *Canada-China News* (Toronto, Canada). He served as the Inspector First Class at the Bureau of International Affairs of National Security in China in 1979-97. His research works include

Reinventing the Cold War; North Korea's Bombs, Spies, and Foreign Policy in the 1990s, "North Korea's Last Secret War: An Inside Story of Pyongyang's Strategic Thinking," and "The Death of the Emperor: Kim Il-Song and His Son."

Xiao-bing Li is an associate professor of History and Geography Department and the associate director of Western Pacific Institute at the University of Central Oklahoma. He is the author, co-author, and co-editor of *Chinese Generals Remember the Korean War* (2000), *Chinese Americans and Their Community* (in Chinese, 1999), *Korea and Regional Geopolitics* (1998), *Social Transition in China* (1998), *Interpreting U.S.-China-Taiwan Relations* (1998), *China and the United States; A New Cold War History* (1997), *U.S. China Policy* (in Chinese, 1997), *Major Events in the 20th Century* (in Chinese, 1994), and *Diplomacy through Militancy* (1993).

Nancy J. Waldenville-Brewer is a research and teaching assistant in the Department of History and Geography at the University of Central Oklahoma. She is the former president of Phi Alpha Theta History Honor Society. Her research interests include China's relations with Taiwan, Korea, and the U.S. She presented her research papers at Phi Alpha Theta Regional conferences, Liberal Arts Symposium, and the Oklahoma Scholar-Leadership Enrichment Program Seminar.

Xiansheng Tian is an assistant professor at the Department of History at Metropolitan State College of Denver. His major teaching and research interests include Sino-American relations in the 1940s-1950s. His article of Hurley's mission to China has been published as a chapter in *China and the United States; A New Cold War History*. Currently he serves as a board member of the Association of Chinese Historians in the U.S.

David Shapard is a history teacher in Oklahoma City Public Schools. He also taught at Oklahoma City University and U.S. Air Force Academy, Colorado Springs. Currently he co-teaches U.S. History classes at the University of Central Oklahoma. In the past 20 years, he have received many honors as the Outstanding Educator, Honors World History Teacher, AP American History Teacher, and Excellent Educator Nominee.

Joan McConnell is an author, lecturer, and professor. For 25 years, she was the Language Program director at the Stanford University Program in Florence, Italy. She also directed the Stanford University Alumni Summer Symposia Series. She is the author of 22 books and numerous articles on linguistic, literature, and cultural issues with a special emphasis on the changing role of English in the 21st century. She has lectured on these topics in the U.S., Europe, and Asia. She has been a guest professor in Japan and Taiwan as well as a guest lecturer at many language conferences in the world.

Charles Henry Winwood, holding a rank of Master Sergeant with the U.S. Special Forces Reserves, is a visiting professor at the University of Jamusi, Heilongjiang, China. He has been teaching and doing research in Chinese universities and colleges in Northeast China in the past three years. His research interests include economic geography in Northeast China, Jewish experience in post-WWII China, and the Korean War's impact on Northeast China.

James Robertson is a graduate student at the University of Central Oklahoma. His research papers have been accepted for presentation at regional academic symposiums. He also presented his paper at the Oklahoma Scholar-Leadership Enrichment Program Seminar on Post-1949 China. His research interests include the Cold War in East Asia and international relations in Asia.

Richard Lee Matthews is a high school teacher of history, government, and geography. Currently he is working on his doctoral degree in higher education at Oklahoma State University. His research interests include historiography, the Cold War, modern history of East and Southeast Asia. His article, "Paranoia, Economics, and the Conflicts in Northeast Asia," has been published as a chapter in *Korea and Regional Geopolitics*.

Ryan Paul Jones is a research and teaching assistant in the Department of History and Geography at the University of Central Oklahoma. His research interests include military history, American combat experience in Asian wars, the Vietnam War, and Weimar and Nazi Germany. He presented his papers at the Asian-Pacific Rim Symposium and the Oklahoma Scholar-Leadership Enrichment Program Seminar.